SANDRA GUSTAFSON'S

CHEAP
SLEEPS IN

Barcelona • Madrid • Seville

SPAIN

**A Traveler's Guide to the
Best-Kept Secrets**

D1023235

CHRONICLE BOOKS
SAN FRANCISCO

Printed in the United States of America

ISBN: 0-8118-2490-X

Book design: Words & Deeds
Author photograph: Marv Summers

Distributed in Canada by
Raincoast Books
8680 Cambie Street
Vancouver, B.C. V6P 6M9

10 9 8 7 6 5 4 3 2 1

Chronicle Books
85 Second Street
San Francisco, CA 94105

www.chroniclebooks.com

For Sue Randerson, a very special friend

Contents

To the Reader

Three Spaniards, four opinions . . .
—Old Spanish Proverb

The modern and medieval blend in today's Spain. Nowhere is this more evident than in Spain's astounding variety of architecture, which is a pastiche of Roman, Christian, Moorish, and Modernist legacies. The country is studded with historic cathedrals, palaces, monuments, and architectural masterpieces—from the Hanging Houses of Cuenca to Gaudí's unfinished cathedral to spectacular modern art museums. In the cities, ancient, narrow, twisting streets feel as though time has stood still since the Middle Ages. Spooky and splendid, drenched in history, Barcelona's Barri Gòtic, or Gothic Quarter, is the oldest part of one of the oldest cities in Europe. The quarter, close to the harbor that made the city a great seaport, was settled by its first wave of inhabitants more than two thousand years ago. In 1992, Barcelona hosted the Olympic Games, and the city received a modern facelift that works in perfect harmony with its ancient past.

By contrast, Seville's old quarter, the Barrio de Santa Cruz, is anything but dark and sinister. It is filled with light and romance, its plazas perfumed by orange trees, its whitewashed houses draped in bougainvillea and brightly blooming flowers cascading from wrought-iron balconies. In the days of Spain's New World explorations, Seville had great importance. Columbus returned here after his first voyage, and as a strategic inland port with ready access to both the Mediterranean and the Atlantic, it attracted fleets of galleons that sailed up the Guadalquivir River to off-load plunder they had taken from the Indian empires. Seville's towering Gothic cathedral—surpassed in size only by St. Peter's in Rome, St. Paul's in London, and a new basilica on the Ivory Coast—contains the tomb of Christopher Columbus, and across the plaza is the fabulous fourteenth-century Alcázar of Pedro the Cruel, a fortified palace built by Mudéjar craftsman.

Madrid, one of Europe's liveliest cosmopolitan capitals, lies at the very heart of Spain. Its pivotal location and status as a transportation hub make it an ideal base for exploring the country's interior, a historic and monumental region that occupies a vast plateau, called the *meseta*, where most of Spain's castles are located. Madrid is a city with two faces. By day, it enjoys more hours of sunshine per year than any other European capital. The city is small enough that visitors can easily walk to almost everything, getting to know its sights, sounds, and a little of her soul as they go. By night, certain parts of Madrid turn into a nonstop party that continues until the first rays of dawn. Visitors will find that the day starts late and ends late, and it's best to adjust to the leisurely flow. Nothing much happens before 10 A.M., and most people aren't ready to go out and begin their evening until 10 P.M.

In the artistic rivalry between Spain's two major cities, Barcelona and Madrid, Madrid has always had the distinct advantage with the Prado, the key member of the "golden mile" trio that includes the Thyssen-Bornemisza and the Centro Reina Sofía. With the 1995 opening of the Contemporary Art Museum and the reopening of the Catalan National Art Museum, Barcelona is rapidly catching up. Madrid and Barcelona are not the only Spanish cities with the means to attract art lovers, however. In the north, Bilbao has the Guggenheim Museum of Modern and Contemporary Art, designed by American architect Frank Gehry. By all accounts, it is *the* museum of the twenty-first century.

Spain is now the number-two travel destination for international tourists, moving ahead of the United States. The reasons for its burgeoning popularity are many. Spain is different, seductive, and affordable. It's filled with colorful fiestas, a vibrant nightlife, dramatic scenery, exciting bullfights, romantic flamenco dancing, and a well-preserved artistic and architectural heritage, both ancient and modern—in short, it provides visitors with a variety that no other European country can match. Spain has entered a golden age of prosperity, and its cities are stylish, sophisticated, and home to a wealth of contemporary art and literature.

Today, travel in Spain is easy, accommodations and food are within almost any budget, and the kind and helpful Spaniards are eager to share their pure joy of living with everyone. To that end, *Cheap Sleeps in Spain* is for those travelers who are looking for the best value for their hotel peseta while staying in Barcelona, Madrid, and Seville. This guide is not, however, for those travelers looking only for the cheapest beds they can find and willing to sacrifice comfort, convenience, and well-being in the bargain. Value is not always measured by how much you spend. There are times when the least expensive option represents the best value available, but at other times, spending a little more can yield much greater comfort and convenience. To achieve this balance, and to get the most out of your trip, it is important that you know what you want—which things you absolutely cannot do without and which ones you can—in order to make the appropriate trade-offs between money and comfort as you evaluate your hotel options. Whatever your budget or desires, *Cheap Sleeps in Spain* will lead you to the best values in every category, from shoestring budget to Big Splurge.

In addition to offering budget-minded travelers the best advice about hotel values, *Cheap Sleeps in Spain* provides Cheap Chic shopping tips for Barcelona, Madrid, and Seville. In the Cheap Chic section, I provide information on the best stores to find local crafts and clothing, special gifts, and hidden bargains—as well as evaluations of each city's outdoor markets—for the smart shopper who feels that no trip is complete without at least a few hours of browsing and buying.

Cheap Sleepers in Spain have a multitude of hotel choices, but you will find that most accommodations don't wallow in nostalgia or display any ruffles or frills. Spain's hotels tend to be simple, basic, sparsely modern, and for the most part hopelessly charmless. Perhaps this is to the good: Life in Spain is too exciting, interesting, and enticing to waste precious vacation hours lounging inside a hotel room. That said, rooms tend to be good sized; they aren't merely spaces wrapped around a double bed with no luggage or living space. Decorating costs have been kept to a minimum, which means bare floors, one chair (perhaps a folding model) per room, and fewer pictures on the walls. In all but the bottom-of-the-barrel budget choices, there will be a television set. Cleanliness is also a strong virtue. However, many of the interior rooms border on the dreary because they have opaque windows opening onto a dark, inside wall that has not seen the light of day for centuries. In the summer, if there is no air-conditioning, your room can become an oven. Rooms with private bathrooms are in good supply, but don't look for baskets of sweet-smelling toiletries. The communal hall facilities may be some of the best you will encounter in Europe. While you should keep these caveats in mind, in the final analysis, if your room is clean, well located, and quiet, allowing you to wake up refreshed and ready for the day ahead . . . what more can you ask for?

Many travelers to Spain are confused about the seemingly endless variety of places to stay. *Cheap Sleeps in Spain* focuses on four main types of accommodations: *pensiones, hostales, hostal residencias,* and hotels, which all receive star ratings in Spain's official classification system (see "Stars and Categories," page 34, for a description of these classifications). I also provide information on staying in apartments, campgrounds, and youth hostels in each city. Most of the *hostales* are small, family-owned operations, and they all offer excellent Cheap Sleeping value for money. If you want to move up a notch or two, you can check into a two- or three-star hotel. However, the star rating system shouldn't be your only guide. Most one-star hotels cost no more than three-star *hostales*—but in many cases they are not nearly as good a value, and many three-star hotels cost more than what their rooms are worth. *Cheap Sleeps in Spain* does not cover the four- and five-star hotels because they are in the luxury class with equally luxurious price tags.

It is very important to know that I do not include any hotel or shop that I have not personally visited. While other guidebooks may send a questionnaire to be filled out by someone at the hotel or *hostal,* and request a series of detailed photographs from which a review will be compiled, I have been to every address in this book—plus hundreds of others that for one reason or another did not make the final cut. When assessing a hotel, I arrive unannounced and uninvited. I begin reviewing the facilities even before I step through the door: Is the exterior well kept? Are the plants alive? Is the paint in good shape, the windows and curtains clean? I look over the lobby and reception area: Are they welcoming, comfortable, nicely furnished? Where is the management? Are they too busy watching television, smoking, or taking care of other business to take care of mine? I ask to see a variety of rooms and avoid using the elevator between floors. This allows me to snoop a bit more, to peek in a room they might not want me to see, or to check out the maids and see how they are going about cleaning the rooms. In each room I am on the lookout for dust, mold, mildew, bugs, thin towels, scratchy or waxed toilet tissue, creaking floors, peeling paint, and cigarette smells or burns on the bedspread. I check the view: Can I see sunshine, or is the place basically a cave? I look for somewhere to put luggage and for enough closet space to hold more than the contents of a small overnight bag. In the bathroom, is there a shelf for a toothbrush and a few cosmetics? A hook on the back of the bathroom door? Are the bathtub and shower in good condition? I turn on the water to check the pressure: If there is a mere trickle, I know that it will be reduced to a drip when two or more guests shower at the same time. My goal is to find out as much as I can about each Cheap Sleep so I can describe it to you in detail, allowing you to make informed choices about one of the major expenses of your trip.

Cheap Sleeps in Spain is a personal guide I wrote for you—not to drum up business for a particular hotel or shop—and I stand behind every write-up. Researching and writing this book was great fun, and hard work, but one of the benefits of my job is discovering wonderful Cheap Sleeps and passing them along to you. During the process, I fell in love with Spain, and I can't wait to go back to do it all over again. In the name of research, I walked hundreds of miles in every type of weather, wore out several pairs of shoes, an umbrella, and most of my clothes. For me, it is the most wonderful job possible . . . I love every minute of it. I hope the first edition of *Cheap Sleeps in Spain* helps make your stay truly special and sets the stage for many return trips. I want to thank the many faithful Cheap Sleepers who have used and enjoyed the other guides in this series and have endorsed my efforts by writing to me and sharing their experiences. Please write to me about your Cheap Sleeps in Spain, whether to disagree with something I have said, or to pat me on the back, or to point me toward some new or special place you want me to check on my next trip. See the Readers' Comments page at the back of the book for an address where you can write to me. Your comments and suggestions are very important; and I read every letter and answer all of my mail personally. In the meantime, I wish you *buena suerta* and *¡buen viaje!*

Tips for Cheap Sleeps in Spain

I thought that I should never return to the country I love more than any other, except my own.
—*Ernest Hemingway*

1. Know your bottom line. That is, know what you need to have in a hotel room, and what you can live without, and make your reservations accordingly.

2. For the best Cheap Sleeps at the lowest prices, go in the off-season when the room rates will be lower, even in the most expensive hotels. But at any time of year, always ask if there are any discounts on the room you might take advantage of. If it's off-season, or simply a slow week, and the hotel is not full, you may get a reduced rate just for the price of asking.

3. Always ask if the price of the room includes the 7 percent IVA tax. In a small, family-run *hostal*, one way to get a slight break on the room price is to offer to pay cash and forego the receipt in exchange for the hotel dropping the 7 percent IVA altogether; in some *hostales*, this is a common practice. However, don't try this in a three-star hotel, as it would be considered *very* bad form.

4. Hotels affiliated with worldwide chains such as Utell or Best Western may not always offer their lowest discounted rates through their toll-free 800 number. For the best discounted price, call the toll-free 800 number first, then call the hotel to see if you can get a better deal.

5. As a general travel rule, stay central to the focus of your activities. It seldom makes Cheap Sleeping sense to stay far from your center of interest in the name of saving a few dollars, since the cost in time, energy, and money spent commuting to and from your hotel usually overshadows any meager savings.

6. Plan ahead. A successful Cheap Sleep within your budget requires some advance homework, and this means making hotel reservations in advance to ensure that you get the hotel of your choice in the location you want and at the price you can afford.

7. In direct contradiction to number 6: Rock-bottom Cheap Sleeps often do not take advance reservations, especially during peak seasons. They will only sell their rooms to someone on the spot.

The good news is that this allows you more flexibility and you can often negotiate the price, but the bad news is that the hotel of your choice may be full by the time you arrive, forcing you to take something you don't like at a price you don't want to pay. If you decide to gamble in this manner, remember to arrive at the hotel before noon, when guests will be checking out, and your chances of snatching something at the last minute will be better.

8. For two people, a room with a double bed (*con una cama grande* or *un matrimonio*) at the back of the hotel with no private facilities will generally be the Cheapest Sleep in the house. The most expensive double will usually be facing front with twin beds (*con dos camas*) and a full bathroom with a bathtub. Somewhere in the middle is a room with a double bed and a bathroom with a shower and toilet. However, sometimes hotels will charge the same price for a room facing the back as one with a sunny balcony and a view. Go figure!

9. Charm, character, comfort, and luxury are not top priorities in Spanish hotels with fewer than three stars. However, the spartan rooms are large and clean.

10. Interior rooms may be more quiet, but you will find them dark, airless, and depressing, thanks to opaque windows opening onto a wall.

11. If you are going in the summer, especially in Madrid and Seville, make sure to get air-conditioning if you can at all afford it. Don't let anyone tell you that you won't need it because your room is on "the cool side of the building," "gets a breeze," "or "doesn't get too hot because the walls are thick." When the temperature is in the triple digits, let's face it, air-conditioning is a necessity, not a luxury. However, not all hotel rooms have individually controlled air-conditioning, and you can sometimes be at the mercy of a very thrifty owner who will turn it on only a few hours during the day. This is also true for heat in the winter.

12. Fabric softener and bleach do not seem to be popular washing aids. As a rule, be prepared to dry off after your bath with some tattle-tale gray towels, which can sometimes be rough and stiff.

13. Check out the room before you check in: Make sure that every-thing works, that it's clean, that there are towels in the bathroom and hangers in the closet, and that it's the location in the hotel you requested. This is the time to reconfirm the room price and discuss extra charges such as telephone calls. Pleading ignorance to extra charges at checkout time is not an excuse to avoid paying them.

14. You can't always judge a Spanish Cheap Sleep by its cover. Some magnificent marble entryways lead to tiny elevators taking you to

some mighty dreary rooms. On the other hand, some *hostales* may have a scruffy entry, but their rooms are neat and clean, reflecting the family's great pride of ownership.

15. Hotel breakfasts are bad buys. Many small hotels in Spain do not serve breakfast at all. If they do, it is overpriced and overrated: usually a roll, coffee, and maybe some juice, or in most three-star hotels, an expensive buffet. You are much better off, and money ahead, going to a corner café or pastry shop.

16. Hotel laundry services, if they even exist in the bottom-end Cheap Sleeps, are sky high. As such, you will often want to wash a few things yourself in your room, but be considerate when you do this. Drip-dry laundries have ruined many hotel floors and carpets, and hotels are generally less than pleased to see wet apparel flapping in the wind in a streetside window. If you need to rinse a few things out, please hang them over a shower or bathtub, or better yet, go to a laundromat and mix with the locals. It might turn into one of your more interesting experiences.

17. BYOL—Bring Your Own Lightbulbs, that is, if you plan on doing much reading or want to work in your room after dark. I always travel with a folding halogen light, but you can increase the wattage by purchasing stronger bulbs locally.

18. Never change money in a hotel, restaurant, or shop. Go to a bank, the nearest American Express office, or use an ATM.

19. I can sum up my advice on travel insurance in two words: Buy it. It may seem like an unnecessary expense, but let me assure you that if you ever need it, you will rejoice that you have it in place. This applies to all types of travel interruption insurance as well as medical insurance (see "Tips on Renting a Spanish Apartment," below, and "Health Matters," page 21).

20. When reserving your Cheap Sleep in Barcelona, Madrid, or Seville, always say that you found the accommodation in *Cheap Sleeps in Spain*. Owners are always happy to know where their business is coming from.

Tips on Renting a Spanish Apartment

1. Most important: *Know the cancellation policy and buy cancellation insurance.* It is beyond the scope of *Cheap Sleeps in Spain* to detail the various apartment rental policies you could encounter, but I can assure you that they are not in your favor and always hit the hardest when the chips are down—when you must change your plans only a few weeks before departure, or worse, in the middle of your stay. To protect yourself, purchase trip insurance. The Automobile Club of America has a list of carriers, some of which are Access America, Inc. 800-248-8300; Carefree Travel Insurance 800-323-3149; and Travel Guard International 800-826-1300, fax: 800-955-8785, Internet: www.noelgroup.com.

2. Before signing on the dotted line, carefully consider all your needs and tell them to the rental agency or apartment hotel. Ask for photos of the apartment you will be assigned. State the size of apartment you want, the number in your party, the types of beds (such as a regular double or twin beds, or will a fold-out sofa bed or futon chair do?). In the bathroom, do you need a shower, or can you live with a little bathtub? Can you exist without CNN, or would you rather work on your Spanish comprehension by having to watch local television? What about stairs, the sophistication of the kitchen, and location? Is it on a busy traffic thoroughfare, close to your center of interest, convenient to grocery shopping and public transportation? Think about every aspect of your stay, and ask questions.

3. Is there a telephone specifically for your unit, and if so, how much will you be charged per call? Spanish telephones are very expense; they can blow a budget right through the roof if you're not careful. Will you be needing to send and receive faxes, hook up a computer, surf the net, use email? If so, consider buying an extension cord, since the distance from the plug to a table can sometimes be too long for your computer cord to reach.

4. In private rentals, it is almost certain that you will pay for all utilities. How much extra will they cost?

5. Ask about maid service: Is it extra or included? Is there a washing machine in your unit or in the building? Who is responsible for washing sheets and towels during, and at the end, of your stay? How is the cleaning deposit handled and how much is the final

cleaning fee? Even if you leave the flat in spotless condition, there will always be a final cleaning fee.

6. Is the apartment appropriate for children or people with special needs?

7. Is there a lift to your flat? While the fourth-floor penthouse will have a fabulous view, do you really want to lug suitcases, as well as daily bags of groceries and shopping finds, up and down four flights of stairs? Think about this issue carefully because stairs can get old fast.

8. If you are renting from an agency, will someone be at the apartment to give you the keys, show you around, and explain how everything works, or do you have to go to an office somewhere to get the keys yourself?

9. Again, if renting through an ageny, make sure you know who the local contact person is, or where the office is located, in case of emergency or repairs. Who do you call when the sink backs up, the appliances won't work, or the maid whom you have paid for in advance doesn't show up. Don't laugh . . . all of these things and more have happened to me many times.

General Information

A traveler without knowledge is a bird without wings.
—Sa'di

WHEN TO GO

The best months to visit Spain are from April through June and from September through October. If I had to pick the very best month, I would select May, when the temperatures have not started to climb dramatically, the days are long, and the nights cool. Unfortunately, I'm not the only one who feels this way, and these months are considered the high season. Low season is from mid-November through mid-March (with the exception of the time around Christmas and New Year's) and all of July and August. To make the most of your Cheap Sleeping dollar, these are the months to travel, but a warning is in order: In July and August, Madrid is unbearably hot, and Seville becomes what is known as "the frying pan of Spain"—and that is not an understatement. In both cities, many of the locals evacuate to cooler climates, leaving skeleton crews in hotels and restaurants, and many shops and museums either close or have shorter hours. The winter months, however, are worth serious consideration, since hotel prices can be dramatically lower, tourist hoards are reduced, and the weather is surprisingly mild in comparison with the rest of Europe. Unless your reservations have already been made, don't even think of arriving is Seville during the Easter celebration of *Semana Santa,* which takes place the week before Easter, or two weeks later during the *Feria de Abril.* Not only are the crowds lethal during these festivals, the prices can escalate by 100 percent.

DISABLED TRAVELERS

Spain is not well known for providing a host of facilities for disabled travelers. Some hotels do have rooms that they say are suitable for the disabled, which in most cases means that the door to the bathroom is wide enough to accommodate a wheelchair, and that the room is located on the ground floor if there is no lift. However, by law, all new public buildings are required to be fully accessible. In 1992, the staging of the Olympics in Barcelona and the Expo in Seville meant improved public facilities in both these cities. Buses and metros are not equipped to handle wheelchairs. For more information, contact one of the organizations listed below.

> Directions Unlimited
> 720 N. Bedford Road
> Bedford Hills, NY 10507
> 800-533-5343

This is a tour operator specializing in custom tours for the disabled.

Society for the Advancement of Travel for the Handicapped, Inc.
347 Fifth Avenue
New York, NY 10016
212-447-7284

Travel Information Service
Moss Rehabilitation Hospital
1200 West Tabor Road
Philadelphia, PA 19141
215-456-9600
They provide telephone information and a referral service.

Twin Peaks Press
Box 129
Vancouver, WA 98666
This group publishes the *Directory of Travel Agencies for the Disabled*, which lists hundreds of agencies around the world.

DISCOUNTS
Hotels

Every *Cheap Sleeps in Spain* hotel listing states if seasonal discounts are offered. The amounts of the discount are not given because they vary with the time of the year, room availability, and often the whim of the owner. In most cases, you can count on a 10 to 15 percent discount in the off-season. Discounts are rarely volunteered, but don't be timid . . . always ask. It is important to stress that discounts are *never* offered during holidays or festivals; in fact, hotel rates can skyrocket, especially in Seville during *Semana Santa* (Holy Week), which runs between Palm Sunday and Easter, and the *Feria de Abril* (April Fair), which is held the last week in April.

Senior Citizens

Sometimes it pays to be older. Today, the largest group of travelers are those over fifty, many of whom have not only more time but more discretionary money in their pockets to spend on traveling. While Spain is not heavily into discounted travel schemes, any person sixty or older is given free or reduced admission to many state and some private museums, national monuments, cultural events, and cinemas. The trick is to ask at the ticket booth and to be prepared to show proof of age with your passport.

These U.S.-based travel organizations aimed at seniors are worth checking into if you are planning any trip, not just one to Spain.

American Association of Retired Persons (AARP)
601 E. Street NW
Washington, D. C. 20049
202-434-2277, 800-424-3410

Elderhostel
75 Federal Street, third floor
Boston, MA 02110
617-426-7788
www.elderhostel.org

Students and Teachers

Those with boundless youth and enthusiasm who are twenty-six years old or younger, or are teachers, qualify for some great discounts.

As for accommodations, sanctioned youth hostels are the cheapest beds, provided you can get one and can stand the mass-sleeping arrangements you often have to endure. To qualify, you will need an International Youth Hostel Association card, which you can get from Hostelling International (HI) at the address listed below. Or, you can wait until you arrive in Spain and purchase it after you have spent a few nights in a hostel, but you are money ahead to get it before you leave because of the additional benefits it allows. To book your bed before you leave, contact the International Booking Network (IBN) at the HI number below, and for a small fee ($5), you can get a confirmed dormitory booking up to six months in advance.

Hostelling International (HI)
733 15th Street, Suite 840 NW
Washington, D.C. 20005
202-783-6161, 202-783-6171 (fax)
Email: hiayhserv@hiayh.org.com
Internet: www.hiayh.org or www.iyhf.org

For discounts on transportation, accommodations, museums, and other attractions, the smart buys are the International Student Identity Card (ISIC) if you are a student of any age and can prove it, or the Go-25 card if you are not a student but still under age twenty-six. There is also a deal for teachers called the International Teacher's Identity Card (ITIC). In the United States, each card costs $20 and is available through Council Travel (see below). One of the best benefits of these cards is the health insurance, which is provided at no additional cost and includes coverage for accidents, hospital visits, emergency evacuation, and accidental death. For more information, brochures, and their *Student Travel* magazine, contact the Council Travel Office:

CIEE headquarters
205 East 42nd Street, sixteenth floor
New York, NY 10017
212-661-1450, 800-2-COUNCIL
www.counciltravel.com

For information about their educational programs, call 888-COUN-CIL. Council Travel has branches in most major U.S. cities; call them for the location nearest you. If you send for the card, allow three weeks; if you go to your local office, it will be issued on the spot.

While the ISIC/ITIC cards are best, it doesn't hurt to get a few more perks if you can. If you are under twenty-six and in Madrid, anyone of any nationality can buy a European Youth Card (*Carnet Joven Europeo*). It costs less than $10 and is good for discounts in museums, theaters, movies, and air and rail tickets throughout Spain and in some other European countries. You can buy this card at Consejería de Educación y Cultura, Calle de Alcalá 31; tel: 91 580 41 96.

HOLIDAYS AND FESTIVALS

No one loves holidays and fiestas more than the Spanish, who have both nationally declared holidays each year plus countless regional celebrations and local festivals. Every city and town, regardless of size, has its local saint's day, which is another holiday. When a holiday falls on a Tuesday or Thursday, the Monday or Friday before or after is also taken as a holiday, which is called a *puente*, literally meaning a bridge, creating a four-day weekend. Regional governments throughout the country set four holidays, and local councils set at least two more. Sometimes the exact dates for regional holidays are not announced until a few weeks before the date, so trying to keep up with all these dates can be a monumental task. As a result, if you are traveling throughout Spain, it is a good idea to keep some money on hand because you may arrive somewhere only to find that all banks and shops are closed. As for longer vacations, Spaniards usually take off the week of *Semana Santa* (right before Easter) and the month of August.

Before leaving for Spain, check with the National Tourist Office of Spain (see page 31) if you want to attend one of these special events. For the regional or city holidays celebrated only in Barcelona, Madrid, or Seville, please refer to the city sections of this book.

National Holidays

New Year's Day	*Año Nuevo*	January 1
Feast of the Epiphany	*Día de los Reyes Magos*	January 6
Good Friday	*Viernes Santo*	March or April
Labor Day	*Fiesta del Trabajo*	May 1
Spain's Patron Saint Day	*Diá de Santiago Apóstol*	June 24
Feast of the Assumption	*La Asunción*	August 15
National Day	*Día de la Hispanidad*	October 12
All Saints' Day	*Todos los Santos*	November 1
Constitution Day	*Día de la Constitución*	December 6
Christmas	*Navidad*	December 25

Local festivals give the natives another excuse to engage in long and colorful partying. Every city and town in Spain has at least one, and most have several, each with its own traditions and pageantry. Many are religious based, but all are high spirited. See the city sections in this book for the major festivals in Barcelona, Madrid, and Seville. If you want to coordinate your trip to coincide with these fiestas, check with the regional tourist office for a list of dates, which are never firmly set from year to year.

HEALTH MATTERS

For medical emergency numbers and hospital locations, turn to the "Medical Problems" section in each city.

Spain is not a difficult place to travel and stay healthy. The main complaints are sunburn, hangovers and/or exhaustion from too much late-night partying, and the usual stomach upsets caused from too much rich food. The water is safe to drink, but I always advise buying bottled water if only because it tastes better. Water from public fountains and spouts is not safe. When in doubt, ask *¿es potable el agua?* If you see the sign *Agua Potable*, it means the water is safe to drink. *Agua No Potable* means you shouldn't drink the water. Of course it is always prudent to pack an extra set of glasses, an adequate supply of whatever medications you are taking, and a copy of prescriptions, perhaps translated into Spanish. Recommended shots are polio, tetanus, and diphtheria. You might also want to check with your doctor about hepatitus shots.

Pharmacies (*farmacias*) can help with many minor medical complaints. A system of on-duty pharmacies ensures that at least one pharmacy in each city area is always open. When a pharmacy is closed, it posts the name of the nearest open pharmacy on a *farmacias de guardia*.

It's very important that you have adequate medical insurance, so check with your medical insurance carrier before leaving home to see what your coverage abroad will be. Most will cover you for a limited period. If you wind up needing medical care in Spain, know that many medical facilities require that you pay for your treatment in full at the time of service, and they won't file claims for you with your medical plan. It will generally be up to you to get your claim processed and be reimbursed, so be sure you get an itemized bill to submit to your insurance company. You may wish to take out additional medical insurance, and if so, contact your own insurance carrier, the American Automobile Association for their list of medical insurance carriers, or Wallach & Company, 107 West Federal Street, P.O. Box 480, Middleburg, Virginia 20118; tel: 800-237-6615; email: info@wallach.com; Internet: www.wallach.com. Another company I have used is Travel Guard. You can call them twenty-four hours a day at 800-826-1399; fax: 800-955-8785; Internet: www.noelgroup.com.

MONEY MATTERS

Until the euro becomes effective as legal tender in July 2002, the basic unit of Spanish currency is the peseta (pta). At press time, one dollar equals 150ptas. Coins come in denominations of 1, 5, 25, 50, 100, 200, and 500ptas. Notes come in 500, 1,000, 5,000, and 10,000ptas.

If you carry traveler's checks, charge big items on your credit card, and use ATMs, you will do well. Also remember to carry some of your own personal checks. If you suddenly run low on funds, you can use them to get cash advances or to buy traveler's checks, provided the credit cards you carry will allow this (American Express will). Travel pundits used to advise getting enough foreign money before leaving home to carry you for a day or two. You can do this, if you want to go to the trouble and expense, but all international airports and most train stations have ATMs that accept U.S. cards. To get some Spanish pesetas before leaving, first check with your local bank and see how long it will take them to get the foreign currency . . . if they can even do so. If you cannot get pesatas in your area, you can order them by telephone for two-day delivery from the Thomas Cook Currency Call Service; tel: 800-287-7362; Internet: www.us.thomascook.com.

In Spain, banks exchange money, and very often at decent rates; they are certainly much better than hotels or exchange offices, which are identified by signs that say "Cambio," "Change," or "Chequepoint." However, as with almost all foreign exchanges, you will pay a commission, so estimate your needs carefully. If you overbuy, you will lose twice, both in buying and in selling back. Every time you change money, someone is making a profit, and it is not you.

Note that Spanish banking hours are from 9 A.M. to 2 P.M., Monday to Friday. Between October 1 and May 31, many branches are also open from 9 A.M. to 1 P.M. on Saturday. Hours vary slightly, and a few banks stay open until 5 P.M. one day a week, usually Thursday. All banks are closed on public holidays, and sometimes on the afternoon before a major holiday. There are also exchange offices at all El Corte Inglés stores, which are open from 10 A.M. to 9:30 P.M., Monday through Saturday.

ATM Cards (*Cajeros Automáticos*)

One of the least-expensive ways to obtain money is through a cash machine or ATM; they are not hard to find in Spain, and they dispense pesetas at any time of day or night. Regardless of the amount you get, your U.S. bank or credit card will charge you for using a foreign ATM (and the foreign bank you are using may add its own fee), but you will be getting a wholesale conversion rate that is better than you will get at a bank or currency exchange office. Check with your bank or credit card to find out if they are part of an internationl ATM network, and if so, then check whether you will need to create a new personal identification number (PIN) for use in Spain (where machines only accept four-digit PINs). Also ask what the withdrawal limits are over what time periods.

Spanish ATM machines work the same way as in the States: You just punch in your PIN and the amount of cash you want. However, most ATMs in Europe automatically select your default account to take money from—they don't give you the option of selecting from different accounts as banks do in the States—so double-check that your default account is the one you want to use. Here are the numbers to call to find out the names of corresponding affiliated cash machine networks in Spain: For Cirrus locations, call 800-4-CIRRUS. For Plus locations, call 800-THE-PLUS. To enroll in the American Express foreign ATM program, call 800-CASH-NOW. You can also ask your bank for a current directory or get worldwide ATM locations on the Internet: www.mastercard.com for Cirrus; www.visa.com for Plus.

Credit Cards

Plastic money has become a way of life in Spain, just as it has almost everywhere else. You can use your cards to pay for just about anything, except the lower-end Cheap Sleep *hostales* and hotels. The most popular cards are Visa and MasterCard (which may be referred to as Carte Bleu and Eurocard, respectively), followed by American Express and Diners Club.

There are many reasons to use credit cards, not the least of which is that they eliminate the need for carrying large amounts of cash. Credit card receipts also provide you with a record of your purchases (and you should save these receipts to check against your credit card bill, since mistakes do occur). Card purchases and cash advances are charged to your account at the time of processing, not at time of purchase, and you often get delayed billing of up to four or six weeks after purchase. However, before using your credit card, it never hurts to ask the store or hotel if there is any discount or incentive to pay in cash.

Note that some card issuers are adding fees on transactions in foreign currencies. As a result, it pays to select your card wisely. Of the major card issuers, Citibank and American Express add a 2 percent surcharge to purchases in foreign currencies, while Diners Club, Visa, and MasterCard levy a 1 percent fee. Others can be as high as 4 percent. Also note that fees for cash advances on credit cards can be even higher; Visa and MasterCard charge fees that can range up to 10 percent.

In some cases you can also get cash by writing a personal check and presenting your credit card. At an American Express office, cardholders can cash a personal check without being charged a commission, but you can also do this with Diners Club, MasterCard, or Visa.

Lost Credit Cards. Keep a copy of all of your credit card numbers with you, and treat them with the same importance you do your passport. Lock them up in the hotel safe—don't keep them in your wallet or purse. If your credit cards get lost or stolen, contact your credit card companies immediately. Here are the U.S. numbers for the major issuers (see the city sections for phone numbers in Spain):

American Express: Toll-free in the U.S., 800-233-5432; collect in the U.S., 336-393-1111; Internet: www.americanexpress.com.

Diner's Club: Toll-free in the U.S., 800-234-6377; collect in the U.S., 702-797-5532; Internet: www.dinersclubus.com.

MasterCard: Toll-free in the U.S., 800-307 7309; collect in the U.S., 314-542-7111; Internet: www.mastercard.com.

Visa: Toll-free in the U.S., 800-336-8472; collect in the U.S., 410-581-9994; Internet: www.visa.com.

American Express Global Assist Program. American Express card members have a host of backup services, including their American Express Global Assist program, which can be reached twenty-four hours a day, seven days a week at 800-554-2639, or collect from abroad at 715-343-7977. This service provides emergency medical, legal, or financial assistance while traveling. Operators at this number will accept collect calls and give information on currency rates, weather, visa and passport requirements, customs, and embassy and consular telephone numbers and addresses. They also will help with urgent message relays, finding lost luggage, prescription assistance, emergency hotel check-in if you have lost your credit card, and provide translations. It is worth having an American Express card just to have this service.

Traveler's Checks

You will get a better rate of exchange with traveler's checks than with cash, and the more traveler's checks you cash, the better the rate. However, this saddles you with carrying large amounts of cash, and unless you have access to a hotel safe, this is not a good idea. The real cost of traveler's checks lies in what you spend to buy the traveler's checks and what commission you pay to cash them. As a rule of thumb, you should never pay more than 1 to 2 percent in purchasing fees.

There are many companies that issue traveler's checks, but American Express is one of the best. Platinum or Gold cardholders can get them free of charge, while Green cardholders and nonmembers must pay a 1 percent commission. American Automoblie Association (AAA) members can purchase American Express traveler's checks commission free from their local AAA branch offices. In Spain, you can exchange American Express traveler's checks to pesetas, commission free, at any American Express office. Consult the city sections of Barcelona, Madrid, and Seville for the office addresses and hours. American Express cardholders can also write a personal check for traveler's checks at any of these offices. For a directory of American Express services and offices, consult their website, www.americanexpress.com, or call 800-673-3782 to order checks or 800-221-7282 to get further information.

Here are the toll-free numbers of some other major issuers of traveler's checks; call for fee and commission information.

Capital Foreign Exchange: 888-842-0880
Citicorp: 800-645-6556
MasterCard/Thomas Cook: 800-CURRENCY; Internet:
    www.usthomascook.com
Visa: 800-227-6811; Internet: www.visa.com

Wiring Money

Sometimes we need a little financial reinforcement from home. When this happens, you can have someone in the States send you a MoneyGram. In the States, call 800-926-9400 (twenty-four hours a day) to find the location nearest you. The sender must go to the Moneygram location with cash in hand—they do not accept checks or credit cards. The limit is $10,000; the minimum is one cent. Fees to Spain run from $20 to $300. The U.S.-based Moneygram office will tell you where the money will arrive in Spain, and the person receiving the money must go to that location with the name of the sender, the reference number of the transaction, and have a valid ID. The money itself takes only ten minutes to send. MoneyGram also offers a free ten-word message and a free three-minute long-distance phone call for the person sending the money.

If you don't use MoneyGram, you can go through Western Union (800-325-6000) or phone 800-CALL-CASH. The advantage of Western Union is that you can use either MasterCard or Visa to send the money. Fees start at $15 and go to $150 for cash transactions; add $10 if you are using MasterCard or Visa. The receiver must have an ID; if this has been lost or stolen, the receiver must have official (that is, police) proof of the loss and provide Western Union with answers to what they call "trick questions," which are intended to prove you are who you say you are.

Tipping and Bargaining

The Spanish are skimpy tippers. In restaurants, menu prices must include the service charge, and what you tip in addition to the bottom line is up to you. As for taxes, there is a variable 7 to 16 percent value-added tax (IVA) applied to most items and services, but most places include this in their prices. When it is not included, particularly in hotels (the amount is 7 percent), it will be clearly marked.

There are no hard and fast rules for tipping, but the following guidelines should take some of the guesswork out of it all.

Restaurants	Round off the total or leave 5 to 10 percent, if you were pleased with the food and the quality of service
Bars	Round off the total or leave a little, whether you sit or stand
Hotel and airport porters	100–500ptas
Taxi	5 percent in general; 10 percent if it is a long trip and luggage is involved
Hairdressers	100–500ptas for everyone who worked on you

The only places bargaining is acceptable are markets and very cheap hotels—and then only if you are staying more than a few nights.

The Euro

The euro became the official currency of the eleven-nation European Union, of which Spain is a part, on January 1, 2000, but euro notes and coins will not be made available until January 2002, when they will be used alongside the national currencies until July 2002. At that point, the euro will become the sole legal tender for the European Union. Until then, travelers can continue to use national currencies (such as pesetas for Spain and francs for France), although you may start to notice prices being displayed in both the national currency and the euro. This is mainly for information and education purposes, to get people used to the new currency. During the transition, while businesses convert to euro pricing, consumers will be able to use euro traveler's checks in denominations of 50, 100, and 200 euros to pay for goods and services. Also during the transition, other traveler's checks can be cashed for local currency, in this case Spanish pesetas.

In *Cheap Eats in Spain,* all prices are in pesetas only.

PACKING

A man wrapped up in himself makes a very small bundle.
—*Benjamin Franklin*

My advice here is simple: Bring as little as possible because everything you pack you are going to have to carry. The best way to pack is to lay out everything you think you are going to need, and then put half of it back in the closet—then wait a few hours or another day if possible and put away half again as much. You will be glad you did this when you are schlepping your bag up six flights of stairs to a charming *hostal* where the elevator is out of service and will remain so during your entire stay. Coordinate your clothes around one color, leave expensive jewelry at home, and use every bit of space to its fullest: stuff your shoes, roll your sweaters and underwear, use plastic garment bags between layers to prevent wrinkling, and pack so things will not slip and slide to one end. Take clothes you would wear to any major metropolitan city. Short shorts, jogging outfits (worn when not actually jogging), and bare midriffs or chests, no matter what the temperature, will label you as a tourist. If you are traveling during the warm months, wear light cottons and comfortable shoes. Synthetics don't breathe and become uncomfortable in the heat. For winter visits, layering makes sense, and so does a lined raincoat, a set of silk long underwear, and a hat (70 percent of body heat goes out through your head). Whenever you go, don't forget an umbrella, an extra pair of walking shoes, a plastic bag for damp or dirty laundry, rubber flip-flops if you are staying in bathless rooms, a money belt you can wear under your clothes, an extra pair of prescription eyeglasses, and all your prescription medications.

Pack your toiletries and cosmetics in a waterproof bag. You only need one experience with the mess caused when the top of your shampoo or nail polish remover is blown off by airplane pressure changes to know what I am talking about.

Remember: You are not going to Mars, but to Spain, where every consumer product is available in a variety of price ranges. If you forget something or run out of toothpaste, you can get more. Besides, part of the fun of traveling is bringing back new things—why not a bottle of shampoo or a new shirt?

The following list of useful items is by no means exhaustive, but is one compiled over the years by a veteran traveler:

- A bar or bottle of bath soap. Many Cheap Sleeps in Spain do not provide soap at all, and if so, it is usually a sliver of something harsh.
- As many moist toilettes as you can fit and/or a bottle of antiseptic hand wash
- Sunscreen lotion
- Dictionary or phrasebook
- Portable radio with earphones
- For walkers, a pedometer to keep track of your miles, so you can impress your friends back home
- Photocopies of your passport, and any other important documents, which if lost or stolen would impede your trip
- A list of your credit card numbers, kept in as safe a place as your passport
- First-aid kit
- Sewing kit, with a pair of decent scissors
- A few wire hangers you can toss out at the end of the trip. You would be surprised at the lack, and condition, of hotel hangers.
- Rubber doorstop as a security measure
- For drip-dry laundries: rubber sink stop, blow-up hangers, clothesline with clothes pins or clothes pins you can hang up, and a small container of spot remover. Don't pack laundry soap, as it's cheap and readily available everywhere.
- Adapter plug for electrical appliances. Spanish current is 220V. With U.S. 110V appliances, you will also need a transformer.
- Suction hook for the back of the bathroom or bedroom door
- Suction-cup magnifying mirror
- Alarm clock
- Mosquito repellent
- Sunglasses
- Flashlight
- Something to read

SAFETY AND SECURITY

Violent crime against visitors in Spain is rare, but petty thievery and purse snatching, unfortunately, are not. The best way to avoid incidents is to use the same good-sense precautions you would in any city. Act purposeful. Don't look at maps at night or wander down dark streets. Spanish men often make comments at women who walk by; this macho male pastime is known in Spain as *piropo,* and while annoying, it is almost never a serious personal threat. Women should avoid public transportation late at night and use taxis instead.

All travelers know that carrying large amounts of cash and a fistful of credit cards is not just risky business but plain stupid. Spain has a bad reputation for its high rate of theft from tourists. According to the Card Protection Plan, no fewer than two hundred thousand credit cards and cash cards were recently stolen in Spain in a four-month period. In 1999, Barcelona was ranked Europe's worst city for card theft, Madrid number three. So it makes travel sense to use the hotel safe, exercise extreme caution, and use a moneybelt when you are out, keeping in it a photo I.D., a bare minimum of cash, and only one credit card.

Here are some other safety tips while traveling in Spain:

- Buy a Spanish morning newspaper, roll it up, and stick in under your arm. You will look more like a local.

- In a café or restaurant, never leave your purse on the floor or on the back of a chair. Hold it in your lap.

- If you carry a purse, wear a shoulder bag with the strap across your body and the bag pulled to your front. If you are wearing a fanny pack, wear it in front, or better yet, under your clothing.

- If you travel by car and have to leave your luggage in the trunk, use parking lots with attendants and never leave anything of value within sight.

- Don't flash cash by paying for things with large bills, and don't wear expensive jewelry.

- Do not participate in any street card or betting games. They are always setups where accomplices pretending to be passersby win all your money.

In addition, watch out in the following situations, which are deliberate tricks designed to rob you. Usually petty thieves are quite crude in their methodology, so forewarned is forearmed.

Street thieves often work in pairs or groups; usually one person asks you for something, bumps into you, or otherwise distracts you while a partner tries to grab your bag or wallet. This basic ruse has a dozen guises, so if someone approaches you too close for any reason . . . keep walking.

A person may offer you flowers on the street, ask you the time to distract you, or move in too close while indicating that you have a stain on your clothing; someone may bump you and hold onto you as if trying to break your fall. If you are driving and stopped at a red light, someone may tell you that you have a flat tire or a burning tire in order to get you out of the car. In all of these situations, be wary.

If you are robbed or attacked, report it to the police (*poner una denuncia*) immediately, or at least within twenty-four hours. You will need an official statement (*denuncia*) to make an insurance claim.

My final safety note has nothing to do with petty theft, but with your physical well-being. Don't stand too close to the curb, especially in Madrid. Buses shoot by at high speeds just inches from curbsides, and drivers are notorious for cutting corners—so stand back, please.

STAYING IN TOUCH

Fax

You can send a fax from most of the better hotels, but find out first what the hidden charges are—and I do mean hidden. I once sent a two-page fax and was charged a $20 "service fee" on top of the charge of the fax. It was my own fault because I had not inquired about any charges other than the cost to send the document. Make sure this does not happen to you. You can send a fax more reasonably from almost all main post offices. One page costs about 350 to 400ptas per page within Spain, around 950ptas to elsewhere in Europe, and up to 2,000ptas to other countries, including the United States. You can sometimes find cheaper rates at shops or offices that have a *Fax Publico* sign.

Email and the Internet

If you are staying in a hotel that has modem-ready rooms, it's easy enough to plug your laptop computer into the phone line and send email and use the Internet. Before you leave home, check with your Internet provider to find out if their services extend to Spain, and the costs. It might be easier, cheaper, and safer to leave the computer at home and go to an Internet café (*café internet*) and access the Internet for a few hundred pesetas per hour. Many of these cyber-cafés offer email services. There are also Internet businesses that rent time on computer terminals by the hour or half hour. Charges start around 600ptas for thirty minutes.

Regular Mail

Main post offices (*oficinas de correos*) in Barcelona, Madrid, and Seville are usually open Monday to Friday from 8:30 A.M. to 8:30 P.M., and on Saturday from 9 A.M. to 1 P.M. All the mail services are available and reliable. It is safe to post your mail in the yellow street postboxes (*buzones*) as well as at the post office directly. Airmail to the United States takes about a week or ten days. Stamps are sold at all post offices and at most *estancos* (tobacconist) shops that display the sign *Tabacos* (in yellow letters on a maroon background).

General delivery mail (*poste restante*) can be addressed to you c/o *lista de correos* anywhere in Spain that has a post office. This is not the fastest way to get mail, but it helps if your surname is written in capital letters and if you include the post code (zip code) in the address. It will be delivered to the city's main post office unless another one is specified in the address. To pick up your mail, take your passport. Here is how your address should read if someone is sending you mail to Barcelona.

Alexander SMITH
Lista de Correos
08080 Barcelona
España

If you have an American Express card, you can use the free client mailing services at all American Express offices in Spain. You will need your passport to pick up your mail. Check with American Express for the locations of their offices in Spain; the city sections in this book give the most central American Express offices.

Telephone

Spaniards love to hate their telephone company (*telefónica*). Rates are high, especially for long-distance calls, though it is about 15 percent cheaper to call after 10 P.M. and before 8 A.M. Monday to Friday, after 2 P.M. on Saturday, and all day Sunday and holidays. Street pay phones, which are painted blue, can be used for both local and international calls. They accept coins and/or phone cards (*tarjetas telefónicas*), and sometimes credit cards. You can buy the phone cards in 1,000 and 2,000ptas denominations at post offices or tobacco shops. You can also use public phones in bars, cafés, or hotels, but they are more expensive than the public phones. At all costs, you should not pick up the phone in your hotel room and make an international call. The hotel surcharge could be 100 percent of the cost of the call.

Domestic Calls

Regular Spanish telephone numbers have seven digits; these can be preceded by a city or area code, which always begins with 9 and consists of two or three digits. All the phone numbers in *Cheap Sleeps in Spain* include the two-digit city code. Madrid is 91, Barcelona is 93, and Seville is 95. You don't need to dial the city code to make a local call within the same city; just dial the seven-digit number. But if you are making a long-distance call in Spain, you do need to dial the area code of the city you're calling. Numbers beginning with 900 are free. For collect calls, dial 009; for directory inquiries, dial 003.

International Calls

The country code for Spain is 34. For calls to Spain from the United States, dial 011+34+the number of the hotel, including the city code (such as, 011-34-93 123 45 67 for Barcelona).

For calls from Spain to the United States without a credit card, dial 07, wait for a new dial tone, then dial the country code (1 for the U.S.), area code, and number. You can do this at a public phone with a prepaid phone card. To make an international collect call, dial 900 99 000 followed by the country code: to connect using AT&T, the U.S. country code is 11, MCI uses 14, and Sprint uses 13. This will get you through to an English-speaking operator. You can also get an English-speaking international operator in Spain by dialing 008 for calls within Europe, or 005 for the rest of the world. For international directory enquiries, dial 025; this costs 150ptas per call (approximately $1).

TIME

Spain is six hours ahead of Eastern Standard Time on the East Coast in the United States, and nine hours ahead of Pacific Daylight Time on the West Coast.

In general, the Spanish have a very relaxed attitude toward time, but those things in life that must happen on fixed schedules—such as buses, trains, soccer matches, bullfights, and theater performances—do so reliably. What is different is how the day is divided and used. The twenty-four-hour clock is used in Spain for official purposes, but not in casual, everyday conversation. The morning is *por la mañana* and the afternoon *por la tarde*. Business hours are flexible: Places stay open in the morning from 9:30 or 10 A.M. until 1:30 or 2 P.M., close for an afternoon siesta, and then reopen from around 5 p.m until 8 or 9 P.M. Major department stores are open all day Monday to Saturday and close late, around 9 P.M. The Spanish afternoon does not start at noon, but after the siesta at 4 or 5 P.M. and goes until 9 P.M. In the summer, life seems to move more than ever into the streets, where it is cooler. On Friday and Saturday nights, barflies are getting a second wind around 2 or 3 A.M., calling it quits after the first light of day.

TOURIST INFORMATION

United States, British, Canadian, or New Zealand citizens need only a valid passport to enter Spain.

Contact one of the Spanish tourist offices to have packets of information sent to you to help in your trip planning. Their website is www.okspain.org, and their toll-free telephone number is 888-OK-SPAIN. Below is a list of Spanish tourist offices in the United States.

New York
665 Fifth Avenue
New York, NY 10002
Tel: 212-265-8822

Los Angeles
8383 Wilshire Boulevard
Beverly Hills, CA 90211
Tel: 323-658-7188

Chicago
845 N. Michigan Avenue, Suite 915E
Chicago, IL 60611
Tel: 312-642-1992

Miami
1221 Brickell Avenue, Suite 1850
Miami, FL 33131
Tel: 305-358-1992

STANDARDS OF MEASURE—METRIC CONVERSIONS

Metric Conversions

	multiply by
inches to centimeters	2.54
centimeters to inches	0.39
feet to meters	0.30
meters to feet	3.28
yards to meters	0.91
meters to yards	1.09
miles to kilometers	1.61
kilometers to miles	0.62

Weight

ounces to grams	28.35
grams to ounces	0.035
pounds to kilograms	0.45
kilograms to pounds	2.20

Volume

U.S. gallons to liters	3.70
liters to U.S. gallons	0.26

Temperature

Centigrade to Fahrenheit	multiply by 1.8 and add 32
Fahrenheit to Centigrade	subtract 32 and multiply by 5/9

How to Use Cheap Sleeps in Spain

ABBREVIATIONS

The following abbreviations are used to denote which credit cards a hotel or shop will accept:

American Express	AE
Diners Club	DC
MasterCard	MC
Visa	V

ADDRESSES

Spanish addresses are written differently than in the United States. Look for the following:

Don Juan Aguilar
C/ de Santa Anna 7, 2° izq
14600 Madrid

This means that Don Juan Aguilar lives at number 7, Santa Anna Street, on the second floor, left side (izq, or *izquierda*). If you saw "2° dcha" (dcha, or *derecha*), it would mean the right side of the second floor, and "C" or "cto" (*centro*) would mean the center. When a building has no street number, usually because it is too big (like a train station), this is written s/n (*sin número*). Addresses in Barcelona are written in Catalan; see the Barcelona section for address terms in that language.

Alameda	Almd
Avenida	Av or Avda
Calle	C/
Callejón	Cllj
Camino	Cno
Carril	Cril
Carretera	Ctra or Ca
Glorieta	Gta
Pasaje	Pje
Pasillo	Pllo
Paseo	Po
Plaza	Pl or Pza
Puente	Pte
Ronda	Rda
Sin número (without number)	s/n

If there are several *hostales* or other business establishments in one building, the floor will be indicated, as well as the location on the floor.

2nd floor, 3rd floor, 4th floor	2°, 3°, 4°
Centro (middle)	C or cto
Derecha (right-hand side)	D or dcha
Izquierda (left-hand side)	I or izq
Interior/Exterior	Int/Ext

If you see the address written Apartado de Correos 510, or Apdo 510, that means the address is a post office box, not a street address.

In written addresses, the word *de* is often omitted from street names. For instance, C/ de Recoletos could be shortened to C/ Recoletos. Addresses in *Cheap Sleeps in Spain* give the full street name.

BIG SPLURGES

Some hotels covered in *Cheap Sleeps in Spain* fall into the Big Splurge category because of their higher prices. These hotels are included for those who have more flexible budgets, exacting tastes, or greater needs. Even though the prices are higher, the hotels all offer good value for your money. It is important to note that many hotels whose prices make them Big Splurges during the high season also offer significantly lower rates during the low season (from mid-November to mid-March, and July through August). In some cases, lower weekend rates are offered year-round. Whenever you are reserving at a more expensive property, remember to ask if any special discounts are being offered—you might be very pleasantly surprised. Throughout *Cheap Sleeps in Spain,* Big Splurge hotels are indicated by a dollar sign ($) to the right of the hotel name. The index lists all the Big Splurges in Barcelona, Madrid, and Seville.

STARS AND CATEGORIES

Spanish hotel accommodations are controlled by a government rating system that ranks them from no stars to five-star deluxe—but please bear in mind that you cannot judge a hotel or *hostal* by its stars. I have seen one-star hotels that are better in every respect than a three-star hotel a block away. The star rating system is concerned solely with the level of amenities offered: It takes into consideration such things as the location of the hotel in the building, whether or not it has a lift, a bar, the number of rooms with or without private facilities, the size of the reception room, and sometimes how many lights are in the room. The difference between a one-star *hostal* and a two-star *hostal* might be something as simple as an elevator. However, the ratings have nothing to do with cleanliness, decor, attitude of management, or views. In addition, each class of accommodation is rated using separate criteria, making it difficult to compare different types of establishments by their stars. My advice is to pay little attention to the star-rating system.

Spain has a wide variety of types of accommodations, all identified by signs outside their establishments, which are marked as follows, from least expensive on up:

F	*fondas*
CH	*casas de huéspedes*
P	*pensiones*
Hs	*hostales*
HsR	*hostal residencias*
H	hotels

Cheap Sleeps in Spain focuses on four main types: *pensiones, hostales, hostal residencias,* and hotels. The first three types can be granted up to three stars in the rating system, and hotels can be granted up to five stars; because of their higher price, four- and five-star hotels do not appear in this guide.

The differences among these types of accommodations is sometimes very slight; for instance, while establishments with a ground-floor entrance are usually classified as hotels, the same rooms with a third-floor entrance would most likely be classified as a *hostal* or *hostal residencia.* Pensiones tend to be very basic accommodations. Most *hostales* are family-run and have basic rooms, either with or without bathrooms; they are usually one or two floors above street level (and may or may not have an elevator), and they seldom serve breakfast. *Hostal residencias* are virtually the same as *hostales.* And hotels usually have better decorated rooms, each with a bathroom and more amenities—satellite TVs, air-conditioning, and so on—someone on the front desk who speaks English, and include breakfast.

RESERVATIONS

One of the most asked questions is: "Do I need reservations if I am only going to be in Barcelona (or Seville or Madrid) for a few days?" The answer is always yes, absolutely, *especially* if you are going to be in one of these cities for a short time. Do you really want to spend valuable vacation time hunting down accommodations in your price range only to find nothing available and subsequently be forced to pay more for a less-than-ideal location? It is not at all unusual for the best Cheap Sleeps in the central parts of these cities to be booked for weeks, sometimes even months, in advance. Today the best way to reserve is by fax or telephone; some places now use email and the Internet to make reservations; and you shouldn't even think about trying to make reservations by writing a letter. The chances of a hotel responding to an old-fashioned written request are about the same as the chances of a revival of the horse-and-buggy: virtually zero.

When making your reservation, keep in mind that in most hotels you pay for the room, not for the number of people in it. The exceptions to this are small doubles that are rented as singles, and doubles that have a sofa bed that can sleep one or two more people. A double sold as a single will cost more than a regular single, but less than a double, and it gets you a slightly better room with more space. It's a good deal if you can afford just a bit more. Double rooms are those with one double bed (*cama de matrimonio*), and they are usually smaller than those with twin beds (*camas gemelas*). If you ask for a room with a private bath, specify if you want a bathtub (*con baño privado*) or will settle for a shower (*con ducha*). Cheap Sleepers all know that a room with a double bed and a shower at the back of the hotel will usually cost less than one with twin beds and a bathtub that has a terrace or balcony at the front. But there are many exceptions to this rule in Spain, so always ask if a room with a view will be the same price as one facing the back.

When making your reservations, the following points should be covered.

1. The dates of the stay, time of arrival, and number of people in the party.

2. The size and type of rooms: double or twin beds, extra beds needed, adjoining rooms, suite.

3. The facilities needed: private toilet and shower or bathtub, or hall facilities, air-conditioning (an essential in the summer).

4. The location of the room: view, on the street, on the courtyard, with a balcony, quiet, inside room on the back of the hotel.

5. The rates: Always confirm the nightly rate and what it includes, such as the 7 percent IVA and/or breakfast.

6. Determine the amount of deposit required and the form of payment. Also inquire about the cancellation policy.

7. Request a written confirmation for both your reservation and your deposit, and carry this confirmation with you to the registration desk when you check in. You may have to prove there is a record of your reservation, or that you are not booked into the most expensive suite . . . or maybe that you are.

Email and Internet

Spain seems to be slowly joining the world of cyberspace, especially in three-star hotels and in those run by anyone under forty, but don't expect to find email and websites for the smaller *madre y padre* Cheap Sleeps in Spain. Whenever applicable, the hotel's email and Internet website have been given. In some cases the hotels subscribe to a general service rather than have their own website. While the concept is gaining ground, it is still in its infancy in comparison to what you routinely find in the States, and you can expect to run into some snafus.

Fax

If you and the hotel both have a fax number, this is the best way to make and confirm a reservation. To send a fax to Spain, use 011-34, then the fax number of the hotel, including the city code.

Telephone

For information on how to call Spain from the United States, or how to call within the country, see the "Staying in Touch" section, page 29. If you are calling for reservations, time the call during the hotel's weekday business hours to avoid talking to a night clerk who has no authority to make any kind of discounts, and who perhaps cannot even accept a telephone reservation from abroad. Before calling, write down all your requests and questions. Ask the hotel to send you a written confirmation (hopefully by fax), and you in turn will send them a confirmation of your conversation with them, outlining your reservation, needs, and requests. Be sure you note the time and date of your conversation and the name of the person who took your reservation. Keep a copy of all such correspondence and carry it with you to the hotel check-in desk.

Making Reservations in Spanish

If the hotel in question has no English-speaking staff, or you just want to try your luck with Spanish, here are a few simple phrases (also see the "Glossary of Spanish Words and Phrase," page 234).

"Do you speak English?"
¿Habla usted Inglés?

"I want to reserve a single/double/triple/suite for_____ people with/without a full bathroom/toilet/shower/for___nights."
Quiero reservar un cuarto con una/dos/tres camas/un appartamento para_____personas con/sin baño completo/servicios/una ducha/por___noches.

"I arrive on____and leave on_____."
Llego el____ y salgo el_____.

"Does the room have: a view to the street/courtyard/a balcony/terrace/air-conditioning/television?"
¿Hay: una vista a la calle/una vista adentro/un balcón/ una terraza/aire a condicionado/una televisión?

"How much does the room cost?"
¿Cuanto cuesta el cuarto?

"Does it include IVA/breakfast?"
¿Está incluido IVA/desayuño?

"Can I guarantee the reservation with my credit card?"
¿Puedo usar una tarjeta de crédito para guarantizar la reservación?

"Please send me a confirmation fax."
Favor de enviarme una confirmación via fax.

"Thank you very much."
Muchas gracias.

DEPOSITS

After making your reservation, most hotels will require a one-night deposit, but not always if you have been a guest there before. This is good insurance for both sides because it means you are guaranteed the room you want for the duration of your stay. The easiest way to handle a deposit is with a credit card. If the hotel does not take credit cards, there are other ways to handle the deposit. You can send an international money order in U.S. dollars. This is easy for you, since it saves you the hassle and expense of getting the money order in pesatas from your bank, but it means the hotel will probably have to pay a commission to convert it into pesetas. Most lower-priced Cheap Sleeps will not do this. They will insist on a deposit made out to them in pesetas. Check with your local bank to find out where you can obtain a foreign-currency money order.

If your local bank cannot provide you with a draft, then contact Ruesch International at 825 14th Street NW, Washington, D.C. 20005, or call 800-696-7990. This currency specialist offers a variety of services, and they have a number of branches in the States and abroad.

CHECKING IN/CHECKING OUT

When reserving, be *very* specific about the type of arrangements you want, get them confirmed in writing, take that confirmation with you to the hotel check-in, and then insist on what you requested when you arrive. Always ask to see the room before accepting it. If you are dissatisfied, ask to see another. It is *your* money, and you should get what you want. After accepting the room, reconfirm the rate and whether or not you will be eating the hotel breakfast (usually it's not a good Cheap Sleeping deal). If not, be sure the breakfast charge is deleted from your bill on a per-person, per-day basis. Also ask about telephone surcharges, air-conditioning charges, and any other hidden extras that might be unpleasant surprises at checkout.

The Spanish hotel day begins and ends at noon, and guests are expected to check out by noon and to check in between noon and 6 P.M. If you have an early-morning arrival flight, and you must have your room before noon, consider booking the room for the day before. Most hotels won't guarantee that your room will be ready before noon, and this will save you from having to hang out in the lobby or wander around in a jet-lagged daze while your room is made available. You should also notify the hotel if you know that you will be late. Even if you have put down a deposit and have a written confirmation, the hotel does not have to hold the room for you beyond 6 P.M. unless they have been advised that you will be arriving late.

If you need a late checkout, this is sometimes granted if the room is not needed immediately. However, in smaller establishments, maids don't work much past 2 or 3 P.M., and the owners of family-run establishments usually don't want to be cleaning rooms late in the day. Some hotels will charge you a day rate for a late checkout. If you are catching a late train or plane, most hotels will hold your luggage at no additional cost and allow you to wait in the lobby. In fact, if you are making some side trips, and do not want to take all the luggage you brought with you, many hotels will, for a nominal fee, store your luggage.

RATES: PAYING THE BILL

Hotel rates, the category of the accommodation, and the number of stars should be posted at every establishment, and the rates should state whether breakfast and taxes are included.

All the rates quoted in *Cheap Sleeps in Spain* are for full price and do not reflect any discounts or special deals. The listings do state, however, if lower off-season rates apply. These special rates can vary widely depending on the time of year, how busy the hotel is, the length of your stay, and, in some smaller hotels, if you pay in cash or by credit card. *No matter what category the hotel may be and no matter when you go, always ask for a discounted rate.* You never know when you will get lucky.

COMPLAINTS BOOK

If you are not happy with a sevice, particularly in a hotel or restaurant, you are entitled to ask for the *Libro de Reclamaciones*. This is an official complaints book for the customer's use, which is theoretically reviewed by local offficials during the year. Only use it when you feel you have been severely cheated, not for minor infractions.

BREAKFAST

Spanish hotel breakfasts are generally not good investments. You are much better off in every respect to go to the corner café, bar, or bakery and rub elbows with the locals over your coffee and toasted roll or sweet pastry. Most *hostales* and small hotels don't serve any breakfast at all. All three-star hotels offer some kind of breakfast—at least a Continental one, consisting of a glass of juice, a white roll, and a cup of strong coffee. Many larger hotels are now offering an overpriced buffet, which is rarely a good deal. It might make sense if you were planning to skip lunch, but remember, most Spaniards eat their main meal around 2 P.M., and dinner is late, usually after 9 P.M. If you do eat breakfast at your hotel buffet, please do not load your purse or sack with enough extra food to make a lunch or dinner picnic. This world-class cheap trick is never anything but a show of poor manners, and hoteliers have very low opinions of those who do it.

ENGLISH SPOKEN

All the listings in *Cheap Sleeps in Spain* tell you whether or not English is spoken. If you can dust off a few Spanish phrases, smile, and display goodwill, you will find that hotel staff will be warm and friendly and go out of their way to accommodate you. However, if you do not speak any Spanish at all, try to make sure someone at the hotel can speak some degree of English. While it is fun to practice your rusty Spanish on the street or in a bar, it is definitely not fun to be unable to communicate when making complicated reservations or when faced with a crisis.

SMOKING/NONSMOKING ROOMS

I wish I could tell you that Spaniards have embraced a healthy attitude and have reduced their smoking habit. If anything, it is on the increase. Everyone smokes . . . even pregnant mothers pushing baby strollers. Chances are excellent that the guests occupying the room before you were heavy smokers. Believe it or not, many maids also smoke—on the job. The pall and odor can be reduced somewhat if the room has bare hardwood or tile floors, few curtains, and easy-wash bedspreads, but exclusive, nonsmoking rooms are very, very scarce. It doesn't hurt to alert the hotel that you want a nonsmoking room, and perhaps the maid will open the window and spray some air freshener before you arrive. In *Cheap Sleeps in Spain,* whenever a hotel has nonsmoking rooms, it is boldly noted in the write-up. Otherwise, *buena suerte.*

FACILITIES AND SERVICES

A brief summary at the end of each hotel listing tells what facilities and services the hotel offers. Generally, the more facilities, the more money you will spend.

NEAREST TOURIST ATTRACTIONS

This section appears at the end of each hotel listing, and it tells you the major tourist attractions that are within a reasonable walking distance.

TRANSPORTATION

In the hotel listings for Barcelona and Madrid, the nearest metro stop is given. Seville has no metro system, and indeed, it is a small city that is best traveled on foot. It is beyond the scope of *Cheap Sleeps in Spain* to cover all the available buses and public transportation alternatives. However, in Barcelona and Madrid, the metro systems are inexpensive, safe, and easy to navigate, and you should not hesitate to use them.

MAPS

The maps in *Cheap Sleeps in Spain* are designed to help the reader locate the hotel and shop listings, but they are not meant to replace fully detailed street maps. If you plan on being in any of the cities for any length of time, I suggest you invest in a proper street map. In *Cheap Sleeps in Spain,* each city has separate maps for hotels and Cheap Chic shops, and each map has its own key. These map key numbers are repeated in the hotel and shop descriptions—they appear in parentheses to the right of the hotel or shop name. If an establishment does not have a number, it is located beyond the boundaries of the map.

BARCELONA

Barcelona . . . a Roman city, a Gothic city, a maritime city and a city of cosmopolitan pleasure. The odd thing is that none of them at first sight looks particularly Spanish.
—Kenneth Tynan, "Barcelona," 1959, in
Tynan Right and Left, *1967*

Barcelona, the heart, soul, and capital of Catalonia, dates back more than twenty-five hundred years when the Phoenicians and Carthaginians settled in the area and operated a commercial port. In the eleventh and twelfth centuries it grew into an important Mediterranean city, but the rapid economic expansion was stopped by the Napoleonic wars. In the early years of the twentieth century, social unrest and tension increased between the rich industrial barons and the working class, but not all was strife and conflict. These were also the years of *modernisme* (the Catalan version of Art Nouveau) and the rise Antoni Gaudí, Barcelona's most famous and brilliant Modernist architect. For those interested in Modernist Barcelona, there is the Modernist Route, *La Ruta del Modernisme,* that identifies fifty of the most important sites. The route begins near the foot of La Rambla at the Palau Güell and ends high above the city at the Park Güell, but no visitor should miss seeing Gaudí's magnificent, still-unfinished cathedral, La Sagrada Familia. The 1992 Olympic Games produced extensive changes to the city and set the stage for the grander expansions and renovations that continue today, especially along the waterfront. The old commercial Port Vell is now a huge entertainment complex, including the Maremagnum center (filled with designer shops and restaurants), the largest aquarium in Europe, an Imax cinema, the Museum of Catalan History, and the Marina Port Vell with more than 410 moorings. The beaches in the Olympic Village and at Port Olympic are the best and most popular in Barcelona.

Barcelona has its own Romance language, Catalan, as well as its own literature, folklore, customs, and personality. For its fifteen million annual visitors, the city is a breath of fresh air and perfectly compact, making it easy to explore on foot, especially along the picturesque streets of the Gothic Quarter. Barcelona is considered Spain's most cosmopolitan, forward-looking city, and certainly one of its richest. It's a museum lover's paradise, with a wide variety of high-quality collections guaranteed to keep visitors occupied for days. The Museu Picasso is Barcelona's most popular museum, but there is also a museum devoted to native son Joan Miró and the striking Museu d'Art Contemporani de Barcelona (MACBA).

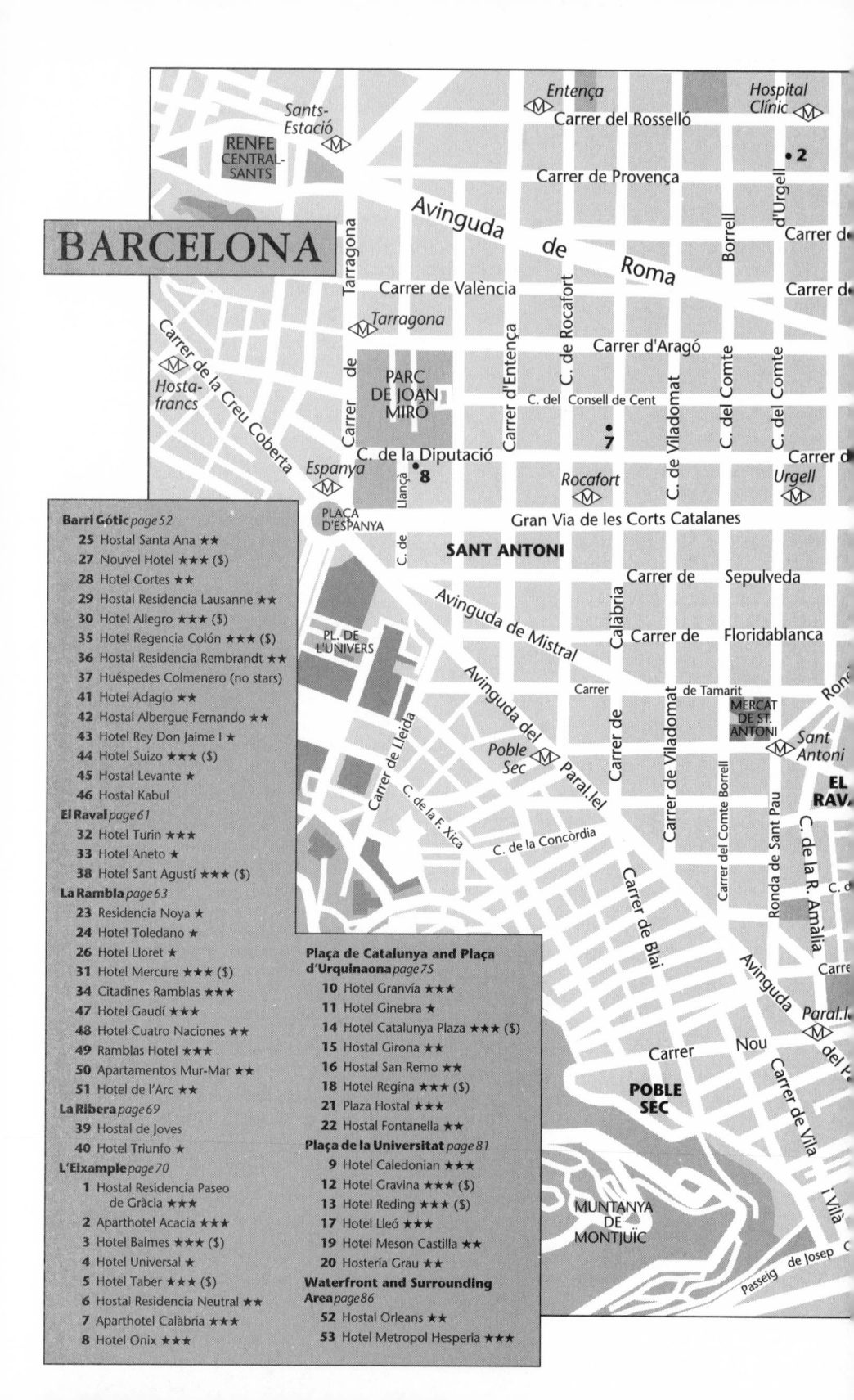

BARCELONA

Sants-
Estació Ⓜ

RENFE
CENTRAL-
SANTS

Entença Ⓜ
Carrer del Rosselló

Hospital
Clínic Ⓜ

• 2

Carrer de Provença

Avinguda

de

Roma

Carrer de

Carrer de València

Tarragona Ⓜ

Carrer d'Aragó

Carrer de

Carrer de la Creu Coberta Ⓜ

Hosta-
francs Ⓜ

PARC
DE JOAN
MIRÓ

C. del Consell de Cent

Espanya Ⓜ
C. de la Diputació

• 8

Llançà

PLAÇA
D'ESPANYA

Rocafort Ⓜ

• 7

Carrer d
Urgell Ⓜ

Gran Via de les Corts Catalanes

SANT ANTONI

Carrer de Sepulveda

PL. DE
L'UNIVERS

Avinguda de Mistral

Calàbria

Carrer de Floridablanca

Avinguda del Paral.lel

Carrer de Tamarit

MERCAT
DE ST.
ANTONI

Sant
Antoni Ⓜ

Poble
Sec Ⓜ

Carrer

Carrer de

EL
RAVA

Carrer de Viladomat

C. de la R. Amàlia

Carrer del Comte Borrell

Ronda de Sant Pau

C. d

C. de la Concòrdia

Carrer de Lleida

C. de la F. Xica

Carrer de Blai

Carrer

Nou

POBLE
SEC

MUNTANYA
DE
MONTJUÏC

Avinguda

Paral.l

del P

Carre

Carrer de Vila

i Vilà

Passeig de Josep C

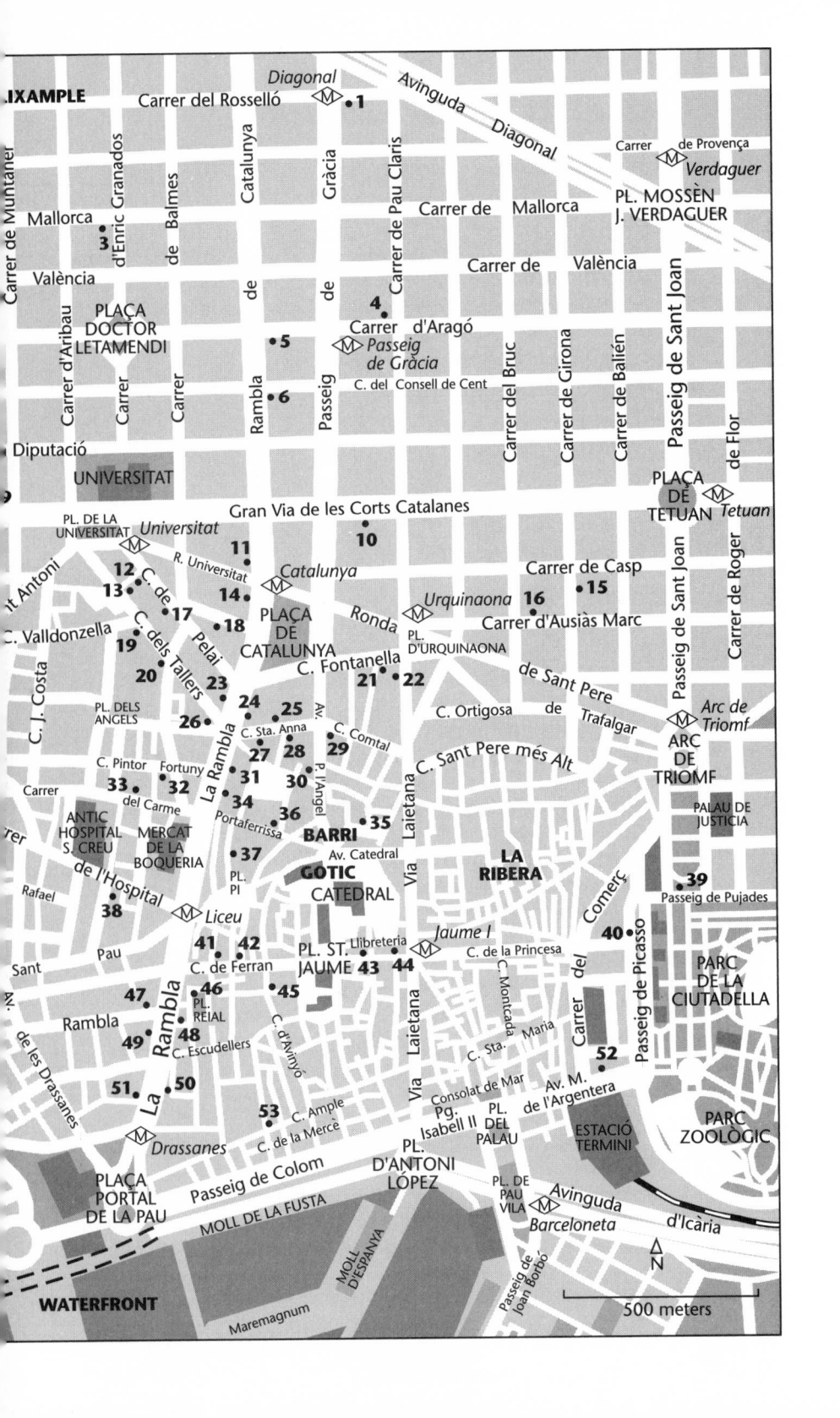

General Information

ADDRESSES

Barcelona addresses appear the same way as in the rest of Spain, but they are written in Catalan, which is also used in this section on Barcelona. Thus, an address written as C/ de Capella 9, 2°, means number 9, Capella Street, second floor. For a complete description of Spanish addresses, see "Addresses" under "How to Use *Cheap Sleeps in Spain*," page 33. The most common Catalan terms and abbreviations are as follows:

avinguda	avda
baixada	bxda
carrer	c/
passeig	pg
plaça	pl
passatge	ptge

BUSINESS HOURS

General business hours are from 9 or 10 A.M. to 1:30 or 2 P.M. and from 4 to 8 P.M. on Monday to Friday. On Saturday, especially during the winter and in tourist-free zones, many shops are only open in the morning. Banks and many government offices, including the post office, close for the day between 1:30 and 2 P.M. Large department stores and shopping malls stay open during the lunch hour, on a few selected Sundays throughout the year, and every Sunday in December. Food markets open between 7 and 8 A.M., and except for the central Boqueria Market on La Rambla, close around 2 P.M. The Boqueria stays open until around 8 P.M. The only food shops open on Sunday are pastry shops (*pastelerías*). Most museums are open on the weekends, but close for one day each week, usually Monday.

CLIMATE

Barcelona has a mild Mediterranean climate. Summers can be hot and humid with 30°C/ 85°F temperatures the norm. Winters are mild, and the rain falls mostly in October, November, March, and April. Humidity is always a factor because of the sea, and in the summer it can be very sticky and uncomfortable, while in the winter, although the temperature never drops too far, the air can be bone chilling.

CONSULATE

The American consulate is at Passeig de la Reina Elsenda de Montcada 23 on the outskirts of Barcelona; tel: 93 280 22 27; hours: Mon–Fri 9 A.M.– 12:30 P.M., 3–5 P.M. If the office is closed, there is an answering machine that will give you emergency contact numbers. There is no Canadian consulate in Barcelona.

DISABLED TRAVELERS

Disabled visitors to Barcelona fare better than in most other Spanish cities, thanks in a large part to the 1992 Olympics. An official guide to disabled transport is available from the transport information office at Metro Universitat; tel: 93 318 70 74. Wheelchair access points are shown on most public transportation maps. The official city organization for the disabled is the Institute Municipal de Disminüits, C/ Compt d'Urgell 240; tel: 93 439 66 00; hours: Mon–Fri 9 A.M.–2 P.M. Special minibus cabs adapted for wheelchairs can be ordered at Barnataxi; tel: 93 357 77 55. There aren't very many of them, so call well in advance to book your time. The fares are the same as for regular cabs.

DISCOUNTS

Barcelona Card

The Barcelona Card is a good deal, offering visitors a number of discounts at seventy of the city's points of interest, some museums, leisure venues, shops, restaurants, and on the Aerobús. The card is personal and nontransferable and can be purchased for durations of 24, 48, and 72 hours for around 3,500, 4,000, and 4,500ptas respectively, with reduced prices for children between the ages of six and fifteen. The card is available at the Centre d'Informació Tursime de Barcelona at Plaça de Catalunya and the Tourist Information office at the Barcelona Sants Railroad Station.

Barcelona Museum Ticket

Another money saver is the Museum Ticket, which is valid for three months for unlimited visits to six museums. There are no time restrictions, and the price depends on how many museums you wish to see. The tickets are available at participating museums. To visit all six museums, the ticket is 2,100ptas, while a percentage discount is taken off at each museum for other tickets. A four-museum ticket provides a 40 percent discount at each museum, three museums provides 30 percent, and two museums 20 percent. Children under four are free.

EMERGENCY NUMBERS

For information on where to go to seek medical treatment in a nonemergency situation, see "Medical Problems," page 47.

Medical Emergencies	061
Ambulance	93 329 9701, 93 300 2020
Dental Emergencies	93 415 99 22
Fire	080
Hospitals	93 441 06 00 (the Centre d'Urgències Precamps)

Pharmacies (24 hours)   010, 93 481 00 60
Poison   91 562 04 20
Police   091 (national), or 092 (local)

HOLIDAYS AND FESTIVALS

The names of the Spanish national holidays are given here in Catalan, plus those holidays and festivals celebrated only in Barcelona.

New Year's Day	*Cap d'Any*	January 1
Three Kings (Epiphany)	*Dia de Reis*	January 6
Easter	*Pasqua*	March/April
Good Friday	*Divendres Sant*	March/April
Easter Monday	*Dilluns de Pasqua Florida*	
Labor Day	*Festa del Treball*	May 1
Whitsun	*Dilluns de Pasqua Granada*	June 1
	Corpus Christi	June (Thursday after the eighth Sunday after Easter)
Summer Solstice	*Sant Joan*	June 24
Feast of St. John the Baptist	*Día de San Juan Bautista*	June 24
Feast of St. James the Apostle	*Día de Santiago Apóstol*	July 25
The Assumption	*L'Assumpció*	August 15
Catalan National Day	*Díada Nacional de Catalunya*	September 11
Our Lady of Mercy	*Festes de la Mercè*	September 24 (a weeklong festival)
Discovery of America	*Día de la Hispanitat*	October 12
All Saints' Day	*Tots Sants*	November 1
Constitution Day	*Día de la Constitució*	December 6
Immaculate Conception	*La Immaculada*	December 8
Christmas Day	*Nadal*	December 25
Boxing Day	*Sant Esteve*	December 26

LOST PROPERTY

At the airport, report any lost property to the Aviación Civil, or call airport information at 93 298 38 38.

If you lose something on public transportation, or in a taxi, contact the Servei de Troballes Ajuntament, Carrer de Ciutat 9; tel: 93 402 31 61; metro: Jaume I, 4; hours: Mon–Fri 9 A.M.–2 P.M. You can also call the city transport authority at 93 318 70 74.

There is no central office for lost property on a train, but you can contact the Atención al Viajero desk or Jefe de Estación office at the main station nearest to where your property was lost. Ask for *objectos perdidos*.

MEDICAL PROBLEMS

The best thing to do in an emergency is to go to the *urgències,* or casualty department, of any major hospital (see "Emergency Numbers," page 45, for immediate care). In the center of Barcelona, near the bottom of La Rambla, go to Centre d'Urgències Precamps, Avinguda de les Drassanes 13-15; tel: 93 441 06 00; metro: Drassanes, 3. This hospital deals only with emergencies. In L'Eixample, go to the Hospital Clínic, Carrer de Casanova; tel: 93 277 54 00; metro: Hospital Clínic, 5. For first aid, you can go twenty-four hours a day to Casc Antic, Carrer de Comtal 24; tel: 93 310 14 21, 93 310 50 98; metro: Catalunya, 1, 3.

Dr. Frances Lynd is a British doctor who is available on Wednesday from 3:30 to 6:30 P.M., or at other times by appointment, at the Centre Mèdic Assistencial Catalonia, Carrer de Provença 281; tel: 93 215 37 93; metro: Diagonal, 3, 5; hours: Mon–Fri 8 A.M.–8 P.M.

For alternative medicine (acupuncture, homeopathy, chiropractors, and so on) head to the Centre de Medicina Integral, Plaça Urquinaona 2; tel: 93 318 30 50; metro: Urquinaona, 1; hours: Mon–Fri 10 A.M.–1 P.M., 4–8 P.M.; closed in August. Some of the staff speak English.

For a full range of dental care, go to Carrer de Calàbria, 251; tel: 93 439 45 00; metro: Entença, 5; hours: Mon–Fri 9 A.M.–9 P.M., Sat 9 A.M.–2 P.M. They accept credit cards (DC, MC, V), and some English is spoken.

Pharmacies

Pharmacies are identified by a large green cross outside. Spanish pharmacies are similar to U.S. pharmacies and carry a large selection of over-the-counter medication for the usual variety of colds, headaches, and other discomforts. If in doubt, ask the pharmacist, who is always knowledgeable. General hours are Monday to Friday 9 A.M.–1:30 P.M., 4:30–8 P.M., Saturday 9 A.M.–1 P.M. At other times a duty pharmacy is open in the neighborhood. The pharmacies marked in blue are open continuously all day Monday to Saturday 9 A.M.–10 P.M., Sunday until 1:30 P.M. Pharmacies marked in red are open twenty-four hours a day.

MONEY

Banking hours are usually from 8 A.M. to 2 or 3 P.M. Monday to Friday; from October 1 to April 30, they are also open on Saturday from 8 A.M. to 1:30 P.M. All banks are closed on Sunday and on all holidays. Most banks readily accept traveler's checks (be sure to bring your passport), but often with high commission rates. The exchange offices scattered around the city *say* they offer commission-free transactions, but believe me, they do not. Thanks to their abysmally low rates they can afford to waive the commission. These are the money changers of last resort—do everything you can to avoid them.

American Express has two centrally located offices: La Rambla, 74; tel: 93 301 11 66; metro: Liceu, 3; and Carrer del Rosselló, 261; metro: Diagonal, 3, 5. Both are open Monday to Friday 9:30 A.M.–6 P.M., and the Rosselló office is also open Saturday 10 A.M.–noon.

Credit cards are accepted in most hotels, shops, and restaurants and many other services, including metro ticket machines. If you have a credit card emergency, contact one of these numbers, all of which have English-speaking staff and are open twenty-four hours a day.

American Express: card emergencies, 91 572 03 03; traveler's checks, 900 99 44 26

Diner's Club: 93 302 14 28, 91 547 40 00

MasterCard and Visa: 93 315 25 12

Wiring Money

Western Union is still one of the fastest and most reliable ways to have money sent to you from abroad. Have the sender in the United States contact a local office for details and prices. In Barcelona, they are at La Rambla 41; tel: 93 412 70 41; metro: Drassanes, 3; hours: Mon–Sat 9:30 A.M.–midnight, Sun 10 A.M.–midnight.

POST OFFICE

The main post office (*correu central*) is at Plaça Antoni López, facing the water at the end of Passeig de Colon; tel: 93 318 35 07; metro: Jaume I, 4; hours: Mon–Fri 8 A.M.–10 P.M., Sat until 8 P.M., Sun (limited services) 9 A.M.–2 P.M. Some branch offices close entirely in August. If all you need are stamps, save yourself the frustration of this huge office and buy them at a tobacconist (*estanco*). The *poste restante* (general delivery) address in Barcelona is:

> The recipient's name
> c/o Poste Restante
> 08080 Barcelona
> Spain

To pick up your mail, you will need to show your passport. If you have an American Express card, you can have mail sent to one of their offices, both of which are more convenient than the main post office. See "Money," page 47, for the addresses of the two American Express offices in Barcelona.

SAFETY AND SECURITY

Barcelona is a safe city and you can walk in most parts with confidence. Violent crime is rare, but purse snatching and pickpocketing does happen, especially around the lower end of La Rambla and Plaça Reial. As in any large city, certain basic precautions should always be taken. If you are robbed or attacked, report the incident immediately to the special Turisme-Atenció at Rambla dels Caputxins, 43; tel: 93 291 50 92; metro: Liceu, 3; hours daily 7 A.M.–10 P.M. This is a special service that has a multilingual staff to assist visitors in any kind of difficulty. Please see "Safety and Security" under "General Information," page 28, for general safety tips in Spain.

TELEPHONE

The country code for Spain is 34. The city code for Barcelona is 93. Numbers beginning with 900 are free. For collect calls, dial 009; for general information, directory inquiries, dial 003. For further information about making international calls and calling within Spain, see "Telephone," page 30.

There are two central *telefónica* offices: Rambla del Caputxins 88; metro: Liceu, 3; hours: daily 10 A.M.–11 P.M.; and in the main hall of Estacio de Sants; metro: Sants Estació, 3, 5; hours: Mon–Sat 8 A.M.–10 P.M., Sun and holidays 9 A.M.–10 P.M.

TOURIST INFORMATION

Barcelona City Hall Tourist Information Office
Barcelona City Hall, Plaça Sant Jaume
No telephone
Open: Mon–Sat 10 A.M.–8 P.M., Sun and holidays 10 A.M.–2 P.M.

Centre d'Informació Plaça Catalunya
Plaça de Catalunya, 17 (underground)
Tel: 93 304 31 34/5; hotel information 93 304 32 32
Metro: Catalunya, 1, 3
Open: Daily 9 A.M.–9 P.M.

This is the main tourist office in the city and has a full information service, money exchange desk, and hotel booking service. Branch offices are at Ajuntament, Plaça Sant Jaume; metro: Jaume I, 4; and at Barcelona-Sants Station, metro: Sants-Estació, 3, 5.

Centre d'Informació de la Virreina
Palau de la Virreina, Rambla de Sant Josep 99
Tel: 93 301 77 75
Metro: Liceu, 3
Open: Mon–Fri 10 A.M.–2 P.M., 4–8 P.M.

The city cultural department office has information on exhibitions, concerts, and theaters. It is the best place to buy tickets for events. In the same building is a bookshop with an extensive selection of books about Barcelona, some in English.

Palau Robert/Oficines d'Informació Turística
Palau Robert, Passeig de Gràcia, 107
Tel: 93 238 40 00
Metro: Diagonal, 3, 5
Open: Mon–Sat 10 A.M.–7 P.M., Sun until 2:30 P.M.

The Catalan government tourist information center is in a turn-of-the-century mansion. While its focus is on the whole of Catalonia, it does have city maps, and it's a worthwhile stop if you're planning any trips outside Barcelona.

Temporary Offices and Red Jackets

In the summer (June 25 to September 25), every day from 10 A.M. to 8 P.M. the Turisme de Barcelona opens this temporary booth located at La Sagrada Familia; it deals with everything a tourist might need to know, with the exception of hotel bookings. At the same time, multilingual information officers called "Red Jackets" in red uniforms roam the Barri Gòtic and along La Rambla and Passeig de Gràcia; they are there to answer any tourists questions.

TRANSPORTATION

Barcelona is an easy city to explore on foot, but there are times when other modes of transportation are necessary. The metro is fast and safe, but buses allow you to see where you are going. A car is a real nuisance in Barcelona, as parking is difficult, not to mention expensive, traffic jams can be daunting, speed limits are ignored, and road rage can run high. The only time to drive a car in Barcelona is when you are leaving town at the end of your stay.

Aerobús

There are three ways to go to and from Barcelona's Aeroport del Prat, which is twelve kilometers south of the city: by bus, train, or taxi. Probably the most convenient way is via the Aerobús, an air-conditioned bus that takes you to and from the airport every fifteen minutes from Plaça de Catalunya, Passeig de Gracia, and Plaça d'Espanya. From the airport, buses pick up outside all the terminals, and take about thirty minutes. A one-way ticket is around 550ptas. A combined three-day ticket for the Aerobús, bus, and metro is 2,000ptas; a five-day ticket is 2,400ptas. This ticket is only available at the airport.

Barcelona Bus Turistic

This tour bus is one of the best and easiest ways to discover the city. You are allowed to get on or off as many times as you like along a route that incudes Barcelona's most characteristic tourist and leisure areas. You can choose between a one- or two-day ticket that includes discount coupons for some attractions along the routes. Some of the buses are open double-deckers, which are great for getting the best panoramic views. The service operates from March 28 to January 6. The first bus leaves from the Plaça de Catalunya stop at 9 A.M., and the complete route lasts around two and a half hours, though you can make it an all-day excursion depending on how many times you get on and off. A one-day ticket costs 2,000ptas, a two-day ticket 3,000ptas. Look for bus no. 100.

Bus

If you want to see the city, and don't want to walk every inch of the way, hop on a city bus. The price is the same as the metro, and you can use tickets for both interchangably. City bus stops are easy to find; most go through Plaça de Catalunya, Plaça de la Universitat, and/or Plaça d'Urquinaona. You board through the front and get off in the middle or rear. Only single tickets can be bought on board. It is better to have a multiple-pass ticket or show your travel card (see "Metro" below).

Metro

Barcelona's subway is one of the best and most modern in Europe. The system's five lines can get you almost anywhere in the city, and the air-conditioned trains are comfortable. The system is clearly signed (lines are identified by color and number), and trains have automated station announcements and illuminated maps that indicate the direction of the train and the next station. You can buy single tickets, but if you are going to use the system at all, it makes better sense to buy a ten-ticket strip called a T1, or *tarjeta,* for around 800ptas, which you can use on both the metro and city buses. There are also one-, three-, and five-day travel cards valid on both the city buses and the metro, and these range from 600 to 2,000ptas. Metro hours are as follows: weekdays 5 A.M.–11 P.M.; Fridays and weekdays preceeding a holiday until 1 A.M.; midweek holidays 6 A.M.–11 P.M.; and Sundays 6 A.M.–midnight. Basic fare for a single ticket on the metro or bus is 150ptas, and each trip costs the same no matter how far your travel. Tickets can be purchased at most city-center metro stations.

Taxis

Taxis are plentiful and uniquely efficient, since they share the same public transportation lanes the buses use, thus avoiding most of the heavy traffic. Barcelona taxis are easy to recognize because they are all black and yellow. They are available if the green *lliure* (or *libre*) light is on. All taxis have a minimum fare that increases with every kilometer traveled. Make sure that when you start your trip the meter is turned on and that you only pay whatever it says, plus any luggage or other extras such as night trips or calling for a taxi. Taxi fares from the airport to central Barcelona should run around 3,000ptas, including an airport supplement. If you are using a taxi from the airport, be sure you use one already in the queue, not a private driver who walks up to you inside the airport. Taxi fares are posted in every taxi, and cheating is rare. If you need a receipt, ask for *un rebut, si us plat* (in Catalan), or *un recibo, por favor* (in Spanish). Special minibus taxis adapted for wheelchairs can be ordered from Barnataxi at 93 357 77 55. Ask for a *Taxi Amic.*

Trains

The main station for trains within Spain is Estació Sants, Plaça dels Països Catalans, s/n; metro: Sants-Estació, 3, 5; hours: Mon–Fri 8 A.M.–8 P.M.; Sat–Sun and holidays 8 A.M.–2 P.M.; and in summer, daily 8 A.M.–8 P.M. For general train information, call 93 490 02 02. For international information and reservations, call 93 490 11 22.

Hotels in Barcelona by Area

BARRI GÒTIC

The Barri Gòtic, or Gothic Quarter, was settled more than two thousand years ago and is the oldest part of the city. Barely half a mile square, it didn't assume its current character—with its storied, almost haunted, narrow twisting streets—until the Middle Ages. Anchoring the maze are the city's two Gothic cathedrals: Santa María del Mar and the thirteenth-century Catedral de Barcelona, a magnificent church that has twenty-nine chapels. The fourteenth-century Santa María del Mar was popular with shipbuilders and sailors, including Christopher Columbus, who attended a Mass of thanksgiving here when he returned from his first visit to the New World. The quarter is famous for its antique shops, art galleries, and booksellers along Carrer de la Palla and Carrer del Banys Nous. In the eleventh century, there was a thriving Jewish ghetto on Carrer del Call and Carrer del Banys Nous, and in Roman times the center of life in the quarter was the Plaça de Sant Jaume, which still houses the government offices for Barcelona. On Sunday morning the *Sardana,* the Catalan folk dance, is performed by anyone who feels like it in the great square in front of the cathedral. Every Thursday the same square is filled with antique dealers, and in the winter, it's lined with stalls selling Christmas decorations.

HOTELS

($) indicates a Big Splurge

HOSTAL ALBERGUE FERNANDO ★★ (42)
C/ de Ferran 31
47 rooms, 40 with shower or bath and toilet

All the laminated furniture is new, and so are the dorm rooms, which house from three to eight snoozers per night. The divided male and female dorms offer travelers a bed, period. You will have to bring your own towels and soap, though you can rent a towel for 200ptas, and you'll have to hope no one pilfers your luggage while you sleep because there are no lockers. The double and triple rooms include soap and towels, are clean, and everything matches, but the bathroom lights are of such low wattage that I think Cheap Sleepers should forget all about private facilities and relish saving money by using the well-lighted hall facilities.

ENGLISH SPOKEN: Yes

FACILITIES AND SERVICES: Lift

NEAREST TOURIST ATTRACTIONS: Can walk to everything in the Barri Gòtic, on La Rambla, and along the water-front

TELEPHONE AND FAX
93 301 79 93

INTERNET
www.barcelona-on-line.es/
fernando

METRO
Liceu, 3

CREDIT CARDS
MC, V

RATES
Single (dorm) 1,750ptas, double 5,600ptas, triple 6,500ptas, 200ptas for a towel in dorm rooms, BYO soap, taxes included

BREAKFAST
Not served

HOSTAL LEVANTE ★ (45)
Baixada de Sant Miquel 2, 2°, off C/ d'Avinyó
40 rooms, 15 with shower or bath and toilet

For a family-run choice in the center of things, it is hard to beat this Cheap Sleep on the second floor of the first telephone building in Barcelona. If you walk up from the ground level, you can appreciate the original woodwork still decorating the hallways. The hostel has been run for over forty years by Manuel Ibánez, who is now ably assisted by his daughter, Lourdes, and to some extent by her two active young boys. If you reserve a double, ask for No. 205, which has thrift-store furniture, a tiled floor, and the only balcony in the place. To watch television, you must journey to the lounge, and to make a telephone call, you will have to stand in the hall. No, it is not fancy, but cheap and clean it definitely is.

ENGLISH SPOKEN: No, but French is

FACILITIES AND SERVICES: Lift to hostel, but must use stairs inside, free use of office safe

TELEPHONE
93 317 95 65

FAX
93 317 05 26

METRO
Liceu, 3, or Jaume I, 4

CREDIT CARDS
MC, V

RATES
Single 3,000ptas, double 4,500–5,500ptas, taxes included

BREAKFAST
Not served

NEAREST TOURIST ATTRACTIONS: Center of Barri Gòtic and within easy walking distance to La Rambla and the waterfront

HOSTAL RESIDENCIA LAUSANNE ★★ (29)
Av. del Portal de l'Angel 24, 1°
17 rooms, 3 with shower or bath and toilet, 4 with a sink and shower

TELEPHONE
93 302 11 39
METRO
Catalunya, 1, 3
CREDIT CARDS
None
RATES
Single from 2,500ptas, double 4,300–6,800ptas, triple 6,200–7,400ptas, taxes included
BREAKFAST
Not Served

The rooms at the Lausanne are welcoming and comfortable for a two-star *hostal residencia*. Most of them have their original tiled floors, a few have balconies, and several overlook a pretty interior courtyard. Room 201 is a bathless double with a courtyard view; it's furnished with one table and a folding chair to complement the double bed. Number 202 is the biggest room. The balcony has a street view, the bathroom is private, and the mustard yellow bedspreads not too hard to live with. Room 206, another double with private facilities, has a small window, two folding chairs, and a multicolored tile floor to offset the white stucco walls. None of the rooms have a television, but you can watch TV with your fellow guests in the lounge, which has a carved and painted ceiling. On warm days, guests congregate on the summer terrace to swap tips about what to see and do in Barcelona.

ENGLISH SPOKEN: Yes

FACILITIES AND SERVICES: Lift, free use of office safe

NEAREST TOURIST ATTRACTIONS: Easy access to everything in the Barri Gòtic and along La Rambla

HOTEL RESIDENCIA REMBRANDT ★★ (36)
C/ de Portaferrissa 23
28 rooms, 8 with shower or bath and toilet

TELEPHONE AND FAX
93 318 10 11
METRO
Liceu, 3
CREDIT CARDS
None, cash only
RATES
Single 3,200–4,200ptas, double 4,900–6,700ptas, triple 6,400–7,900ptas; suite: for two 8,400ptas, for three 10,000ptas, for four 16,000ptas; apartment for 2–6 from 10,000ptas per day, monthly rates on request; all rates are plus 7 percent tax
BREAKFAST
450ptas per person

If it is charm and character you want, the Rembrandt has it in spades. Granted, it is a little frayed around the edges, but it has soul, and that is what sets this Cheap Sleep apart. The charm starts the minute you walk up the steep steps and are greeted by the lovely English-speaking receptionist, Dana, who handles everything with style and grace. It is obvious that the owner, whose paintings you see hanging throughout the hotel, has a sense of artistic style, which is also on display in each of the individually decorated rooms. The suite is naturally the best room, thanks to its fireplace, TV, and very nice bathroom. Room 15, which used to belong to the owner's daughter, opens onto a flower- and plant-filled courtyard, fitted with a table and chairs. The room itself has an upholstered armchair and a bathroom with a circular tub that is perfect for long bubble baths. I like No. 23, a corner, beamed room with two of almost everything: windows, balconies, chairs, and bedside tables, as well as a wash basin trimmed in gold tiles. Number 1 is a bright corner choice that is large enough for a sofa, chair, and wardrobe, but for the moment is bathless. Room 19 has a private bathroom, a sunny balcony, and matching curtains and spreads on twin beds. Number 4 has a pretty tiled floor, twin beds, and a shower in the corner, but there isn't even enough room for a chair, and No. 28 is an old, bathless room on the back with an interior view. Breakfast, if you opt for it, is served in the mosaic-tiled patio in the summer or inside in the dining room, which (except for the suite) has the only television set in the hotel.

The hotel also has an apartment located a few blocks away that can accommodate up to six people. When I saw it, students were living in it, each with his own messy area staked out. Despite the overwhelming clutter, I could see that the apartment had great appeal, provided you don't mind the sixty-six-step climb to reach it, and the fact that there is no telephone.

ENGLISH SPOKEN: Yes, very well

FACILITIES AND SERVICES: Fans available (400ptas per day), free office safe, TV in suite, desk open from 9 A.M.– 11 P.M.

NEAREST TOURIST ATTRACTIONS: Easy access to everything in the Barri Gòtic, along La Rambla, and the waterfront

HOSTAL SANTA ANA ★★ (25)
C/ de Santa Anna 23
15 rooms, 3 with shower or bath and toilet

The Santa Ana is run by Maria Pampin, her two daughters, Sonia and Yolanda, and their three cats: Fernando, Amelio, and Curro. It has only fifteen rooms located up a flight of stairs, and is not exactly a plush Cheap Sleep. However, it is a clean one, and room prices won't put a big dent in your budget. If you insist on your own bathroom, there are three rooms that have them, including No. 203, a double with a balcony that overlooks an inside courtyard. Otherwise, you will save money by using the well-kept hall facilities and reserving the bathless No. 202, which has a terrace and can sleep four in bunk beds.

TELEPHONE
93 301 22 46

METRO
Catalunya, 1, 3

CREDIT CARDS
None, cash only

RATES
Single 2,600ptas, double 4,100–6,100ptas, triple 6,100ptas, tax included

BREAKFAST
Not served

ENGLISH SPOKEN: Yes

FACILITIES AND SERVICES: Free use of office safe

NEAREST TOURIST ATTRACTIONS: Can walk along La Rambla and to the Barri Gòtic, near the big El Corte Inglés department store

HOTEL ADAGIO ★★ (41)
C/ de Ferran 21
38 rooms, all with shower or bath and toilet

TELEPHONE
93 318 90 61

FAX
93 318 37 24

METRO
Liceu, 3

CREDIT CARDS
AE, DC, MC, V

RATES
Single 7,700ptas, double 9,700ptas, triple 12,400 ptas, plus 7 percent tax

BREAKFAST
Continental included

If a two-star hotel is on your horizon, this one is lower priced than much of its competition. The focus here seems to be on business travelers who expect the basics (such as a satellite television) in a comfortable room and someone at the front desk who speaks English and can take messages. You will have it all in Room 401, a twin-bedded choice that overlooks the street. The furniture would be perfect in any student dorm, but at least the spreads match, the hardwood floor is clean, and there is a picture over the beds and lamps beside them. The television is perched so high on the wall you will probably have to watch it lying flat on your back in bed. The polished gray-tiled bath has a good mirror, nice tub, and a hair dryer. Towels are thin. The multipurpose lobby doubles as a reception area and morning breakfast room. Changing art exhibitions featuring local artists add color and interest.

ENGLISH SPOKEN: Yes

FACILITIES AND SERVICES: Air-conditioning, direct-dial phones, hair dryer, lift, office safe (400ptas per day), satellite TV

NEAREST TOURIST ATTRACTIONS: Everything in the Barri Gòtic, easy walk to the waterfront and along La Rambla

HOTEL ALLEGRO ★★★ (30, $)
Av. del Portal de l'Angel 17
74 rooms, all with shower or bath and toilet

TELEPHONE
93 318 41 41

FAX
93 301 26 31

EMAIL
cataloni@hoteles-catalonia.es

INTERNET
www.hoteles-catalonia.es

METRO
Catalunya, 1, 3

CREDIT CARDS
AE, DC, MC, V

If the Allegro looks like a palace, that's because it once was. Built in 1872 by the Rocamora family, the historic building underwent a massive renovation in 1998, and is now one of the most stunning three-star hotel choices in Barcelona. Because it is a listed architectural site, certain features have been beautifully preserved, most notably the facade and the impressive interior marble staircase and floors. A new glass dining room and lobby bar are welcome additions to the public areas. A royal blue and golden yellow color scheme has been used throughout the hotel and bedrooms, creating a serene sense of unity and contemporary style. The rooms are spacious, with the latest in bathroom fixtures. Number 221 has a balcony and a sitting area large enough to accommodate a sofa bed and chair. Number 207 is a large, quiet choice with a sunny balcony, and the good news is that the hotel has twelve other rooms just like it. Finally, the hotel's location couldn't be better— close to the top edge of the Gothic Quarter, the famed La Rambla, and many excellent Cheap Eats restaurants, and only a few minutes' walk from the elegant boutiques and shops that line the streets above Plaça de Catalunya.

ENGLISH SPOKEN: Yes

FACILITIES AND SERVICES: Air-conditioning, bar, conference room, direct-dial phone, hair dryer, laundry service, lift, minibar, restaurant, room service, room safe (300ptas per day), satellite TV

NEAREST TOURIST ATTRACTIONS: Shopping, La Rambla, Barri Gòtic

RATES
Single 22,000ptas, double 24,000ptas, triple 27,000ptas, plus 7 percent tax

BREAKFAST
Buffet 1,300ptas per person

HOTEL CORTES ★★ (28)
C/ de Santa Anna 25
43 rooms, all with shower or bath and toilet

The Hotel Cortes occupies a favorable location close to almost everything on a visitor's itinerary in Barcelona. It is no more than a five- to fifteen-minute walk in any direction to the Gothic Quarter, along the length of La Rambla, and in the other direction, to the boutique-lined shopping streets of Passeig de Gràcia, Carrer de Pau Claris, and Rambla de Catalunya. The rooms are nothing special, decorated in the basic, Motel 6 style— that is, functional but without personality. Number 306 is one of the best twins, with two windows letting in plenty of light, a desk, and a luggage rack. Number 108 is a double with a pink bathroom, which has good counter space and a separate toilet. Unless No. 107 has been repainted and the peeling ceiling in the bathroom fixed, I would avoid it. The hotel has a restaurant open to the public that offers a 10 percent discount to hotel guests. The food matches the hotel: functional.

ENGLISH SPOKEN: Yes

FACILITIES AND SERVICES: Bar, direct-dial phone, laundry service, lift, office safe (250ptas per day), restaurant (10 percent discount for hotel guests), TV

NEAREST TOURIST ATTRACTIONS: An easy walk to the Barri Gòtic, La Rambla, and L'Eixample

TELEPHONE
93 317 91 12

FAX
93 302 78 70

METRO
Catalunya, 1, 3

CREDIT CARDS
AE, DC, MC, V

RATES
Single 6,500ptas, double 10,700ptas, triple 14,500ptas, tax included

BREAKFAST
Continental included

HOTEL REGENCIA COLÓN ★★★ (35, $)
C/ dels Sagristans 13/17
55 rooms, all with shower or bath and toilet

TELEPHONE
93 318 98 58
FAX
93 317 28 22
METRO
Catalunya, 1, 3, or Jaume I, 4
CREDIT CARDS
AE, DC, MC, V
RATES
Single 9,800–13,000ptas,
double 16,400ptas, extra bed
3,500ptas, plus 7 percent tax
BREAKFAST
Buffet 1,200ptas per person

All rooms face out at the Regencia Colón, the three-star sister hotel to the more luxurious four-star Hotel Colón. Of course, at the Hotel Colón you can have a room facing the dramatic Barcelona cathedral square, but smart Cheap Sleepers know that, since the Regencia Colón is only a half block or so away, they can get the same view by walking to the square themselves and enjoying all the activity from the comfort of an umbrella-shaded café chair. The Regencia Colón is an older hotel, but still nicely maintained and staffed. When booking, request a renovated room on the second, fourth, or fifth floors. Five of these rooms are doubles with cathedral views. If you want more space, ask for No. 561, a larger twin choice with a table and two chairs, full closet with drawers and hanging space, and a bright bathroom with plenty of sink area and its own window. Solo Cheap Sleepers will like No. 552, with its coordinated wall and bed coverings, cushioned chair, and enclosed stall shower. It also can be joined to the room next door, an attractive feature if you are traveling with older children.

ENGLISH SPOKEN: Yes

FACILITIES AND SERVICES: Air-conditioning, direct-dial phone, hair dryer available, laundry service, lift, minibar, parking (2,200ptas per day), restaurant for breakfast and light lunch, free office safe, room safe (200ptas per day), satellite TV

NEAREST TOURIST ATTRACTIONS: As central as you can get, Barri Gòtic, La Rambla

HOTEL REY DON JAMIE I ★ (43)
C/ de Jaume I 11
30 rooms, all with shower or bath and toilet

TELEPHONE AND FAX
93 310 62 08
METRO
Jaume I, 4
CREDIT CARDS
AE, DC, MC, V
RATES
Single 4,650ptas, double
6,850–7,200ptas, plus
7 percent tax
BREAKFAST
Not served

The Hotel Rey Don Jamie I has a pivotal location next to the Plaça de Sant Jaume that puts Cheap Sleepers within easy access to everything in the Barri Gòtic, including a large number of recommended Cheap Eats. While this is a one-star hotel—so you cannot expect the works—each room is spotless and has its own bathroom, and many have balconies overlooking the busy street below. Room 304 has whitewashed walls, mustard yellow curtains, and a balcony. The blond furniture consists of a double bed with a brown spread, two chairs, and a wardrobe with drawers. The bath is tiny, the towels acceptable. A better choice is No. 212, a double with a built-in armoire, desk, luggage rack, and bathroom with a tub and shower plus plenty of sink space to spread out your toiletries.

ENGLISH SPOKEN: Yes

FACILITIES AND SERVICES: Direct-dial phones, lift, free use of office safe

NEAREST TOURIST ATTRACTIONS: Centrally located near the Barri Gòtic, La Rambla, and the waterfront

HOTEL SUIZO ★★★ (44, $)
Pl. de l'Ángel 12, off C/ de Jaume I
50 rooms, all with shower or bath and toilet

Hotel Suizo is part of the Gargallo Group, a national chain of three- and four-star hotels in Spain. This means that guests can expect a certain level of quality and service, and the hotel succeeds as a typical midcity hotel with a multilingual staff that caters to small groups and business travelers. This is a busy street, so noise will be part of your daily, and nightly, life if you opt for a front-facing room with a balcony. All the white-walled rooms are created equally: They have dark, laminated, burled walnut built-ins, bedside lights, one chair, one step stool, and a tiled bathroom with an assortment of toiletries. The only rooms I would definitely avoid are the eight or nine that have no windows, only skylights. Their redeeming feature is that they are quiet, but you would have to stand on something to see outside. There are two restaurants: one a casual cafeteria that serves breakfast and light snacks, and the other a more formal restaurant that I found dreary.

ENGLISH SPOKEN: Yes

FACILITIES AND SERVICES: Air-conditioning, bar, conference room, direct-dial phone, hair dryer in some rooms (and available by request), laundry service, lift, minibar, cafeteria and restaurant for all meals, room safe (250ptas per day), TV

NEAREST TOURIST ATTRACTIONS: Close to everything in Barri Gòtic, Museu Picasso, Museu Textil, La Rambla, and the waterfront

TELEPHONE
93 310 61 08

FAX
93 315 04 61

METRO
Jaume I, 4

CREDIT CARDS
AE, DC, MC, V

RATES
Single 12,500ptas, double 16,500ptas, triple, 22,000ptas, suite 24,000ptas, plus 7 percent tax

BREAKFAST
Continental 1,000ptas per person, buffet 1,500ptas per person

HUÉSPEDES COLMENERO (no stars, 37)
C/ de Petritxol 12, 2°, north of Plaça del Pi
7 rooms, 2 with shower or bath and toilet

TELEPHONE
93 302 66 34

METRO
Liceu, 3

CREDIT CARDS
None, cash only

RATES
Single 2,000–3,200ptas, double 5,000–6,000ptas, triple 6,000–7,000ptas, tax included

BREAKFAST
Not served

Seven rooms, two with baths, in a second-floor walk-up on one of the more interesting streets in the Gothic Quarter (and located across the street from one of the best pastry shops in town) pretty much sums up Rosa Aliaga's cozy Cheap Sleep in Barcelona. True, you will have to climb the steps of the marble stairway to reach the door of the pension, but you will be rewarded with small, clean rooms that display a mélange of vintage furniture. I like No. 1, a single with its own bathroom and a plant-filled balcony overlooking the street. Number 2 is a bathless double, but the hall facility is just outside the door and will probably be used only by you. It has a pair of marble-topped bedside tables, and a direct view of the street and of Xocoa, which is the only place you should head for breakfast, and not just because Rosa does not serve it. Xocoa is my favorite pastry shop, with a bakery on one side and a chocolate shop on the other, and it's open every day, enticing you with its beautiful windows filled with magnificent sweet temptations (see *Cheap Eats in Spain*).

ENGLISH SPOKEN: Very limited, but the owner speaks French

FACILITIES AND SERVICES: None

NEAREST TOURIST ATTRACTIONS: Everything in the Barri Gòtic, an easy walk down La Rambla to the waterfront

NOUVEL HOTEL ★★★ (27, $)
C/ de Santa Anna 18-20
69 rooms, all with shower or bath and toilet

TELEPHONE
93 301 82 74

FAX
93 301 83 70

METRO
Catalunya, 1, 3

CREDIT CARDS
AE, DC, MC, V

RATES
Single 12,200ptas, double 17,900ptas, minisuite or triple 22,000ptas, plus 7 percent tax

BREAKFAST
Buffet included

Built in 1917, a year before the Ritz was completed in Paris, the Nouvel is a beautiful example of the rich Spanish *modernista* style of architecture so famous in Barcelona. The owner, Gabriel Mercadal, has painstakingly restored the hotel and its restaurant to its former glory, making it one of the best hotels for the money in this part of the city. Many rooms have beautiful wrought-iron balconies, high ceilings, and their original tile floors. Those in the back, with no balconies and no views, are more modern and a bit quieter. Room 492 is a sunny twin with a *Rear Window*-style view from the balcony; there are two chairs, a desk, marble floors, and a decent bathroom. For an increase in space and ambience, reserve No. 121, the twin-bedded minisuite, which has a comfortable sitting area, a bathroom with a Jacuzzi, a double mirrored wardrobe, and a view to the pedestrian-only street in front of the hotel. By contrast, No. 122 is the smallest single, but still nice, thanks to its view of the street. You will sacrifice a view in No. 135, but it is a larger single with a nice bathroom.

ENGLISH SPOKEN: Yes

FACILITIES AND SERVICES: Air-conditioning, bar (planned), conference room, direct-dial phone, hair dryer, laundry service, lift, restaurant, free office safe, room safe (250ptas per day), one handicapped bathroom, satellite TV

NEAREST TOURIST ATTRACTIONS: Close to Plaça de Catalunya, Barri Gòtic, and La Rambla

EL RAVAL

El Raval is a diverse, multicultural area that was home to many immigrants and refugees in the years between the two world wars. Today it is a blue-collar neighborhood and home to the fabulous Mercat de la Boqueria, as well as to lots of interesting, small workshops and supply stores (such as a place that sells only shoelaces). The area experienced something of a face-lift for the 1992 Olympics in Barcelona.

HOTELS

Hotel Aneto ★	**61**
Hotel Sant Agustí ★★★ ($)	**62**
Hotel Turin ★★★	**63**

($) indicates a Big Splurge

HOTEL ANETO ★ (33)
C/ del Carme 38, 1°
27 rooms, all with shower or bath and toilet

Cheap Sleepers in Barcelona take note: The Hotel Aneto is a one-star hotel with more features for the money than you will find in the majority of one-star picks, let alone many two-star choices. What are these good features? First, the rooms are fully air-conditioned. Second, there is a lift. Third, the rooms come equipped with a direct-dial phone and a TV. And finally, the prices include both breakfast and the 7 percent IVA. On the downside, the instant, prepackaged breakfast is

TELEPHONE
93 301 99 89, 93 310 90 64

FAX
93 301 98 62

METRO
Catalunya, 1, 3, or Liceu, 3

CREDIT CARDS
AE, DC, MC, V

RATES
Single 5,500ptas, double 8,000ptas, tax included

BREAKFAST
Prepackaged Continental
breakfast included

hardly the stuff of gourmet dreams, consisting of instant coffee, cocoa, or a tea bag and a cellophane-wrapped pastry. Another drawback is that there is no safe, and English is definitely limited. If you can live with these limitations, ask for a room with a view of the square below; you will be rewarded with a clean, light space with matching bedspreads, desk and luggage space, tile floors, and inset marble sinks in the bathrooms.

ENGLISH SPOKEN: Limited

FACILITIES AND SERVICES: Air-conditioning, direct-dial phone, lift, TV

NEAREST TOURIST ATTRACTIONS: Central location near La Rambla, Plaça de Catalunya, and Barri Gòtic

HOTEL SANT AGUSTÍ ★★★ (38, $)
Plaça de Sant Agusti 3, corner C/ de l'Hospital
77 rooms, all with shower or bath and toilet

TELEPHONE
93 318 16 58
FAX
93 317 29 28
INTERNET
cartur@redestb.es
METRO
Liceu, 3
CREDIT CARDS
AE, DC, MC, V
RATES
Single 11,500ptas, double 15,500ptas, triple 18,500ptas, suite 19,000ptas, plus 7 percent tax
BREAKFAST
Buffet included

History pervades this area: The street dates from the first century when it was the principal road out of Barcelona, and the seventeenth-century building originally was the Sant Augustin convent. In 1849 it became a hotel that weathered gracefully until its radical renovation in 1992, just in time to cash in on the Olympics. Fortunately, only good things can be said about the renovation, which preserved the heart and soul of the graceful building by keeping the lovely arches on the first floor and many of the beamed ceilings through-out the rest of the hotel. A very attractive bar overlook-ing the leafy Plaça de Sant Agustí adds even more charm. Almost all of the rooms are nice, but I think the most interesting are Nos. 401-408, which are on the top floor and have pitched windows that afford some views. I also like No. 363, with hardwood floors, two windows, and two balconies. For a sunny twin, request No. 345 with a rooftop vista and good closets. There are three rooms that have bathrooms fitted for handicapped guests, three more that are family-sized, and several on the lower floors with balconies overlooking the square. The only ones on my reject list are No. 343, an inside viewless room, and No. 220, with the oldest bathroom in the hotel.

ENGLISH SPOKEN: Yes

FACILITIES AND SERVICES: Air-conditioning, bar, confer-ence room, direct-dial phone, hair dryer, rooms for handicapped guests, laundry service, lift, some minibars, room service, room safe (200ptas per day), radio, satellite TV

NEAREST TOURIST ATTRACTIONS: La Rambla, Barri Gòtic

HOTEL TURIN ★★★ (32)
C/ del Pintor Fortuny 9-11
59 rooms, all with shower or bath and toilet

The modern, identically outfitted rooms are impersonal yet clean, functional but filled with the usual three-star perks. Each one is spacious enough to allow you to live comfortably without crawling over beds and suitcases to get to the closet or out the door. The older-style bathrooms have shelves, a tray of complimentary toiletries, and some of the best towels in Barcelona. Rooms on the back are light and quiet and have views of apartment buildings, allowing you a peek into the everyday life of the people living there. In the morning, a buffet breakfast is served in a brick room with framed pictures of Spanish caricatures on the walls. Rounding out the experience is the pleasing desk staff.

ENGLISH SPOKEN: Yes

FACILITIES AND SERVICES: Air-conditioning, bar, direct-dial phones, laundry service, lift, parking (2,000ptas per day), restaurant (lunch only, otherwise for groups by prior arrangement), free room safe, satellite TV, piped-in room music

NEAREST TOURIST ATTRACTIONS: La Rambla, Barri Gòtic

TELEPHONE
93 302 48 12

FAX
93 302 10 05

EMAIL
hotelturin@icab.es

METRO
Catalunya, 1, 3

CREDIT CARDS
AE, DC, MC, V

RATES
Single 11,000–14,000ptas, double 16,500ptas, triple 17,500ptas, quad 18,500ptas, plus 7 percent tax

BREAKFAST
Buffet 1,300ptas per person

LA RAMBLA _____

One of the first things visitors do in Barcelona is to stroll along La Rambla, the wide, mile-long boulevard that has been the heart and spirit of the city for centuries. Beginning at the top end by Plaça de Catalunya and leading to the waterfront, the tree-lined thoroughfare actually is five separate streets strung together, starting with Rambla de Canaletes, Rambla dels Estudis, Rambla de Sant Josep, Rambla dels Caputxins, and finally Rambla de Santa Mònica. La Rambla bisects the middle of the old city and is filled with historic and artistic monuments, but its main charm lies in the surge of humanity who meet here daily, sit at umbrella-shaded cafés, and slowly meander by the dozens of colorful flower sellers, bird stalls, portrait painters and caricaturists, newsstands selling everything from international newspapers to hard-core porn, and the buskers, human statues, puppeteers, dancers, and musicians hustling for your change. Not to be missed is the most colorful market in the city, the Mercat de la Boqueria at Rambla de Sant Josep 85-89, where animated sellers offer every type of fresh produce, meat, fish, and cheese imaginable. For a typical Barcelona breakfast, stop at the zinc counter near the entrance and order a *café con leche* and the Catalan specialty *pa amb tomaquet*—a thick slice of bread rubbed with fresh tomato and topped with slices of Serrano mountain ham.

HOTELS

OTHER OPTIONS
Residence Hotels

($) indicates a Big Splurge

HOTEL CUATRO NACIONES ★★ (48)
Rambla dels Caputxins 40
47 rooms, all with shower or bath and toilet

TELEPHONE
93 317 36 24
FAX
93 302 69 85
EMAIL
h4n@h4n.com
INTERNET
www.h4n.com
METRO
Liceu, 3
CREDIT CARDS
AE, DC, MC, V
RATES
Single 6,500ptas, double 8,500ptas, triple 11,000ptas, plus 7 percent tax

The hotel dates from 1849, and for years was considered Barcelona's best. Now well past its prime and stellar reputation, it offers simple, clean, charm-free rooms, but only travelers who won't be bothered by the round-the-clock fun and merrymaking that takes place on the busy Ramblas should consider them. Besides being clean, rooms come with a bidet in the bathroom, luggage racks, mosaic-tiled floors, and air-conditioning, a godsend in Barcelona when the temperature soars . . . or the noise on the street below reaches a crescendo.

ENGLISH SPOKEN: Yes

FACILITIES AND SERVICES: Air-conditioning, bar, direct-dial phone, hair dryer available, laundry service, lift, office safe (150ptas per day), satellite TV

NEAREST TOURIST ATTRACTIONS: La Rambla, Barri Gòtic

HOTEL DE L'ARC ★★ (51)
Rambla de Santa Mònica 19
46 rooms, all with shower or bath and toilet

Three or four years ago the Hotel de l'Arc was a run-down hostel. Now it is a renewed and recommendable Cheap Sleep, on the lower part of La Rambla near the waterfront. The forty-six rooms are sizable and spotlessly clean. If you want to escape the incessant noise from pedestrians along La Rambla, book a room at the back. From No. 402, a twin with pink floral tile accents in the bathroom, you will face a fire escape, but what you sacrifice in a view will be made up in a restful night's sleep. Number 401 promises a double brass bed and two reasonably comfortable chairs in a spacious, tile-floored room, again with no view but with the promise of a better night's sleep than in those facing front. Then again, if you want to be front and center for all the La Rambla action, you will like No. 301, a double with a mirrored backdrop behind the bed and a plain but serviceable bathroom.

ENGLISH SPOKEN: Yes

FACILITIES AND SERVICES: Air-conditioning in some rooms, bar, conference room, hair dryers in some rooms, laundry service, lift, free office safe, satellite TV

NEAREST TOURIST ATTRACTIONS: La Rambla, waterfront, Barri Gòtic

HOTEL GAUDÍ ★★★ (47)
C/ Nou de la Rambla 12
73 rooms, all with shower or bath and toilet

Directly across the street from the hotel is Gaudí's Palau Güell, built between 1886 and 1888 as a residence for Antoni Gaudí's patron, Eusebi Güell. Daily tours of the Palau Güell allow visitors to view the fortresslike building, which has its lavish wooden ceilings, stone pillars, and many of the original pieces of furniture still in place. There are sweeping views over the city from the roof terrace, which is ringed with imaginatively decorated chimneys.

The hotel takes its decorating cue from the Palau Güell, especially in the marble-tiled lobby with a Gaudíesque waterfall nestled against the staircase. The large

---

BREAKFAST
Buffet 550ptas per person

TELEPHONE
93 301 97 98, 93 301 41 04,
93 317 05 37

FAX
93 318 62 63

INTERNET
www.madeinspain.net/
hotelesbarcelona/arc

METRO
Drassanes, 3

CREDIT CARDS
AE, MC, V

RATES
Single 7,500ptas, double
10,700ptas, extra person
3,500ptas, plus 7 percent tax

BREAKFAST
Continental 800ptas per person,
buffet 1,000ptas per person

TELEPHONE
93 317 90 32

FAX
93 412 26 36

EMAIL
gaudi@hotelgaudi.es

INTERNET
www.hotelgaudi.es

METRO
Liceu, 3

CREDIT CARDS
AE, DC, MC, V

RATES
Single 10,000–12,500ptas,
double 12,500–15,500ptas,
triple or suite 15,500–
18,500ptas, plus 7 percent tax
BREAKFAST
Buffet 1,000ptas per person

sitting room, with cigar brown leather seating, has a breakfast area beyond it with interesting abstract murals and watercolors. The side street location, less than a block from La Rambla, is just far enough away from all the noisy action to ensure some degree of quiet. The rooms are modern, with built-ins that allow more actual living space. A few Cheap Sleepers might be put off by the ugly brown spreads and curtains in some, or they may wonder where the chairs are in others. No one, however, can fault the cleanliness in every room. Many, like No. 423, have sunny terraces with wraparound views of the Palau Güell and beyond to the mountains. Number 316 also has a terrace, but it doesn't have the same exceptional view.

ENGLISH SPOKEN: Yes

FACILITIES AND SERVICES: Air-conditioning, bar, direct-dial phone, hair dryer, laundry service, lift, parking (2,000ptas per day), room safe (400ptas per day), satellite TV

NEAREST TOURIST ATTRACTIONS: Across the street from Gaudí's Palau Güell, La Rambla, Barri Gòtic, the waterfront

HOTEL LLORET ★ (26)
Rambla de Canaletes 125
52 rooms, all with shower or bath and toilet

TELEPHONE
93 317 33 66
FAX
93 301 92 83
METRO
Catalunya, 1, 3
CREDIT CARDS
AE, MC, V
RATES
Single 6,000ptas, double
8,300ptas, triple 9,300ptas,
quad 10,300ptas, tax included
BREAKFAST
Buffet 450ptas per person

The sixty-five-year-old hotel is on the first floor of a grand old building at the Plaça de Catalunya end of La Rambla. Facing La Rambla are two main sitting areas with broken-in leather sofas and armchairs. Breakfast is served on marble-topped tables in a pretty dining room with Art Deco ceiling fixtures; it also has a collection of black-and-white photos of La Rambla around the turn of the nineteenth century, which shows that even then selling colorful songbirds was a viable occupation. The larger-than-average rooms offer good value, good housekeeping, and furnishings that vary from nondescript modern to rustic, country-style copies. Bathrooms have those half-tubs with a wide step that can double as a seat if you want to sit while rinsing off with the handheld shower hose.

ENGLISH SPOKEN: Yes

FACILITIES AND SERVICES: Air-conditioning, direct-dial phone, lift, free office safe, TV

NEAREST TOURIST ATTRACTIONS: La Rambla, shopping, Barri Gòtic

HOTEL MERCURE ★★★ (31, $)
Rambla dels Estudis 124
80 rooms, all with shower or bath and toilet

From its excellent post on La Rambla, the Hotel Mercure is well suited for the Big Splurge traveler who wants both maximum comfort and value for money. The worldwide Mercure group of hotels commands a loyal following who appreciate the nonsmoking rooms, the luxurious suites and superior doubles with Jacuzzis, and the tastefully color-coordinated rooms. The second floor has been painstakingly restored and is where I will reserve my next room, perhaps No. 208, a quiet superior twin overlooking a private garden. I also like No. 416, a standard double with a balcony overlooking La Rambla. The beautiful bathroom has a combination shower and tub, good sink space, and enough light to see what you are doing. If you are lucky enough to occupy Suite 515, you will enjoy a bright sea green, sponge-painted entry, a large room with recessed lighting, a king-size bed, a round table with four chairs, and a window view of La Rambla. The hotel is perfectly positioned within easy walking distance of excellent shopping and everything La Rambla and the Gothic Quarter have to offer.

ENGLISH SPOKEN: Yes

FACILITIES AND SERVICES: Air-conditioning, bar, conference room, direct-dial phone, hair dryer, laundry service, lift, minibar, parking (2,200ptas per day), nonsmoking floor, room safe (300ptas per day), satellite TV, Jacuzzis in superior rooms

NEAREST TOURIST ATTRACTIONS: La Rambla, Barri Gòtic

TELEPHONE
93 412 04 04
FAX
93 318 73 23
EMAIL
montecarlobcn@abaforum.es
METRO
Catalunya, 1, 3
CREDIT CARDS
AE, DC, MC, V
RATES
Single 10,500–16,600ptas, double 17,500–20,600ptas, club room 24,200ptas, suite 27,000ptas, plus 7 percent tax
BREAKFAST
Buffet 1,500ptas per person

HOTEL TOLEDANO ★ (24)
Rambla de Canaletes 138
17 rooms, all with shower or bath and toilet

The Toledano is a hard-core Cheap Sleeping choice on La Rambla near Plaça de Catalunya. It is a handy location near this transportation hub: The Blue Aerobús leaves from Plaça de Catalunya, as does the metro and almost every major bus in the city. And you can take care of all your shopping needs, from food to fashion, at the enormous El Corte Inglés department store. The typically pared-down rooms are also budget priced and clean, but have worn carpets and walls in need of repainting or repapering. Some of the Formica-topped furniture has nicks, and the closets are certainly not designed to please

TELEPHONE
93 301 08 72
FAX
93 412 31 42
EMAIL
toledano@idgrup.ibernet.com
INTERNET
http://fast.to/hotel_toledano
METRO
Catalunya, 1, 3
RATES
Single 3,900–4,200ptas, double 5,600–7,200ptas, triple 8,900ptas, quad 10,000ptas, plus 7 percent tax

BREAKFAST
Not served

fashion mavens. The Hostal Residencia Capitol is also owned by the Toledano, but it is not recommended.

ENGLISH SPOKEN: Yes

FACILITIES AND SERVICES: Direct-dial phone, lift, free office safe, satellite TV

NEAREST TOURIST ATTRACTIONS: La Rambla, shopping, Barri Gòtic

RAMBLAS HOTEL ★★★ (49)
Rambla dels Caputxins 35
70 rooms, all with shower or bath and toilet

TELEPHONE
93 301 57 00

FAX
93 412 25 07

METRO
Liceu or Drassanes, 3

CREDIT CARDS
AE, MC, V

RATES
Single 12,500ptas, double 14,600ptas, extra person 5,000ptas, plus 7 percent tax

BREAKFAST
Buffet included

A mirrored elevator brings guests to the second-floor reception area, which has polished tile floors, a bar with rattan-backed stools, purple barrel chairs around four tables, an upright piano, and windows overlooking La Rambla. The breakfast room is lined with photos of Gaudí's most famous Barcelona landmarks. The seventy modern rooms are above average with good bathrooms, space, views, and innerspring mattresses. Single Cheap Sleepers will like No. 702, which has a sunny view of the city and blond furnishings. It hasn't much personality, but all the basics are here, including luggage space and a nice bathroom. Number 811 is another sunny room that can sleep up to three. It has only one chair in the room, but there are two chairs and a table on the balcony, which provides a view of Barcelona and La Rambla.

ENGLISH SPOKEN: Yes

FACILITIES AND SERVICES: Air-conditioning, bar, conference room, hair dryer available, laundry service, lift, minibar, room safe (400ptas per day), satellite TV

NEAREST TOURIST ATTRACTIONS: La Rambla, Barri Gòtic, the waterfront

RESIDENCIA NOYA ★ (23)
Rambla de Canaletes 133, 3°
15 rooms, none with shower or bath and toilet

TELEPHONE
93 301 48 31

METRO
Catalunya, 1, 3

CREDIT CARDS
None

RATES
Single 2,200–2,400ptas, double 3,800–4,200ptas, extra person 2,000ptas, tax included

BREAKFAST
Not served

The best rock-bottom Cheap Sleep on La Rambla is the Residencia Noya. Your budget won't get a workout here, but you will, every time you hike up the steep marble stairway to the third-floor location. Forget ruffles and flourishes, but the rooms are habitable and some facing La Rambla have little balconies. The communal bathrooms are kept clean by the owner, Adela Gil, who is so nice and helpful that you will almost forget that she doesn't speak much English.

ENGLISH SPOKEN: Very little

FACILITIES AND SERVICES: Free office safe

NEAREST TOURIST ATTRACTIONS: La Rambla, shopping, moderate walk to Barri Gòtic

LA RIBERA

The dominant attractions of La Ribera are the Parc de la Ciutadella and the Museu Picasso. The Parc was built in 1887 on the ruins of an old military arsenal and is the largest open green space in Barcelona. It contains the zoo, the Botanic and Modern Art Museums, the Catalan Parliament, and lovely fountains and ponds. The Museu Picasso, which displays a fascinating collection of the artist's earliest paintings, drawings, watercolors, and pastels, is in one of a succession of palaces dating from the Middle Ages that line the Carrer Montcada.

HOTELS
Hotel Triunfo ★   **69**

OTHER OPTIONS
Youth Hostels
Hostal de Joves   **98**

HOTEL TRIUNFO ★ (40)
Passeig de Picasso 22 (just beyond C/ de la Princesa)
20 rooms, all with shower or bath and toilet

Hotel Triunfo is across the street from the Parc de la Ciutadella, the zoo, and several other museums, which is appealing to many Cheap Sleepers who don't mind otherwise being on the edge of things in order to save on accommodation costs. Amenities are slim, but so are the prices. Many of the clean, recently redone rooms, including all of the singles, also have balconies facing the Parc. All are cheerfully done with blue floral quilted spreads, air-conditioning, a television, and a private bathroom with a half-tub and handheld shower. Given the nicer alternatives, I would not book No. 17, since it has a dismal view.

TELEPHONE AND FAX
93 315 08 06

CREDIT CARDS
AE, DC, MC, V

METRO
Arc de Triomf, 1

RATES
Single 6,100ptas, double 9,100ptas

BREAKFAST
Not Served

ENGLISH SPOKEN: Yes

FACILITIES AND SERVICES: Air-conditioning, direct-dial phone, lift, office safe, radio, TV

NEAREST TOURIST ATTRACTIONS: Across the street from the Museu de Geologia in the Parc de la Ciutadella, walking distance to the Barri Gòtic and the waterfront

L'EIXAMPLE

The splendor of the Barcelona bourgeoisie at the turn of the century is reflected in the beauty of the buildings and streets of L'Eixample, which has the largest concentration of Modernist architecture in the world. *Modernisme,* the Catalan variety of Art Nouveau, is reflected throughout the area in countless shopfronts, doorways, stained-glass windows, and, of course, in the great buildings of the foremost architect of the movement, Antoni Gaudí. The privileged area of L'Eixample, known as the "golden square," is also where you will find the highest concentration of art galleries, beautiful boutique shops, and fine restaurants.

HOTELS

OTHER OPTIONS
Residence Hotels

($) indicates a Big Splurge

ASTORIA HOTEL ★★★ ($)
C/ de París 203, at the corner of C/ d'Enric Granados
117 rooms, all with shower or bath and toilet

TELEPHONE
93 209 83 11; toll-free in the U.S., Utell 800–448-8355

FAX
93 202 30 08

EMAIL
info@derbyhotels.es

INTERNET
www.derbyhotels.es

METRO
Diagonal, 3, 5

CREDIT CARDS
AE, DC, MC, V

An impressive entry with four pillars supporting a dramatic ceiling mural of three dolphins sets the discreetly elegant tone of the Astoria Hotel, located in a residential quarter of Barcelona. To the left of the entry is a sitting room with comfortable green leather sofas and chairs as well as a dining room with two brass chandeliers that highlight the hand-painted blue irises on the wall. A circular marble stairway leads to marble-floored hallways lined with gold mirrors and framed oil and watercolor paintings. The normal singles and doubles are very nice, but I recommend upgrading to one of the stunning suites or studios. In Suite 727, you have your own black-and-white-tiled sitting room with its own terrace and television set. Just off the large, double-windowed bedroom is a dressing area with two wardrobes, a minibar, and room safe. The bathroom has two sinks, a bidet, and a deep bathtub with a shower. Monogrammed towels and plenty of sink space complete the sophisticated picture. The single and double studios with private terraces are also in great demand, even though you are required to walk up a few stairs to reach them. Finally, if you do reserve a regular double, ask for No. 527, which is a twin-bedded room with an entry with a sofa, extra luggage space, a desk, good closet space, and a view of the street. Single Cheap Sleepers should avoid No. 520, which has only one window with opaque pebbled glass. Why? The window opens onto an interior well with no view of anything but cement walls.

ENGLISH SPOKEN: Yes

FACILITIES AND SERVICES: Air-conditioning, bar, conference room, direct-dial phones, hair dryers in most rooms (or available by request), laundry service, lift, minibar, parking (2,350ptas per day), pets allowed, free room safe in some rooms, free office safe, satellite TV

NEAREST TOURIST ATTRACTIONS: Must use public transportation

RATES
Single 13,150–17,900ptas, double 21,250ptas, suite 24,200ptas, plus 7 percent tax

BREAKFAST
Buffet 1,500ptas per person

HOSTAL RESIDENCIA NEUTRAL ★★ (6)
Rambla de Catalunya 42, corner of Consell de Cent
32 rooms, all with shower, 20 also with toilet

The Hostal Residencia Neutral opened during World War I, and for business reasons the owner wanted to declare to the world that he was "neutral" about the outcome. The thirty-two-room pick is still aptly named, as it is a nondescript, neutral, and economical choice in a neighborhood not well known for anything that even hints at the word *budget*.

From the lounge, guests can walk out to a small roof terrace that has great views of the wide avenue below. Many of the rooms also have views and retain their original multicolored mosaic-tiled floors. Other than the painted ceiling in the breakfast room, I saw nothing else that puts the hotel into any category but neutral. Besides being clean and cheap for the area, the rooms have enough space to allow for actual living. Those on the back are quiet but dark, a few have ugly cigar-colored spreads, and those with only a shower have it

TELEPHONE
93 487 63 90

FAX
93 487 40 28

METRO
Passeig de Gràcia, 3

CREDIT CARDS
MC, V

RATES
Single 3,350ptas, double 5,600–5,900ptas, triple 7,200ptas, quad 8,200ptas, plus 7 percent tax

BREAKFAST
Continental 500ptas per person

stuck in a corner of the room. The receptionist, Fernando, speaks excellent English and is very pleasant and helpful to everyone. In my opinion, he is reason enough to stay here.

NOTE: The Hotel Universal, page 74, is under the same ownership.

ENGLISH SPOKEN: Yes

FACILITIES AND SERVICES: Direct-dial phones, fans, lift, room safe (200ptas per day)

NEAREST TOURIST ATTRACTIONS: Elegant shopping, *modernista* buildings

HOSTAL RESIDENCIA PASEO DE GRÀCIA ★★★ (1)
Passeig de Gràcia 102, 2°
33 rooms, all with shower or bath and toilet

TELEPHONE
93 215 58 28

FAX
93 215 37 24

METRO
Diagonal, 3, 5

CREDIT CARDS
AE, DC, MC, V

RATES
Single 6,800ptas, double 8,600ptas, triple 11,800ptas, plus 7 percent tax

BREAKFAST
Continental 300ptas per person

For a Cheap Sleep in a luxurious part of Barcelona, book a top-floor room here with a sweeping terrace view of the city and the hills beyond. One of the best of these is No. 308, with twin beds and good light. The other rooms, which are scattered on several floors, are comfortably furnished and have city views. Number 101 on the sixth floor has a large balcony where you can sit on a bus-stop-type bench and admire the view. The old bathroom has a pedestal sink and a window. The hotel appeals to older, international guests who have been coming to Barcelona for years and remember the *hostal residencia* in its heyday, when guests arrived with trunks and stayed for months at a time.

ENGLISH SPOKEN: Yes

FACILITIES AND SERVICES: Air-conditioning, direct-dial phones, lift, free office safe, TV

NEAREST TOURIST ATTRACTIONS: Gaudí's Casa Milà, other *modernista* buildings, La Sagrada Família (twenty-five-minute walk)

HOTEL BALMES ★★★ (3, $)
C/ de Mallorca 216
100 rooms, all with shower or bath and toilet

TELEPHONE
93 451 19 14; toll-free in the U.S., Utell 800-448-8355

FAX
93 451 00 49

EMAIL
info@derbyhotels.es

INTERNET
www.derbyhotels.es

METRO
Passeig de Gràcia, 3

Comfort and service are the hallmarks of this Big Splurge hotel in the middle of L'Eixample. Built in the early 1990s, the hotel displays modern good taste throughout. Marble and copper pillars are reflected in the mirrors of the turquoise, Art Deco–theme bar. Copper is used again with the steel along the curved stairway that leads downstairs to the skylighted dining room, which has linen-covered tables overlooking an interior atrium. Three duplex rooms have their own terraces, and all the backside rooms on the second through sixth floors overlook a small swimming pool. All the rooms are decorated in monochromactic shades of beige accented by plain brown-and-white-striped spreads and curtains. The rooms all have desk space, simulated wooden floors, and marble bathrooms with good light, mirrors, and complimentary toiletries. As you can imagine, management is on its toes, from the front desk staff, which includes a bellboy, to the platoon of uniformed maids.

ENGLISH SPOKEN: Yes

FACILITIES AND SERVICES: Air-conditioning, bar, direct-dial phone, hair dryers in most rooms (or available by request), laundry service, lift, minibar, pets accepted, restaurant, room service, free room safe, small swimming pool, satellite TV

NEAREST TOURIST ATTRACTIONS: Expensive residential/business area, good shopping, *modernista* architecture

CREDIT CARDS
AE, DC, MC, V

RATES
Single 14,000–20,500ptas, double 22,700ptas, suite 25,500ptas, plus 7 percent tax

BREAKFAST
Buffet 1,600ptas per person

HOTEL ONIX ★★★ (8)
C/ de Llançà, 30, at corner of C/ de la Diputació
80 rooms, all with shower or bath and toilet

When it comes to value for money, the Onix has it all, including great weekend discounts, provided you can time your stay *not* to coincide with a holiday or large exhibition. It is across the street from the four-city-block Parc de Jean Miró, built in 1979 on the site of an old slaughterhouse. The large dirt space displays Miró's sculpture *Dona I Ocell,* which rises out of a pool in the center of the park. The well-appointed hotel is also close to Plaça d'Espanya (Barcelona's Trade Fair and Congress Center) and has easy access to the Sants Central train station and the airport. The Edward Hopper prints and other modern art paintings lend the hotel a cool, contemporary feel, and the small, rooftop pool and lounging area is a welcome oasis on hot Barcelona days. You can't see much through the block-glass windows in the breakfast room, but you certainly can if you are in any of the rooms on the fifth floor, or in the twenty front rooms, whose balconies face the old Arenas bullring. All the rooms have marble bathrooms with good towels, lights, mirrors, and a basket of toiletries. Twin-bedded rooms are the largest, with double wardrobes, built-in headboards, and desks.

ENGLISH SPOKEN: Yes

TELEPHONE
93 426 00 87

FAX
93 426 19 81

METRO
Espanya, 1, 3

CREDIT CARDS
AE, DC, MC, V

RATES
Single 10,500ptas, double 13,500ptas, triple 17,000ptas, plus 7 percent tax; significant weekend discounts, except on holidays or during major exhibitions

BREAKFAST
Buffet 1,100ptas per person

FACILITIES AND SERVICES: Air-conditioned, baby cribs, bar, conference rooms, direct-dial phone, rooms with handicapped access, hair dryer, laundry service, lift, minibar, parking (1,900ptas per day), piped-in music in the rooms, room safe (600ptas per day), satellite TV, rooftop swmming pool open in the summer

NEAREST TOURIST ATTRACTIONS: The Arenas bullring (not in use), Parc de Joan Miró

HOTEL TABER ★★★ (5, $)
C/ d'Aragó 256, at Rambla de Catalunya
93 rooms, all with shower or bath and toilet

TELEPHONE
93 487 38 87; toll-free in U.S.,
Utell 800–448-8355

FAX
93 488 13 50

INTERNET
www.softly.es/turismo/sercotel

METRO
Passeig de Gràcia, 3

CREDIT CARDS
AE, DC, MC, V

RATES
Single 15,000ptas, double 18,000ptas, suite 22,000ptas, plus 7 percent tax

BREAKFAST
Buffet 1,700ptas per person

The Hotel Taber has all the extras we expect in a city hotel. What is lacking is personality, especially in the lobby and hallways, but who cares if you can sleep well in a comfortable bed and your attractive room has enough space for both you and your luggage? Soft salmon is the color of choice in the rooms, which have chairs, a desk, luggage space, bedside reading lamps, and double closets with private safes. I can recommend the singles, especially No. 803, thanks to its private terrace and marble-tiled bathroom. Duo Cheap Sleepers can stay next door in No. 804, which also has a private rooftop terrace.

ENGLISH SPOKEN: Yes

FACILITIES AND SERVICES: Air-conditioning, bar, conference room, direct-dial phone, hair dryer, laundry service, lift, minibar, parking (2,000ptas per day), room safe (600ptas per day), satellite TV

NEAREST TOURIST ATTRACTIONS: Elegant shopping, *modernista* architecture

HOTEL UNIVERSAL ★ (4)
C/ d'Aragó 281, 2°
18 rooms, all with shower or bath and toilet

TELEPHONE
93 487 97 62

FAX
93 487 40 28

METRO
Passeig de Gràcia, 3

CREDIT CARDS
AE, DC, MC, V

RATES
Single 4,900ptas, double 6,500ptas, triple 8,000ptas, plus 7 percent tax

BREAKFAST
Not served

The Hotel Universal is a Cheap Sleep for the area. Air-conditioning and private safes are the two big draws in the clean, simple, monotonous white rooms that have cocoa brown fringed spreads, a desk and chair, and indoor-outdoor floor coverings. Bathrooms have tubs and/or showers. Rooms 107, 108, 208, 209, and 210 are five interior rooms that have absolutely no view, but they are quiet, and this is worth remembering because the second-floor hotel is in a corner office building on a wide street with four lanes of traffic whizzing by around the clock. Also under the same ownership is the two-star Hostal Residencia Neutral, page 71.

ENGLISH SPOKEN: Yes

FACILITIES AND SERVICES: Air-conditioning, direct-dial phone, room safe (200ptas per day), TV

NEAREST TOURIST ATTRACTIONS: Elegant shopping, *modernista* architecture

PLAÇA DE CATALUNYA AND PLAÇA D'URQUINAONA

Plaça de Catalunya is the city's transportation hub. At the intersection of La Rambla and Passeig de Gràcia, it connects the historical center of the city with the nineteenth-century Eixample. The wide avenues converging on the square are all busy commercial streets. Plaça de Catalunya serves as the central axis for most major bus routes, including those going to the airport, and it has two metro lines, a main line RENFE railway station, and the city's main tourist office, the Centre d'Informació Plaça de Catalunya.

Plaça d'Urquinaona, just east of Plaça de Catalunya, is another of the city's transportation hubs.

HOTELS

Hostal Fontanella ★★	**75**
Hostal Girona ★★	**76**
Hostal San Remo ★★	**77**
Hotel Catalunya Plaza ★★★ ($)	**77**
Hotel Ginebra ★	**78**
Hotel Granvía ★★★	**78**
Hotel Regina ★★★ ($)	**79**
Plaza Hostal ★★★	**80**

($) indicates a Big Splurge

HOSTAL FONTANELLA ★★ (22)
Via Laietana 71, 2°, corner of C/ Fontanella
10 rooms, 2 with shower or bath and toilet

Owner Encarna Olid wants to please her guests, and in an effort to do so asks for their written comments at the end of their stay. After you read through a recent stack of testimonials—such as, "You offer a special temporary home to travelers," "Thank you very much for making our stay in Barcelona special," and "Very nice

TELEPHONE AND FAX
93 317 59 43

METRO
Catalunya, 1, 3, or Urquinaona, 1, 4

CREDIT CARDS
AE, DC, MC, V

RATES
Single 3,200–4,000ptas, double
5,000–6,800ptas, triple 6,900–
9,450ptas, plus 7 percent tax

BREAKFAST
Not served

compared to every place we have stayed so far"—it is easy to see that guests appreciate the friendly, family atmosphere she provides. When you arrive, you will be welcomed by Encarna and her mascot dog, Benjy. The reception area and hallways are dotted with her dried floral arrangements and an impressive collection of framed Olympic posters. The furniture and accessories in the ten immaculate rooms flow together nicely. I like No. 1, a double or triple with its own bathroom and balcony. Room 7 has its own bathroom, but no view through the opaque windows. In Rooms 5 and 6, you might encounter some noise and you will have to share the facilities across the hall with three other rooms. No breakfast is served, but the area is filled with more cafés and bakeries than you could sample in a week.

ENGLISH SPOKEN: Some

FACILITIES AND SERVICES: Direct-dial phone, fans, laundry service, lift, free office safe, TV on request (500ptas per day)

NEAREST TOURIST ATTRACTIONS: Excellent shopping, *modernista* architecture, ten- to fifteen-minute walk to Barri Gòtic and La Rambla

HOSTAL GIRONA ★★ (15)
C/ de Girona 21, 2°, between C/ d'Ausiàs Marc and C/ de Casp
8 rooms, all with shower, 4 also with toilet

TELEPHONE
93 265 02 58

FAX
93 265 85 32

METRO
Urquinaona, 1, 4

CREDIT CARDS
V

RATES
Single 2,700ptas, double 5,700ptas, tax included

BREAKFAST
Not Served

The quiet, nontouristy neighborhood is lined with magnificent *modernista* buildings, and this eight-room family-run *hostal* is in one of the most beautiful of all. To reach the second-floor *hostal,* you can either take a black cage elevator or walk up a beautiful marble staircase. The *hostal* itself has lovely turn-of-the-nineteenth-century furnishings in the reception area, along the hallway, and sprinkled throughout the rooms. The four double rooms have private showers and toilets, but the singles come equipped only with a basin and shower. Ask for a room with a balcony, since those on the interior are dark. Even though the owner does not speak much English, she is sweet and very patient with those who have to rely on dusty high school Spanish to get by.

ENGLISH SPOKEN: Very limited

FACILITIES AND SERVICES: Bar, lift, TV

NEAREST TOURIST ATTRACTIONS: *Modernista* architecture, shopping, half-hour walk to Barri Gòtic

HOSTAL SAN REMO ★★ (16)
C/ d'Ausiàs Marc 19, 1°, corner C/ del Bruc
7 rooms, all with shower or bath and toilet

This is another family-run choice just far enough off tourist central to keep it quiet and unknown. It is owned by Señora Rosa, who redid the rooms when she bought it about three years ago. Now they all have central heating, air-conditioning, double-glazed windows, a television, and nice bathrooms, which are a real bonus for a Cheap Sleep at this price. Number 4 is a sweet twin with a balcony, view, and the original tile floor still in place. Another twin, No. 7, is equally nice and has a balcony but not much view. The only room I would absolutely refuse is the airless, windowless cubicle next to reception that is marked with a *P*; it is in reality nothing more than a closet with an air vent over the door.

ENGLISH SPOKEN: Very limited

FACILITIES AND SERVICES: Air-conditioning, lift, free office safe, TV, desk open 8 A.M.–11 P.M.

NEAREST TOURIST ATTRACTIONS: Excellent shopping, half-hour walk to La Rambla and Barri Gòtic

TELEPHONE
93 302 19 89

FAX
93 301 07 74

METRO
Urquinaona, 1, 4

CREDIT CARDS
MC, V, but prefers cash

RATES
Single 4,200–5,200ptas, double 5,700–6,200ptas, triple 7,700ptas, tax included

BREAKFAST
Not served

HOTEL CATALUNYA PLAZA ★★★ (14, $)
Plaça de Catalunya 7
46 rooms, all with shower or bath and toilet

This heart-of-the-city location can't be topped. If you can't walk to virtually everything on your Barcelona must-see list, then there is either a metro or bus that will take you there from the Plaça de Catalunya. The hotel was opened for the 1992 Olympic Games and is a typical, big-city hotel with all the whistles and bells professional travelers demand, yet small enough to make guests feel important and cared for. The hotel overlooks the Plaça de Catalunya and has a large terrace and two conference rooms along the front. The dining room ceiling, decorated with large moldings and figures that symbolize the four seasons, is especially beautiful. Simulated burled walnut doors lead to the well-constructed bedrooms, each of which has a lighted work area, excellent closet space, and well-equipped bathrooms. Each floor has its own sitting area and many rooms look onto a plant-hung interior atrium. Others have balcony views of the fountains in the Plaça de Catalunya. Number 313 is one of my favorites, mostly because I appreciate the desk space conveniently placed along one wall, the balcony with double windows, and the great closet space.

TELEPHONE
93 317 71 71

FAX
93 317 78 55

EMAIL
catalunya@city-hotels.es

METRO
Catalunya, 1, 3

CREDIT CARDS
AE, DC, MC, V

RATES
Single 20,000ptas, double 23,000ptas, triple 26,000ptas, plus 7 percent tax

BREAKFAST
1,600ptas per person

ENGLISH SPOKEN: Yes

FACILITIES AND SERVICES: Air-conditioning, bar, conference room, direct-dial phone, hair dryer, laundry service, lift, minibar, restaurant, room service, room safe (350ptas per day), satellite TV

NEAREST TOURIST ATTRACTIONS: Central Barcelona, within a thirty-minute radius to almost everything

HOTEL GINEBRA ★ (11)
Rambla de Catalunya 1, 3°
12 rooms, all with shower or bath and toilet

TELEPHONE
93 317 10 63
FAX
93 317 55 65
METRO
Catalunya, 1, 3
CREDIT CARDS
DC, MC, V
RATES
Single 5,000ptas, double 8,300ptas, triple 10,500ptas, plus 7 percent tax
BREAKFAST
Continental 400ptas per person

The Ginebra is on the third floor of a beautiful building across from the Plaça de Catalunya in the center of Barcelona. It is owned by Juan Herrera and his family, who also do all the work that comes with maintaining a smooth-running hotel. Breakfast is served in what feels like their family dining room, and in the rest of the hotel, pictures and plants add further warming touches. There is no getting around the noise coming from Barcelona's busiest square, but the third-floor site and double windows in the air-conditioned rooms certainly cut down on some of it. As for the best rooms, try No. 412. Even though it doesn't have a balcony, it's a good double-bedded pick with the most space, a wall of wardrobes, a comfortable chair, and a sizable bathroom with a tub. Number 402, a twin with a balcony, is furnished in simulated pine with two chairs, a small table, a wardrobe, and a framed picture of a Japanese geisha. The bathroom has a half-tub and shower and small window. Speaking of small, that doesn't even begin to describe the room next door, No. 403, which is so tight that you have to crawl over the bed to get to the bathroom.

ENGLISH SPOKEN: Yes

FACILITIES AND SERVICES: Air-conditioning, direct-dial phone, hair dryer, lift, free office safe, satellite TV

NEAREST TOURIST ATTRACTIONS: Central Barcelona, within a thirty-minute radius to almost everything

HOTEL GRANVÍA ★★★ (10)
Gran Via de les Corts Catalanes 642
53 rooms, all with shower or bath and toilet

TELEPHONE
93 318 19 00
FAX
93 318 99 97
METRO
Catalunya, 1, 3
CREDIT CARDS
AE, DC, MC, V

The ornate rococo-style hotel began life in the nineteenth century as an elegant townhome on this fashionable avenue in the center of Barcelona. When it was converted to a hotel in 1936, the grandiose rooms, winding stairway, arcaded gallery, and colonnades on the first floor were all kept in place. Breakfast is served in a grand salon that would not be out of place in any Spanish palace. The imposing room, with a huge circular balcony, has three crystal chandeliers, matching wall sconces, and a domed stained-glass skylight. The main sitting room is furnished in gold and opens onto a bricked terrace. Unfortunately, the mirrored-glass vitrines displaying T-shirts, bottles of scotch, and various liqueurs seem horribly out of place and mar the atmosphere.

With few exceptions, most of the rooms lack the character of the public areas. If you really want to revel in the past, reserve the Chapel Room, but be aware you will not be able to see the light of day through the opaque pebbled-glass windows. Maybe you won't need to, since the hand-painted furniture, two red highback chairs, and the screen by the entrance might be enough to keep you visually interested during your stay. The bathroom does have a window, along with a bidet and plenty of space. Bring earplugs if you plan to get much sleep in No. 301, a front-facing twin furnished in semi-antiques. The room has livable space, but I can't say the same for the dimly lit bathroom. Quieter rooms are on the terrace side of the hotel.

ENGLISH SPOKEN: Yes

FACILITIES AND SERVICES: Air-conditioning, conference room, direct-dial phones, hair dryer available, laundry service, lift, minibar, parking by arrangement (2,300ptas per day), room safe (350ptas per day), TV

NEAREST TOURIST ATTRACTIONS: Excellent shopping, La Rambla, a twenty-minute walk to Barri Gòtic

RATES
Single 9,500ptas, double 13,000ptas, triple 16,500ptas, plus 7 percent tax

BREAKFAST
Continental 650ptas per person

HOTEL REGINA ★★★ (18, $)
C/ de Bergara 4
103 rooms, all with shower or bath and toilet

For four-star comforts and amenities at three-star prices, check into the Hotel Regina, a centrally located choice next to the Plaça de Catalunya, which is within easy walking distance to most of the interesting monuments, museums, churches, and elegant shops Barcelona is famous for. The hotel has an interesting history. In 1909, Francisco Recasens Bella bought a boardinghouse here for 5,300ptas—which is less than a single room costs today!—and over the years expanded his holdings to what finally became the Hotel Regina. By 1920, the Regina was one of three hotels in the city that could

TELEPHONE
93 301 32 32; toll-free in U.S., Best Western 800-528-1234

FAX
93 318 23 26

EMAIL
reservas@reginahotel.com

INTERNET
www.reginahotel.es

METRO
Catalunya, 1, 3

CREDIT CARDS
AE, DC, MC, V

RATES
Single 14,500ptas, double
22,000ptas, plus 7 percent tax

BREAKFAST
Buffet 1,600ptas per person

boast that every room had a complete bathroom. The other two were the Ritz and Oriente. Since then, the hotel has continued to maintain its reputation as a distinguished hotel that offers its guests fine accommodations and services.

The reception and lobby is a modern oasis with a soothing waterfall along the back wall. An abstract mural of a Spanish city highlights the rest of the room, which has large overstuffed chairs nicely placed for quiet conversations. The modern theme is continued in the small dining room, which has a sleek chrome-and-wood bar. All the rooms are exceptional, especially Nos. 118 and 119, both large twin suites with a closet-lined entryway and a sitting room with well-lit desk space, a sofa bed, and overstuffed chair. Each has a super bathroom, with a separate stall shower and double-mirrored sink. Cheap Sleepers will be glad to know that these two suites are the same price as a regular twin-bedded double! If the suites are booked, don't dispair, as the regular large twin rooms are very, very nice, especially No. 102, which is quiet even though it has a small balcony. The room itself is spacious enough to have a sofa bed and comfortable chair, and the large bath has a bidet and a stretch sink backed by mirrors.

NOTE: The hotel has ten rooms reserved for nonsmoking guests.

ENGLISH SPOKEN: Yes

FACILITIES AND SERVICES: Air-conditioning, baby cots, bar, conference room, direct-dial phone, hair dryer, laundry services, lift, minibar, restaurant, room service, room safe (300ptas per day), ten nonsmoking rooms, satellite TV, pay-per-view videos

NEAREST TOURIST ATTRACTIONS: Central Barcelona, close to the Barri Gòtic, La Rambla, shopping, and *modernista* buildings

PLAZA HOSTAL ★★★ (21)
C/ Fontanella 18, 1°
14 rooms, all with shower or bath and toilet

TELEPHONE AND FAX
93 301 01 39

EMAIL
Plazahostal@mx3.redestb.es

INTERNET
www.redestb.es/Personal/
PlazaHostal

METRO
Catalunya, 1, 3, or
Urquinaona, 1, 4

The Plaza Hostal is owned and operated by an enthusiastic Hispanic-American family that includes their two dogs (a Samoyed named Snow and a Yorkie named Sophie) and assorted birds who live in three cages in the reception area. Before returning to Barcelona to run their hotel, the family lived in the States in Miami and Houston, so they are well aware of what most Americans expect in a hotel. Along with the basics, they offer lots of extras: Internet usage (on a half-hour fee basis), free use of a microwave and refrigerator, a TV lounge, laundry service, and tons of information on what to see and do in Barcelona. Robin's egg blue doors lead to the fourteen clean and generally well-maintained rooms, pleasantly done in bamboo and wicker furnishings, with plastic chairs and wire racks for extra hanging space. Some have pebbled windows and no view, others have balconies with street views. The only one I found lacking was No. 58, a double with a balcony and two pictures of Marilyn Monroe on the wall. The problem here is that there is no place to put anything except on the bed, which means that you would have to transfer any books and belongings to the floor at night, unless you wanted to sleep with them.

ENGLISH SPOKEN: Yes, fluently

FACILITIES AND SERVICES: Fans, hair dryer available, laundry service, lift, free office safe, Internet usage (600ptas per half hour), use of refrigerator and microwave

NEAREST TOURIST ATTRACTIONS: Good shopping, walking distance to La Rambla and Barri Gòtic

CREDIT CARDS
AE, DC, MC, V

RATES
Single 5,000ptas, double 8,000ptas, triple 11,000ptas, plus 7 percent tax

BREAKFAST
Not served

PLAÇA DE LA UNIVERSITAT _____

Plaça de la Universitat is a large square linking a portion of old Barcelona to the elegant L'Eixample neighborhoods. While the tourist attractions may be a bracing walk or a Metro stop away, the area affords visitors a quiet and peaceful stay in a beautiful part of the city.

HOTELS

Hostería Grau ★★	82
Hotel Caledonian ★★★	82
Hotel Gravina ★★★ ($)	83
Hotel Lleó ★★★	84
Hotel Meson Castilla ★★	85
Hotel Reding ★★★ ($)	86

($) indicates a Big Splurge

HOSTERÍA GRAU ★★ (20)
C/ de les Ramelleres 27, at C/ dels Tallers
26 rooms, 15 with shower or bath and toilet

TELEPHONE
93 301 81 35
FAX
93 317 68 25
EMAIL
hgrau@lix.intercom.es
INTERNET
www.intercom.es/grau
METRO
Universitat, 1, 2, or
Catalunya, 1, 3
CREDIT CARDS
AE, DC, MC, V
RATES
Single 3,750–6,000ptas, double
5,400–7,500ptas, plus
7 percent tax
BREAKFAST
Extra charge, per person: El
Rapido 400ptas, Continental
600ptas, French 750ptas,
English 800ptas

Besides price, the two-star Hostería Grau has a lot going for it. First of all, there's the owner, Felix, who lived in New York City, and his charming daughter, Monica, who loves to travel and has made several trips to the States. Both are multilingual and full of great information about what to see and do in Barcelona. They also know about restaurants and gave me several insider tips that you will find in *Cheap Eats in Spain*. The location is another point in its favor. From the front door, you are minutes from La Rambla and less than an hour from the airport if you use the Aerobús. They offer four reasonably priced breakfasts, all of which are available until noon and served in their downstairs dining room, which has a working fireplace and a big satellite television, or in the little first-floor sitting room. If you want only tea or coffee and a croissant, order the *Rápido*. The Continental adds a glass of orange juice. The *Francés* is an omelette served with toast, orange juice, and tea or coffee, and the *Inglés* offers the works: a fried egg, sausage, toast, orange juice, and coffee or tea.

The room prices vary depending on the level of plumbing. There are four new rooms, Nos. 232 (no balcony), 234, 236, and 238. This is not to suggest that the older rooms are not accceptable; they are, especially No. 224, which has a streetside balcony, two metal-framed beds, and a gray-tiled bathroom with an enclosed stall shower and good towels. Number 218 is sold as a triple, but I think it is too constricted to house three with any degree of comfort. Also to be avoided are the interior rooms, which are dark and stuffy.

ENGLISH SPOKEN: Yes

FACILITIES AND SERVICES: Bar, fans, hair dryer available, laundry service, free office safe

NEAREST TOURIST ATTRACTIONS: La Rambla, Barri Gòtic

HOTEL CALEDONIAN ★★★ (9)
Gran Via de les Corts Catalanes 574, between C/ de Muntaner and C/ de Casanova
51 rooms, all with shower or bath and toilet

TELEPHONE
93 453 02 00
FAX
93 451 77 03
INTERNET
www.arrakis.es/~reservar
METRO
Universitat, 1, 2

A stay at the Hotel Caledonian promises a modern room at a fair price in a hotel that has all the extras. The small reception area has a turquoise-colored suede sectional couch and a balcony draped in fake greenery, and another sitting area and bar has gold, pounded-metal tabletops and more artificial plants. Watercolors on the walls and polished hardwood floors add a needed touch of class. The bedrooms are uniformly done, and offer work space, mirrored wardrobes, and bathrooms with sink space and good towels. None of the rooms faces a wall, and all have clear glass windows you can actually see out of, two features that many Spanish hotels lack Another winning feature for many Cheap Sleepers is that the airport buses arrive and depart from Plaça de la Universitat, which is only two blocks from the hotel.

ENGLISH SPOKEN: Yes

FACILITIES AND SERVICES: Air-conditioning, bar, direct-dial phone, hair dryer, laundry service, lift, minibar, parking (1,500ptas per day), room safe (500ptas per day), satellite TV

NEAREST TOURIST ATTRACTIONS: Excellent shopping, twenty minutes to Barri Gòtic, fifteen to La Rambla

CREDIT CARDS
AE, DC, MC, V

RATES
Single 11,000ptas, double 17,500ptas, triple 22,000ptas, suite 19,500ptas, plus 7 percent tax

BREAKFAST
Buffet 1,100ptas per person

HOTEL GRAVINA ★★★ (12, $)
C/ de Gravina 12, at C/ de Pelai
86 rooms, all with shower or bath and toilet

The building was the home of Captain Gravina, a Spanish naval hero who fought against Britain's Admiral Nelson. All that remains of the original structure is the facade and, above the entrance, the stone lion that served as the captain's mascot. Today the building houses a beautiful three-star hotel that offers more than most four-star hotels. Not only is there an Internet hookup available, but one entire floor is reserved for nonsmoking guests, and there is a special lift to take handicapped guests to their designated rooms. Whether you check into a standard double, or the grand suite, your stay will be exceptional and the service from the thirty-plus staff always polite and efficient.

Since the hotel is on a small side street, noise is kept to a minimum. Most of the uniformily attractive rooms along the front have a balcony, and three back rooms on each floor also have balconies. The bedrooms are simply decorated with gray carpeting, blue sponge-painted walls, and matching spreads. Each has a comfortable chair, a luggage rack, desk space, and reading lights. You will love the spacious pink-marble baths, which have a selection of toiletries, glass shower guards on the tubs, magnifying mirrors, and excellent towels. If you reserve one of the suites, you will not only have great

TELEPHONE
93 301 68 68; toll-free in the U.S., Best Western 800-528-1234

FAX
93 317 28 38

EMAIL
Gravina@Smc.es

INTERNET
www.bestwestern.com/thisco/bs/92187/92187_b.html.

METRO
Universitat, 1, 2

CREDIT CARDS
AE, DC, MC, V

RATES
Single 14,000–17,000ptas, double 17,500–22,500ptas, junior suite 26,000–29,000ptas, grand suite (up to 5 people) 30,000–37,000ptas, plus 7 percent tax

BREAKFAST
Continental 1,000ptas per person, buffet 1,500ptas per person

space but soft terrycloth robes to put on after relaxing in your Jacuzzi bath. As one guest aptly put it, "I recall with pleasure everything the hotel offered me, which was without a doubt much more than three stars." I agree, and I know you will, too.

ENGLISH SPOKEN: Yes

FACILITIES AND SERVICES: Air-conditioning, bar, conference room, direct-dial phone, hair dryer, Internet hookup available on request, laundry, lift, minibar, Jacuzzis and terry robes in the suites, parking (1,600ptas per day), restaurant, room service, one nonsmoking floor, rooms with handicapped access, room safe (250ptas per day), satellite TV, pay-per-view video

NEAREST TOURIST ATTRACTIONS: Excellent shopping, La Rambla, within twenty minutes to Barri Gòtic

HOTEL LLEÓ ★★★ (17)
C/ de Pelai 22–24
83 rooms, all with shower or bath and toilet

TELEPHONE
93 318 13 12

FAX
93 412 26 57

INTERNET
www.hotel-lleo.es

METRO
Universitat, 1, 2

CREDIT CARDS
AE, MC, V

RATES
Single 11,000ptas, double 15,500ptas, triple 18,500ptas, plus 7 percent tax

BREAKFAST
Buffet 1,200ptas per person

The Hotel Lleó is a city-center hotel that offers comfort and convenience without the element of surprise. The lobby and sitting area has an interesting display of faux cacti, which look as though they have just been transplanted from the American Southwest. The breakfast room has a garden theme, and in the morning, they serve a huge hot and cold buffet breakfast. The rooms are all acceptable—and there are nonsmoking rooms on the third floor—but I would have to give the edge to the new rooms on the fifth floor, as well as to Nos. 312 and 313. Number 312 is a big double with a sitting area that has an interesting view of some older apartments. The bathroom is a winner, with two sinks, a magnifying makeup mirror, bidet, and separate toilet. Number 313 is another large room with the same view, but it has the advantage of two work areas, two double beds, as well as a sitting area and spacious bathroom. If you are traveling alone, be advised that No. 309 is quiet, but the opaque window opens onto a gray wall.

ENGLISH SPOKEN: Yes

FACILITIES AND SERVICES: Air-conditioning, bar, conference room, direct-dial phones, laundry service, lift, minibar, restaurant, room service, nonsmoking rooms on third floor, room safe (200ptas per day), satellite TV, pay-for-view videos, piped-in music in room

NEAREST TOURIST ATTRACTIONS: La Rambla, shopping, Barri Gòtic

HOTEL MESON CASTILLA ★★ (19)
C/ de Valldonzella 5
56 rooms, all with shower or bath and toilet

For my Cheap Sleeping money, one of the best two-star hotels in Barcelona is the Hotel Meson Castilla. Not only is it loaded with charm and character, reflecting the gracious good taste of the delightful owner, but the well-being of guests is always uppermost in the minds of her pleasant staff. All the first-floor reception rooms have original beamed ceilings, hand painted with the coats of arms of major Spanish cities. Large armchairs covered in leather and floral fabrics provide comfortable seating. The dining room is magnificent, with seven arched windows overlooking a circular outdoor terrace, which is lined with plants, covered in mosaic tiles, and sports views over Barcelona. A buffet breakfast is served inside or on the terrace. Around the room is a series of photos documenting the life of this hotel, which has been family owned and operated since 1952. Many of the photos show the owner and employees in native Castilian dress, and they reveal that nothing at the hotel has changed much over the years, except that the roof has been improved and what is now the salon was once the dining room. On the landing of every floor is a comfortable place to sit and current periodicals to leaf through.

The rooms are individually furnished in the typically ornate, multicolored Spanish style of the area. Those on the second, third, and fifth floor have private terraces with views of the nearby Museu d'Art Contemporani and the rooftops of Barcelona. I especially like Room 126, with a bay window and nice bathroom. Number 464 is a beautiful twin with a little sitting area, rooftop view, and a small bathroom with shelves and its own window. If you need more space, book Room 253, which has a terrace and can be joined with No. 252 next door for a nice family-style accommodation.

ENGLISH SPOKEN: Yes

FACILITIES AND SERVICES: Air-conditioning, direct-dial phone, hair dryers in some room (or available by request), lift, some minibars, parking (2,000ptas per day), free office safe, satellite TV

NEAREST TOURIST ATTRACTIONS: Musée d'Art Contemporani, walking distance to La Rambla, about twenty minutes to Barri Gòtic

TELEPHONE
93 318 21 82

FAX
93 412 40 20

EMAIL
depcomcen@husa.es

INTERNET
www.husa.es

METRO
Universitat, 1, 2

CREDIT CARDS
AE, DC, MC, V

RATES
Single 10,800ptas, double 13,800ptas, triple 18,200ptas, plus 7 percent tax

BREAKFAST
Buffet included

HOTEL REDING ★★★ (13, $)
C/ de Gravina 5–7, at C/ dels Tallers
44 rooms, all with shower or bath and toilet

TELEPHONE
93 412 10 97

FAX
93 268 34 82

EMAIL
reding@occidentalhoteles.com

INTERNET
www.occidentalhoteles.com

METRO
Universitat, 1, 2

CREDIT CARDS
AE, DC, MC, V

RATES
Single 16,500ptas, double 21,000ptas, suite 3,000ptas extra per person, plus 7 percent tax

BREAKFAST
1,500ptas per person

Barcelona is one of Europe's most popular trade-fair locations, and the Hotel Reding is ready, willing, and able to attend to fairgoers' needs. The El Prat International airport is only twelve kilometers from the hotel, and the airport bus arrives and departs from the Plaça de la Universitat, about two blocks from the hotel. In addition to the usual business perks, rooms can be equipped with a fax, and modems are planned for the year 2000. Four rooms—two doubles and two singles—boast their own terraces. All the color-coordinated, carpeted doubles, and two singles, have either king or twin beds, work space, and beautiful marble baths with ample sink space and well-lighted mirrors. Some conserve space with attractive walnut built-in furniture, others are large enough for a good-size table. There's also a restaurant where you can order everything from a light snack to a full meal.

ENGLISH SPOKEN: Yes

FACILITIES AND SERVICES: Air-conditioning, bar, conference room, direct-dial phone, hair dryer, laundry service, lift, minibar, parking (2,200ptas per day), restaurant, room safe (370ptas per day), satellite TV, piped-in room music

NEAREST TOURIST ATTRACTIONS: Museu d'Art Contemporani, Trade Fairground, La Rambla

WATERFRONT AND SURROUNDING AREA

Barcelona has a seafront that's equalled by few other European cities. Before the 1992 Olympic Games, the waterfront was a busy Mediterranean port with a lively fishing community called Barceloneta jutting out beside it. In anticipation of the millions of television viewers tuning into Barcelona for the Games, the area was cleaned up in a massive scheme of brilliant urban renewal, and the Olympic Port has become one of the most popular areas of the city. Today, it contains seafood restaurants, bars, leisure activities, shopping complexes, Europe's largest aquarium, and a big-screen Imax cinema.

HOTELS

HOSTAL ORLEANS ★★ (52)
Avda. Marquès de l'Argentera 13, 1°
26 rooms, all with shower, 12 also with toilet

Josephine Ibañez's hostal across the street from the Estació Termini Railway station provides a mixed bag of Cheap Sleeps for budgeteers wanting to be close to the train station and the waterfront. Most important: Special rates can be arranged for weekly stays and for triple and quad rooms. The best choices are on the top floors. The decor in the twenty-six clean rooms, furnished in rattan and wicker, won't require blinders or incite nightmares. They each contain a desk and chair, wardrobe space that includes hanging and drawer space, and a TV. Many rooms have balconies, but you can expect noise in these. The rooms with only a basin and shower have portable shower booths right in the room, and some beds sag. However, Josephine is very sweet and tries very hard to please, and for many, that is worth a great deal.

ENGLISH SPOKEN: Yes

FACILITIES AND SERVICES: Direct-dial phones in rooms with bathrooms, TV

NEAREST TOURIST ATTRACTIONS: Waterfront, walk to Barri Gòtic

TELEPHONE
93 319 73 82

FAX
93 319 22 19

METRO
Barceloneta, 4

CREDIT CARDS
AE, DC, MC, V

RATES
Single 3,200–4,700ptas, double 5,200–6,700ptas, triple 6,700–7,700ptas, quad 7,200–8,700ptas, tax included

BREAKFAST
Not served

HOTEL METROPOL HESPERIA ★★★ (53)
C/ Ample 31
71 rooms, all with shower or bath and toilet

Built for the 1992 Olympics, the Hotel Metropol Hesperia offers attentive and personal service in a modern, hospitable atmosphere with enough pleasing extras to ensure that guests enjoy their stay. The lobby, reception, and breakfast areas are soberly done with black leather upholstery on low-rise sofas and chairs. While I cannot say much for the drab white stucco halls carpeted in cheap grass-green indoor/outdoor floor covering, I can assure you that the rooms are much better than this would lead you to expect. All of the rooms facing the street have balconies. No matter where you land, you will be in a uniformly done, air-conditioned room with luggage and closet space, a framed art print on the wall, and a marble bathroom with plenty of towels.

TELEPHONE
93 301 51 00

FAX
93 319 12 76

EMAIL
hhes@hoteles-hesperia.es

INTERNET
www.hoteles-hesperia.es

METRO
Drassanes, 3

CREDIT CARDS
AE, DC, MC, V

RATES
Single 13,000ptas, double 14,500ptas, triple 16,500ptas, plus 7 percent tax

BREAKFAST
Buffet 1,100ptas per person

ENGLISH SPOKEN: Yes

FACILITIES AND SERVICES: Air-conditioning, conference room, direct-dial phone, hair dryer available, laundry service, lift, minibar, room safe (300ptas per day), radio, satellite TV

NEAREST TOURIST ATTRACTIONS: Waterfront, La Rambla, Gothic Quarter

Other Options

If living in a hotel is not for you, there are several other options that make Cheap Sleeping sense in Barcelona. For the Cheapest Sleep of all, you can commune with nature and pitch a tent on the outskirts of the city. For students or young-at-heart travelers, youth hostels will save you considerable money. For a more intimate experience than a hotel, reserve your room in a private bed and breakfast. Finally, if you want to feel like you are a part of the city, consider the many benefits of renting your own apartment, from having more space to the adventure of interacting with local merchants while shopping for life's necessities in your own Barcelona neighborhood. See "Tips on Renting a Spanish Apartment," page 15, for more details about this.

Apartment Rental Agencies

EL SOL VACATION VILLAS
P.O. Box 329
Wayne, PA 19087

From an economical studio to an elegant apartment or country chateau, Mary Vaira's El Sol Vacation Villas can point you in the right direction for whatever accommodation your heart or budget desires. In addition to properties in the cities and countryside of Spain, Mary and her staff can put a roof over your head in Portugal, Italy, France, Great Britain, the Caribbean, Mexico, and Hawaii. For further information about your specific needs, visit their website, or contact them directly by telephone.

TELEPHONE
610-687-9066

FAX
610-687-9056

EMAIL
mvaira@aol.com

INTERNET
www.elsolvillas.com

CREDIT CARDS
MC

RATES
From $650 for small studios and up, depending on size and location

VILLAS INTERNATIONAL
950 Northgate Drive, Suite 206
San Rafael, CA 94903

TELEPHONE
415-499-9490, 800-221-2260

FAX
415-499-9491

EMAIL
villas@best.com

INTERNET
www.villasintl.com

CREDIT CARDS
None, cash only

RATES
Vary by location and type; prices begin around $650 per week for two in a small, fully equipped studio

Villas International offers a wide selection of rental properties of all types for independent travelers who want more than a large city hotel can offer. Property locations and prices vary from city center studios and apartments to seaside villas and country estates in almost every European country, Mexico, the Caribbean, and Hawaii. For information about specific locations, visit their website or contact their San Francisco office.

Bed and Breakfast in a Private Home

FAMILY HOUSE-CAL JOSEP
C/ de Rogent 56, 5°
9 rooms, none with shower or bath and toilet

TELEPHONE
93 246 67 45

FAX
93 232 92 81

EMAIL
barcelona@housefamily.com

INTERNET
www.housefamily.com

METRO
Clot, 1

CREDIT CARDS
None, cash only

RATES
Minimum stay 3 nights; single room 13,000ptas, with half board 15,000ptas; double room 12,000ptas per person, with half board, 13,500ptas per person; rates vary depending on type of accommodation, length of stay, and number of people in room; all rates include taxes

BREAKFAST
Continental included; half board (dinner) 1,000ptas per person, per night, or less if requested at time of reservation

Montserrat and Josep Moix offer visitors single, double, and triple guest rooms and a penthouse apartment in their home. They live in a large apartment, about a thirty- to forty-minute commute to the center of Barcelona. The overall neighborhood could be considered dull by some standards, but as a traveler, I always find it interesting to get a glimpse at how the average person lives in the cities I visit. The Moix's fifth-floor apartment has been their family home for years, so you can expect an array of proudly displayed mementos and knickknacks. Most of the guests are students here for various language courses or couples who like this type of warm and fuzzy international living. Guests are invited to gather in the living room to watch television, or to sit on the large terrace, which has a view of the tip of Gaudí's La Sagrada Familia. Breakfast is included in the rate, and a home-cooked dinner is available on a half-board basis. On Friday the popular menu is always the same: paella and sangría. The neighborhood has few restaurants, so unless you eat somewhere else in the city, dinner here is a convenient option—unless you take advantage of the refrigerator and microwave to prepare your own light meals.

If you plan on spending much time in your room, I strongly recommend you book one that faces out—it will be noisier, but you will avoid the dark interior views of dank walls or flapping lines of laundry. Number 8, a twin or triple, has a balcony and is on a quiet side street. Number 6, a double or triple, also faces out, and so does No. 3: from its window you can see La Sagrada Familia, but the room is so small that it only has enough space for the bed, one wooden chair, and a fold-down table. I like No. 2 because it has a corner view from its terrace and better wardrobe and drawer space. The penthouse apartment has two double bedrooms that can sleep six. You will have your own kitchen and washing machine, but no television and no telephone. Otherwise, rooms to avoid are No.1, a cramped, dark, interior single; No. 4, a depressing double; No. 5, with nice furniture, but poor light and another horrible view; No. 7, because it looks directly onto lines of laundry; and No. 9, because you can't see out of the opaque window.

ENGLISH SPOKEN: Yes, and French and German

FACILITIES AND SERVICES: Airport pickup (10,000ptas), laundry service, use of refrigerator and microwave, TV lounge

NEAREST TOURIST ATTRACTIONS: None, must use public transportation

Camping

The closest campsite is seven kilometers from Barcelona. However, if you want to combine a beach stay along with your trip to Barcelona, camping may be the way to go.

Albatros	**91**
Cala Gogó	**92**
El Toro Bravo	**92**
Masnou	**93**

ALBATROS
Autovia de Castelldefels, 08850, Gavà

The campground on the beach at Gavà has everything a vacationer could want, including a reasonably close location to Barcelona. In addition to a bar, restaurant, store, hairdresser, and laundry on the premises, you can rent a mobile home, play tennis or miniature golf, engage in watersports in the sports center, watch free videos in English, join excursions to Barcelona, or send your children to take part in their own activities.

TELEPHONE AND FAX: 93 633 06 95

METRO: Bus 95 from Ronda Universitat in Barcelona stops 250 meters from the entrance

OPEN: May–Sept; office hours 8 A.M.–10 P.M.

CREDIT CARDS: None, cash only

RATES: Per person, per night: 700ptas; under 10 years 500ptas, plus extra charges for cars, motorcycles, caravans, tents, and electric hookup, plus 7 percent tax

ENGLISH SPOKEN: Limited

CALA GOGÓ
Carretera de la Platja, 08820, El Prat de Llobregat

This is the closest campground to Barcelona, and it can accommodate 4,500 happy campers. There is a market, bar, restaurant, and swimming pool at the campground, and nearby, there's fishing, the beach, and tennis courts.

TELEPHONE: 93 379 46 00

FAX: 93 379 47 11

METRO: Bus 65 from Plaça d'Espanya

OPEN: Mar 15–Oct 15; office hours 9 A.M–2 P.M.

CREDIT CARDS: MC, V

RATES: Per night: Mar–June, Oct 1,500ptas with electricity, plus 500ptas per adult, 350ptas per child under 9; June–Sept 2,100ptas with electricity, plus 700ptas per adult, 500ptas per child under 9; all rates plus 7 percent tax

ENGLISH SPOKEN: Limited

EL TORO BRAVO
Autovia de Castelldefels, 08840, Viladecans

If you don't have a car, you'd better forget about this campsite, unless you don't mind a six-mile hike from the main road bus stop to the campground. It is open year-round and has spaces for 3,500 campgoers. The seaside location offers a hairdresser, swimming pools, and tennis courts.

TELEPHONE: 93 637 34 62

FAX: 93 637 21 15

METRO: Bus 95 from Ronda Universitat

OPEN: All year; office hours June-Aug 8 A.M.–8 P.M., Sept–June 8:30 A.M.–1:30 P.M., 4–6 P.M.

CREDIT CARDS: AE, MC, V

RATES: Per person 850ptas, children under ten 550ptas, plus charges for cars, tents, caravans, and electricity; all rates plus 7 percent tax

ENGLISH SPOKEN: Limited

MASNOU
Carretera N-11, 08320, El Masnou

The smallest and most rural of the campgrounds, Masnou has spaces for only 120 nature lovers. You can pitch a tent under a tree, rent a cabin for four people, and take a free shower. There is a bar, restaurant, market, children's playground and swimming pool, and a beach with diving and sailing nearby.

TELEPHONE AND FAX: 93 555 15 03

METRO: RENFE train to Masnou from Plaça de Catalunya

OPEN: All year; office hours 8 A.M.–9 P.M.

CREDIT CARDS: None, cash only

RATES: Per person 800ptas, children under ten 700ptas, plus extra charges for vehicles, caravans, tents, and electricity; cabins 3,200ptas per person, per day, minimum 4 people; all rates plus 7 percent tax

ENGLISH SPOKEN: Limited

Residence Hotels

Some lucky Cheap Sleepers in Barcelona require a home base for a week or more. Renting a serviced apartment in a residence hotel may at first glance seem expensive, but when you cost it out per person, consider the increase in space, general comfort, and amenities, plus the cost-saving convenience of your own kitchen, it oftens turns out to be a very smart Cheap Sleeping option. In addition, you will have all the front desk staff and support you would have in a hotel, and in some cases more business facilities. Best of all, the longer the stay, the better the price, especially in the low season. For more details, see "Tips on Renting a Spanish Apartment," page 15.

APARTHOTEL ACACIA ★★★ (2)
C/ del Comte d'Urgell 194
26 apartments, all with shower or bath and toilet and fitted kitchen

TELEPHONE
93 454 07 37

FAX
93 451 85 82

METRO
Hospital Clínic, 5

CREDIT CARDS
AE, DC, MC, V

RATES
Single 16,000ptas, double 18,000ptas, extra person 3,000ptas, plus 7 percent tax

BREAKAST
Continental 1,000ptas per person

The Acacia is a sleek and modern complex with twenty-six excellent apartments that have marble floors and stainless-steel kitchens outfitted with attractive dishes and cooking utensils. Living space is ample, with enough work room to spread out and complete a project; the storage space for your luggage and clothes is also excellent. To relax, just turn on the television set or pop in a video. Bathrooms are beautiful, all marble with good lighting, wide mirrors, and shower shields. While it is not centrally located from a tourist's standpoint, public transportation is very good, and the Eixample neighborhood is attractive, safe, and offers an interesting glimpse into the everyday life of upscale Barcelonans.

NOTE: These apartments can also be booked through Villas International, page 90.

ENGLISH SPOKEN: Yes

FACILITIES AND SERVICES: Air-conditioning, direct-dial phones, hair dryer, fitted kitchen, laundry service, lift, parking (1,500ptas per day), room safe (300ptas per day), handicapped access, satellite TV, video

NEAREST TOURIST ATTRACTIONS: None, must use public transportation

APARTHOTEL CALÀBRIA ★★★ (7)
C/ de Calàbria 129–131
72 apartments, all with shower or bath and toilet and fitted kitchens

TELEPHONE
93 426 42 28, 93 426 74 85

FAX
93 426 76 40

METRO
Rocafort, 1

CREDIT CARDS
AE, MC, V

RATES
Single 10,000ptas, double 12,000ptas, extra person 3,800ptas, plus 7 percent tax

The Calàbria serviced apartments are three metro stops from Plaça de Catalunya in a quiet corner of L'Eixample, and it's convenient for those visitors attending trade fairs and conventions. The functionally modern studios on the top floor (Nos. 707, 708, and 709) are the best picks because they are larger and have better terraces. Discounts are offered only for stays of one month or more.

NOTE: These apartments can be booked through Villas International, page 90.

ENGLISH SPOKEN: Yes

FACILITIES AND SERVICES: Air-conditioning, direct-dial phone, hair dryer available, fitted kitchens, laundry service, lift, daily maid service included, parking (1,500ptas per day), room safe (250ptas per day), handicapped access, TV

NEAREST TOURIST ATTRACTIONS: None, must use public transportation

APARTAMENTOS MUR-MAR ★★ (50)
Rambla de Santa Mònica 34
33 apartments, all with shower or bath and toilet and fitted kitchens

The apartments have a late-1940s feel to them, but they are saved because of their location and the Cheap Sleeping–friendly prices. The units themselves are huge, and so are the old-fashioned kitchens, which are serviceable but would still inspire me to eat out as often as possible. Beds range from two bunks piled on top of each other to make a day-bed sofa to proper twins and doubles. Advantages are daily maid service and linen changes three times a week. For the best experience at the Mur-Mar, book Nos. 1, 2, 3, 4, 71, or 81, which all have wraparound terraces with beautiful views of Barcelona. There is also a restaurant and outdoor café in connection with the apartment/hotel, but like the hotel, I found the food to be serviceably routine.

ENGLISH SPOKEN: Yes

FACILITIES AND SERVICES: Air-conditioned, direct-dial phone, laundry service, lift, daily maid service, office safe (150ptas per day), radio, TV

NEAREST TOURIST ATTRACTIONS: La Rambla, waterfront, Barri Gòtic

TELEPHONE
93 318 26 12

FAX
93 412 50 39

METRO
Drassanes or Liceu, 3

CREDIT CARDS
AE, DC, MC, V

RATES
Single 6,700ptas, double 9,200ptas, triple 11,200ptas, quad 13,500ptas, plus 7 percent tax

BREAKFAST
Continental 500ptas per person

CITADINES RAMBLAS ★★★ (34)
Rambla dels Estudis 122
131 studios and apartments, all with shower or bath and toilet, most with fitted kitchens

The Citadines Barcelona lives up to its motto: "At Citadines, you are at home far from home." You can't top the location, the services, and the layout of each unit, whether it is one of the hotel rooms or suites (which don't have kitchens) or one of the apartments, which range in size from commodious studios to two-room suites and all have fitted kitchens. From here you can walk to almost everything, including Barcelona's fabulous covered food market, wander the crooked streets of the Barri Gòtic, or stroll along La Rambla. The rooms are decorated in blue and yellow with smart built-in desks and large workspaces. Those on the front face La Rambla and can be noisy. Beds are excellent, lighting more than adequate, and the compact kitchens outfitted with attractive china, glassware, and cooking utensils.

TELEPHONE
93 270 11 11

FAX
93 412 74 21

EMAIL
citadbcn@globalnet.es

INTERNET
www.citadines.com

METRO
Catalunya, 1, 3

RATES
Hotel: single 14,000–16,500ptas, double 16,000–18,500ptas, suite 21,000–23,650ptas, extra bed 2,500ptas, dog 750ptas; apartment: studio (2 people) 13,000–13,500ptas, 2-room apartment (2 to 4 people) 18,500–20,000ptas; all rates plus 7 percent tax

BREAKFAST
1,155ptas per person

I also love the mirrored, marble bathrooms, which have more space than you will need, even if you move in for two months . . . as I did when I was in Barcelona to research both *Cheap Eats* and *Cheap Sleeps in Spain.*

NOTE: All the rates vary by season. You can also book your Citadines Ramblas accommodation through Villas International, page 90.

ENGLISH SPOKEN: Yes

FACILITIES AND SERVICES: Air-conditioning, conference room, direct-dial phone (with private number), hair dryer, laundry service, coin-operated washer and dryer, lift, daily maid and linen service in hotel, weekly maid and linen change in apartments, kitchens in apartments, parking (2,700ptas per day), free office safe, room safe (300ptas per day), handicapped access, satellite TV, solarium

NEAREST TOURIST ATTRACTIONS: La Rambla, Barri Gòtic

Youth Hostels

Youth hostels appeal to anyone looking for a Cheap Sleep and willing to endure bunk beds and bootcamp-style dorm rooms that can house up to ten or fifteen other budget-minded sleepers. There are institutional bathrooms on each floor, privacy is not a consideration, and neither is much comfort. You must be a member of Hostelling International (HI), which costs less than a cheap burger and a beer and gives you access to a worldwide network of Cheap Sleeps and provides endless opportunities to make contact with like-minded budget-conscious travelers. See the "Students and Teachers" section under "Discounts," page 19, for the contact information in the United States.

The Hostelling International Booking Network (IBN) Booking Office in Barcelona for onward reservations is Tujuca Central Reservations, Rocafort 116-122, tel: 93 483 83 63, fax: 93 483 83 50.

ALBERG PERE TARRÉS
C/ de Numància 149–151
96 beds, no private facilities

There are no single or double rooms at this ninety-six-bed hostel in the northern part of Barcelona, about a half hour from the city center. Rooms hold from four to twenty-six others, and in the morning lines often form at each of the five bathrooms, which you will share with twenty others. Meals can be provided for groups of twenty-five or more, otherwise you must prepare your own in the communal kitchen. There are some strict rules, some that will probably be welcomed by many: There is no smoking or alcohol permitted in the dorms, and no eating or drinking allowed outside of the dining room.

TELEPHONE: 93 410 23 09

FAX: 93 419 62 68

EMAIL: alberg@peretarres.org

INTERNET: www.peretarres.org

METRO: Maria Cristina, 3

CREDIT CARDS: MC, V

RATES: With HI card, under 25 years 1,700ptas, over 25 years 1,900ptas per night; without HI card, add 400ptas per night, sheets 400ptas, all rates taxes included

BREAKFAST: Continental incuded

ENGLISH SPOKEN: Yes

FACILITIES AND SERVICES: Kitchen priviledges, coin laundry, free lockers, parking for cars (1,300ptas per day) and motorcycles (700ptas), TV lounge

NEAREST TOURIST ATTRACTIONS: None, must use public transportation

ALBERG MARE DE DÉU DE MONTSERRAT
Passeig de la Mare de Déu del Coll 41–51
185 beds, no private facilities

The hostel is HI sanctioned and requires a membership to stay here, and in high season, your stay is limited to five nights. Dorm rooms house from four to twelve Cheap Sleepers. Half- or full-board might make Cheap Eating sense for some who don't want to commute into Barcelona for meals.

TELEPHONE: 93 483 83 63

FAX: 93 483 83 50

METRO: Vallcarca, 3

CREDIT CARDS: MC, V

RATES: Over 25 years: bed and breakfast 2,500ptas, half board 3,500ptas, full board 4,300ptas; under 25 years: bed and breakfast 2,100ptas, half board 2,650ptas, full board 3,400ptas, taxes included

BREAKFAST: Continental included

ENGLISH SPOKEN: Yes

FACILITIES AND SERVICES: Auditorium, coin laundry, handicapped access, TV/video lounge

NEAREST TOURIST ATTRACTIONS: None, must use public transportation

HOSTAL DE JOVES (39)
Passeig de Pujades 29
68 beds, no private facilities

The Hostal de Joves is the oldest hostel in Spain, and despite renovation a few years ago, it looks it. The office is open from 7 to 10 A.M. and 3 P.M. to midnight, and all Cheap Sleepers are required to vacate the premises between 10 A.M. and 3 P.M. There is a midnight curfew, but if you miss it, the door is opened for five minutes again at 1 A.M. and 2 A.M. The dorm rooms are nonsmoking, but not the TV lounge. You can only stay five nights, and you must have an HI membership card.

TELEPHONE AND FAX: 93 300 31 04

METRO: Arc de Triomf, 1

CREDIT CARDS: None, cash only

RATES: Over 25 years 1,800ptas, under 25 years 1,600ptas, sheets 225ptas, blankets 125ptas, towels 125ptas, taxes included

BREAKFAST: Continental included

ENGLISH SPOKEN: Yes

FACILITIES AND SERVICES: Coin laundry, lockers (200ptas per day), TV lounge

NEAREST TOURIST ATTRACTIONS: Parc de la Ciutadella, moderate walk to Barri Gòtic

HOSTAL KABUL (46)
Plaça Reial 17
140 beds, no private facilities

Cheap Sleepers either love or hate the Kabul, a laid-back crash pad right on the Plaça Reial. It is privately owned and belongs to the same group as the Three Ducks in Paris and The Generator in London, both listed in *Cheap Sleeps* for those cities. Rooms can sleep from two to twelve, and the best ones are those overlooking the Plaça, provided you can sleep through the continual noise. Nonsmokers beware: Everyone seems to chain smoke, including the desk staff.

TELEPHONE: 93 318 51 90

FAX: 93 310 40 34

EMAIL: kabul@kabul-hostel.com

INTERNET: www.kabul-hostel.com

METRO: Liceu, 3

CREDIT CARDS: None, cash only

RATES: 1,700ptas per bed, 1,100ptas for a key, sheets 200ptas, taxes included

BREAKFAST: Continental 250–400ptas, bacon and eggs 500ptas

ENGLISH SPOKEN: Yes

FACILITIES AND SERVICES: Coin laundry, office safe (150ptas per day), TV lounge

NEAREST TOURIST ATTRACTIONS: Heart of Barri Gòtic, La Rambla, waterfront

Glossary of Catalan Words and Phrases

Catalan is its own language, and it is spoken in Barcelona, along with Castilian Spanish. Those with a little knowledge of French or Spanish grammar will be able to pick up Catalan without too much trouble. Although half the population of Barcelona is not of Catalan origin, most understand and speak it, if only because all the public signs and maps are exclusively written in Catalan. Also, all radio and television stations must broadcast at least half their programs in Catalan, and children are taught it in school. Locals do not expect tourists to know Catalan, but if you make a goodwill attempt at speaking either Catalan or Spanish, and add gestures, you will get by. If you are trying to win someone's heart, "I love you" in Catalan is *t'estimo*. On the other side of the coin, *ves-te'n a la merda* means "go to hell." Below are a few helpful Catalan words and phrases to get you started. For a list of Catalan shopping terms, please see the "Glossary of Cheap Chic Words and Phrases," page 232. For the main, Castilian glossary, see page 234.

General Phrases

please	*si us plau*
thank you (very much)	*(moltes) gràcies*
You are welcome.	*De rés.*
yes/no	*sí/no*
hello/(on the phone)	*hola/digui'm*
How are you?	*¿Com estás?*
good morning, good day	*bon dia*
good afternoon, good evening	*bona tarda*
good night	*bona nit*
good-bye	*adéu*
See you later.	*Fins després.*
Do you speak English?	*¿Parla anglés?*
I am sorry I do not speak Catalan.	*Ho sento, no parlo català.*
I don't understand.	*No entenc.*
How do you say that in Catalan?	*¿Com se diu això en Català?*
What is your name?	*¿Com se diu?*
Sir/Madam/Miss	*senyor/senyora/senyoreta*
girl/boy/child (affectionate)	*una noia/un noi/nen(a)*
excuse me/sorry	*perdoni/disculpi*

excuse me, please	*escolti*
Why?	*¿Perqué?*
When?	*¿Quan?*
Who is it?	*¿Qui és?*
What time is it?	*¿Qué hora és?*
Where is . . . ?	*¿On és . . . ?*
good	*bo/bona*
very good, great	*molt bé*
bad	*dolent/a, malament*
nothing	*res*
a lot/a little	*força/un mica*
Stop, enough!	*Prou!*

At the Hotel

How much is it?	*¿Quant és?*
expensive/cheap	*ar/a, barat/a*
with	*amb*
without	*sense*
I like.	*M'agrada.*
I would like.	*Vull.*
I do not want.	*No vull.*
What do you want?	*¿Que vols?*
small	*petit*
big	*gran*
price	*preu*
free	*gratuit/de franc*
more	*més*
less	*menys*
more or less	*més o menys*

Signs

entrance	*entrada*
exit	*sortida*
open	*obert(a)*
closed	*tancat*

Getting Around

a ticket/metro ticket	*un billet/tarjeta*
return	*d'anada I tornado*
card expired (metro)	*teitol esgotat*

left/right	*esquerre(a)/dret(a)*
here/there	*aquí/allí*
straight ahead/at the corner	*tot recte/a la cantonada*
near/far	*a prop/lluny*
Is it far?	*¿És lluny?*
boat	*vaixell*
bus	*autobús*
car	*cotxe*
direction	*direcció*

Places

beach	*platja*
block	*illa*
bullring	*plaça de braus*
building	*edifici*
bus stop	*parada*
church	*esglesia*
district	*barri*
garden	*jardí*
museum	*museu*
park	*parc*
station	*estació*
theater	*teatre*

Time

morning	*el mati*
midday	*migdía*
afternoon	*a tarda*
evening	*el vespre*
now/later	*ara/més tard*
yesterday/today/tomorrow	*ahir/avui/demà*
tomorrow morning	*demá pel matí*
day before tomorrow	*abans d'ahir*
day after tomorrow	*demà passat*
At what time?	*¿A quina hora?*
in an hour	*en una hora*
sometimes	*a vegades*
never	*mai*

Days, Months, Seasons

Monday	*Dilluns*
Tuesday	*Dimarts*
Wednesday	*Dimecres*
Thursday	*Dijous*
Friday	*Divendres*
Saturday	*Dissabte*
Sunday	*Diumenge*
weekend	*cap de setmana*
January	*Gener*
February	*Feber*
March	*Març*
April	*Abril*
May	*Maig*
June	*Juny*
July	*Juliol*
August	*Agost*
September	*Setembre*
October	*Octobre*
November	*Novembre*
December	*Desembre*
spring	*primavera*
summer	*estiu*
autumn/fall	*tardor*
winter	*hivern*
Christmas	*Nadal*
holiday	*festa*
holidays	*vacances*

Numbers

0	*zero*
1	*un, una*
2	*dos, dues*
3	*tres*
4	*quatre*
5	*cinc*
6	*sis*
7	*set*
8	*vuit*

9	*nou*
10	*deu*
11	*onze*
12	*dotze*
13	*tretze*
14	*catorze*
15	*quinze*
16	*setze*
17	*disset*
18	*divuit*
19	*dinou*
20	*vint*
21	*vint-i-u*
22	*vint-i-dos, vint-i-dues*
30	*trenta*
40	*quaranta*
50	*cinquanta*
60	*seixanta*
70	*setanta*
80	*vuitanta*
90	*noranta*
100	*cent*
200	*dos-cent, dues-cents*
1,000	*mil*
1,000,000	*un milló*

MADRID

It may truly be affirmed that as God worked six days, and rested on the seventh, Madrileños rest the six, and on the seventh . . . go to the bull fight.
—*H.O'Shea,* A Guide to Spain, *1865*

Madrid is a city of more than three million people and known for its cosmopolitan lifestyle and world-famous art museums, including the renowned golden triangle—the Museo del Prado, Museo Thyssen-Bornemisza, and the Museo Nacional Centro de Arte Reina Sofía. The world-famous Prado houses the most important schools of painting from the twelfth to the nineteenth centuries and is widely considered one of the world's richest collections for its quality and variety. The Thyssen-Bornemisza includes eight hundred paintings spanning the great masters and schools from the thirteenth century to the present day, making the collection an incomparable survey of the history of Western art. The Reina Sofía is an impressive collection of twentieth-century Spanish art, including masterpieces by the great geniuses of the Spanish avant-garde: Picasso, Miró, and Dalí. Picasso's famed *Guernica* occupies a place of honor in the collection because of its historic and artistic importance.

Except for five years in the early 1600s, Madrid has been the capital of Spain since Philip II moved his court here in 1561, and it is the country's geographic, administrative, and financial center. To say that Madrileños take pride in their city is an understatement. There is a local saying, *Madrid es el puerta del cielo*, which means Madrid is the door to heaven. A great deal of Madrid life takes place out of doors, on the streets, especially on the weekends and during the hot months, when there seems to be an unwritten law that no one can go to bed before daybreak. Madrid really comes into its own during the May festivities, especially the celebrations in honor of the city's patron saint, San Isidro Labrador (May 15). During this time there are open-air dances, all-night parties, and the most famous bullfighting festival in the world, *Madrid en Danza*.

When it comes to Madrid hotels, you are paying for location, not charm and amenities. Noise from the street can be a nightly problem. In the Cheaper Sleeps, you probably won't be served breakfast or be able to get a room with air-conditioning, but you might be able to negotiate paying for your stay in cash, thus avoiding the added 7 percent IVA (value-added tax).

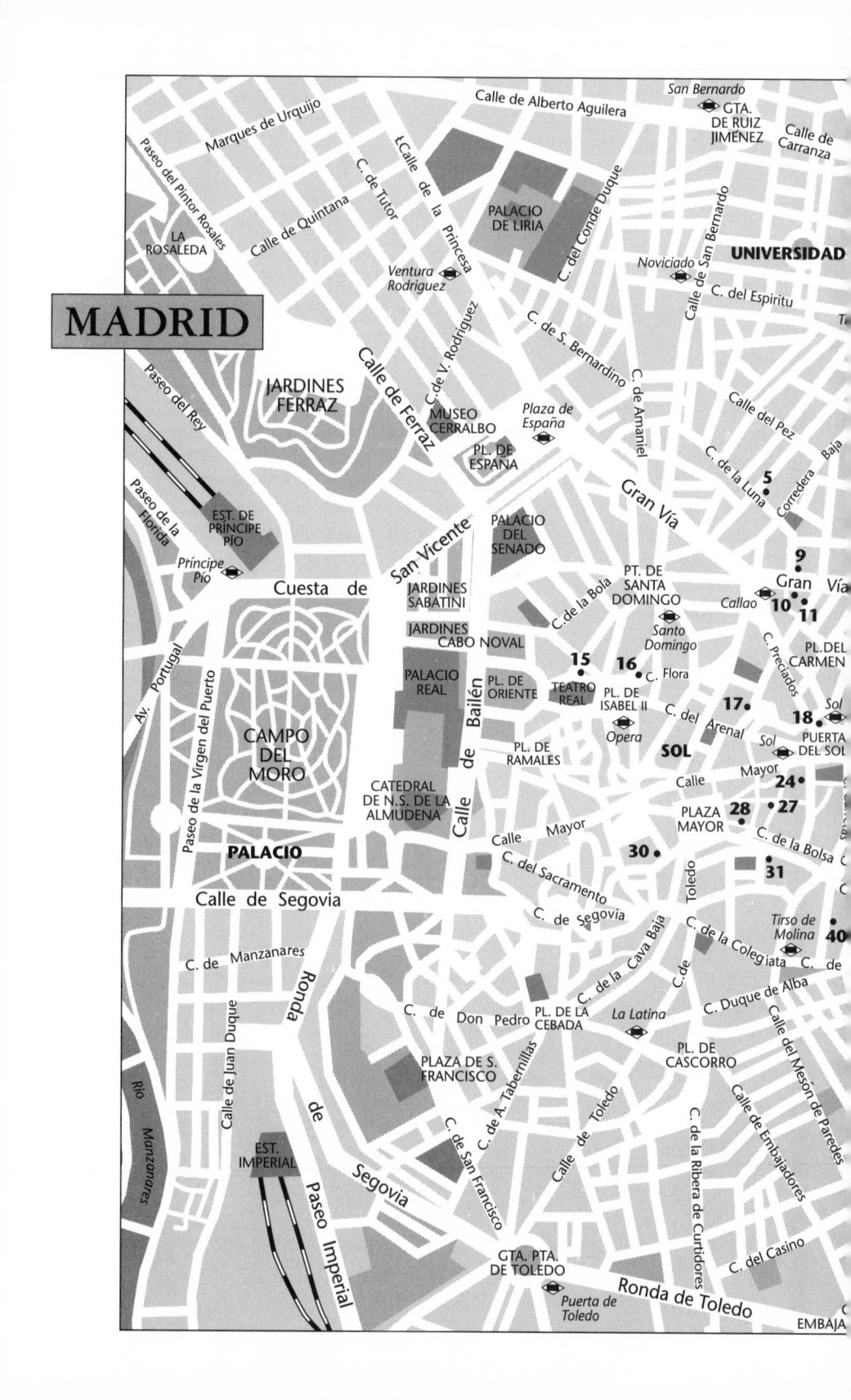

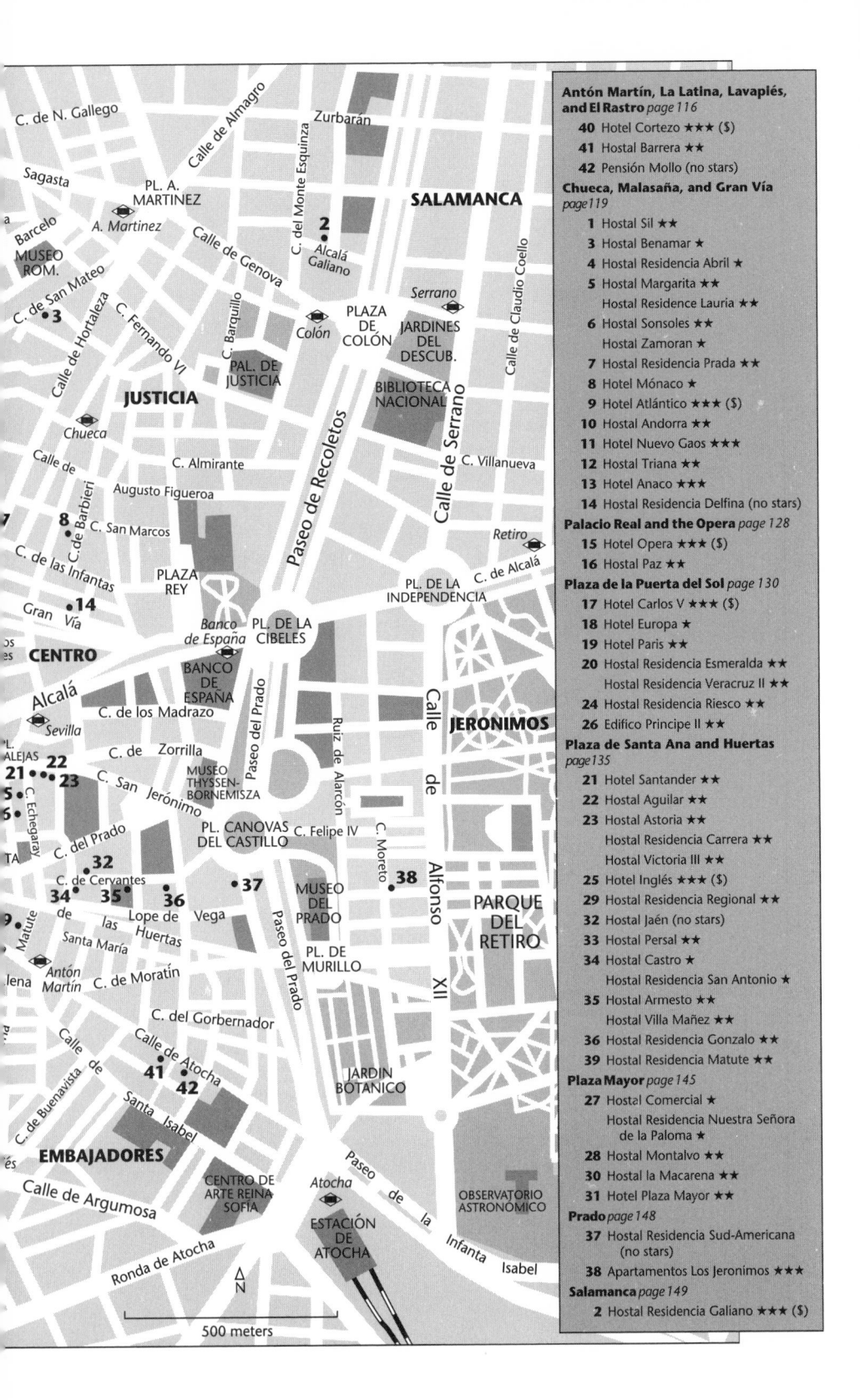

General Information

ADDRESSES

Addresses in Spain are written differently than those in the States. For a description of how to decipher Madrid addresses and of their many abbreviations, please see the "Addresses" section, page 33, under "How to Use *Cheap Sleeps in Spain.*"

BUSINESS HOURS

Business hours are from Monday to Friday from around 9:30 or 10 A.M. to 2 P.M., then from 5 P.M. to 8 or 8:30 P.M. Most shops observe the same morning hours on Saturday and close in the afternoon. El Corte Inglés department stores remain open from about 10 A.M. to 9 P.M., Monday to Saturday. Banks are open Monday to Friday from 9 A.M. to 2 P.M., and from October to May on Saturday until 1 P.M. Lunch usually begins around 2 P.M. and dinner around 9 or 10 P.M., even later in the summer.

In the summer, Madrid just about shuts down, or so it seems. From mid-July until the first of September, many bars, restaurants, and offices are closed. However, if you are here during that time of sweltering heat, you'll find that the nightlife lasts longer, there are some special music programs, hotel prices can be discounted, and the city can seem calm and almost peaceful—since half its residents have abandoned the town and fled to the Costa del Sol.

Most museums and many bars and restaurants close on Monday. Major museums that are open on Monday are the Reina Sofía and the Palacio Real.

CLIMATE

Madrid is cold and reasonably dry in the winter; lovely but full of pollen in the spring; almost unbearably hot and dry in the summer; and warm and pleasant in the fall. As such, the best times to go are either in the spring or fall, trying to avoid November and April, which are the rainy months. Average seasonal temperatures are as follows: spring, 6.5° to 18.5°C (44°–65°F); summer, 15.5° to 40°C (60°–104°F); fall, 7.5° to 20.5°C (45.5°–69°F); and winter, .5° to 10.5°C (33°–51°F).

DISABLED TRAVELERS

For more information about negotiating Madrid if you have a disability, contact the Organizacíon Nacional de Ciegos de España, Calle de Prado 24; tel: 91 589 4,600 or 91 577 37 56. Wheelchair-accessible taxis, called *Eurotaxis*, are available from Radio Taxi; tel: 91 547 82 00. Fares are the same as for regular taxis.

EMBASSIES

There is an American Embassy in Madrid at Calle de Serrano 75; tel: 91 577 40 00; metro: Rubén Daríol, 5; hours: Mon–Fri 9 A.M.–12:30 P.M., 3–5 P.M.; the visa section is open 8:30–11 A.M.

The Canadian Embassy is at Calle de Núñez de Balboa 35; tel: 91 431 43 00; metro: Velázquez, 4.

The British Embassy is at Calle de Fernando el Santo 16; tel: 91 319 02 00; metro: Alonso Martínez, 4, 5, 10; hours: Mon–Fri 9 A.M.–1:30 P.M., 3–6 P.M.

EMERGENCY NUMBERS

For information on where to go for medical treatment in a non-emergency situation, see "Medical Problems," page 110.

Ambulance	061, 91 588 45 00, 91 522 22 22
Fire	080
Pharmacies	010, 098
Police	091 (national), or 092 (local)

HOLIDAYS AND FESTIVALS

For a complete list of national holidays, see "Holidays and Festivals," page 20. Listed below are the regional and city holidays and festivals celebrated in Madrid.

Three Kings Day	*Reyes Magos*	January 6
Maundy Thursday	*Jueves Santo*	Day before Good Friday
Madrid Day	*Día de la Comunidad de Madrid*	May 2
Madrid's Patron Saint's Day	*San Isidro*	May 15
San Isidro Festival	*Fiestas de San Isidro*	Third week in May
	Corpus Christi	June
Feast of St. John the Baptist	*Día de San Juan Bautista*	June 24
Feast of St. James the Apostle	*Día de Santiago Apóstol*	July 25
	Virgen de la Paloma	August 15
	Virgen de la Almudena	November 9
Immaculate Conception	*La Immaculada Concepeción*	December 8

LOST PROPERTY

If you lose something at the airport, report it to the Aviación Civil office or call 91 393 60 00 and ask for *objetos perdidos* (lost objects).

If the loss happens on a bus, report it to the EMT, Calle de Alcántara 24-26; tel: 91 401 31 00; metro: Lista, 4; hours: Mon–Fri 8 A.M.–2 P.M.

If you are on the Metro or in a taxi, contact the Negociado de Objetos Perdidos, Plaza de Legazpi 7; tel: 91 588 43 46; metro: Legazpi, 3, 6; hours: Mon–Fri 9 A.M.–2 P.M. (till 1:30 P.M. in the summer).

Finally, if you lose something at a railway station, look for the *Atención al Viajero* desk or the *Jefe de Estación* office.

MEDICAL PROBLEMS

The best thing to do in an emergency is to go to the *urgencias,* or casualty department, of any major hospital (see "Emergency Numbers," page 109, for immediate care). Two of the larger hospitals with emergency units are the following: Hospital Clínico San Carlos, Plaza de Cristo Rey; tel: 91 330 37 47; metro: Moncloa, 6; and Hospital Gregorio Marañón, Calle Dr Esquerdo 46; tel: 91 586 80 00; metro: O'Donnell, 6.

Unidad Médica Angloamericana is a British-American clinic that has a bilingual staff, will make house calls, and offers a full range of medical services, including dentistry. They are at Calle del Conde de Aranda 1; tel: 91 435 18 23; metro: Retiro, 2; hours: Mon–Fri 9 A.M.–8 P.M., emergencies only on Sat 10 A.M.–1 P.M., closed Sun and holidays. In August, they have abbreviated weekday hours (10 A.M.–5 P.M.).

The Instituto de Medicina Natural is a clinic offering acupuncture, homeopathy, chiropractors, and other forms of alternative health care. Some English is spoken. They are at Plaza de la Independencia 4; tel: 91 576 26 49; metro: Retiro, 2; hours: Mon–Fri 9 A.M.–9 P.M., Sat–Sun 9 A.M.–2 P.M.

If you need a dentist, the Clínica Dental Cisne offers free consultations in Spanish, but consultations cost 3,000ptas in English. They are at Calle de Magallanes 18; tel: 91 446 32 21; metro: Quevedo, 2; hours: Mon, Thur 10 A.M.–1:30 P.M., 3–8 P.M.; Tues, Wed, Fri 2–8 P.M. Call to check if they are open in August; they don't take credit cards.

Pharmacies

You can recognize a pharmacy by the large green cross in front. Hours are generally from 9:30 A.M. to 2 P.M., and 5 to 8 P.M., but every district has a pharmacy that is open all night and on Sunday. Call 010 or 098 for information in Spanish, or look on the door of your local pharmacy for the name and address of the nearest open one.

There are two twenty-four-hour pharmacies: Farmacia Central, Paseo de Santa María de la Cabeza 64; tel: 91 473 06 72; metro: Palos de la Frontera, 3; no credit cards. And Farmacia Lastra, Calle del Conde de Peñalver 27; tel: 91 402 43 63; metro: Goya, 2, 4; credit cards: AE, DC, MC, V.

MONEY

Most of Madrid's banks are on Calle de Acalá and Gran Vía. See "Money Matters," page 21, for a discussion of changing money at banks. If you are stuck, and have no choice but to change money at an exchange office, try Chequepoint, Plaza de Callao 4; metro: Callao, 3, 5; hours: daily twenty-four hours. American Express has a main office at Plaza de las Cortes 2 (entrance on Marqués de Cubas); tel: 91 322 54 40, 91 322 54 55; metro: Sevilla, 2; hours: Mon–Fri 9 A.M.–5:30 P.M., Sat until noon.

If you are faced with a credit card emergency, contact one of the numbers below, all of which have English-speaking operators and are open twenty-four hours daily.

American Express	Credit card emergencies, 91 572 03 20, 91 572 03 03; traveler's check emergencies, 91 900 994 426
Diner's Club	91 547 40 00
MasterCard	91 900 971 231, 91 519 21 00
Visa	91 900 974 445

Wiring Money

Western Union is the quickest way to have money sent to you abroad. It should arrive about one hour after being sent. The commission is paid by the sender. You can do this at Change Express, Gran Vía 16; tel: 91 900 633 633 or 91 523 45 31; metro: Gran Vía, 1, 5; hours: daily 10 A.M.–10 P.M.

MUSEUM DISCOUNTS

There are several ways to reduce the cost of visiting Madrid's splendid art galleries and museums. The best way is to time your visit during the free admission times. If you are under eighteen or over sixty-five, you will not pay Saturday afternoon from 2 to 9 P.M. On Sunday admission is free for everyone, regardless of age, and the lethal crowds this draws means you have to arrive *early* to avoid spending all your time standing in line.

Another excellent option is the Paseo del Arte ticket, which is available for Madrid's Big Three—the Museo del Prado, Museo Thyssen-Bornemisza, and the Museo Nacional Centro de Arte Reina Sofía. The cost is 1,050ptas. After visiting one musum with the ticket you must visit the other two within a calendar year. If you won't be here on a Sunday, or don't want to fight the crowds, this ticket makes lots of sense. Strangely enough, there is not much publicity about this, and you may have to ask for it, but it is sold at the ticket desks in all three museums. A year's ticket for unlimited visits to either El Prado or the Reina Sofía costs 4,000ptas. A yearly ticket to both and a series of nine other museums throughout Spain is 6,000ptas. These tickets are also sold at the respective museums.

POST OFFICE

The main post office is the Palacio de Comunicaciones, Plaza de la Cibeles; tel: 91 537 64 94 or 91 521 65 00; metro: Banco de España, 2. Stamps are sold Monday to Friday 8 A.M.–10 P.M., Saturday 8:30 A.M.– 8 P.M. Packages are sent from Puerta N on the south side of the building.

There is also a low-priced packing service. The package section is open Monday to Friday 8 A.M.–9 P.M., Saturday until 2 P.M. To send an express letter, say you want it sent *urgente*.

Letters sent *poste restante* (general delivery) should be addressed as follows:

> Your name
> c/o Lista de Correos
> 2800 Madrid, España

To pick up a letter sent this way, you must show your passport. Go to window No. 18 at the Post Restante section in the main post office. Hours are Monday to Friday 8 A.M.–8 P.M., Saturday until 2 P.M.

Branch offices are open Monday to Saturday 9 A.M.–2 P.M. One of the most convenient is at El Corte Inglés, Calle de Preciados; metro: Sol, 1, 2, 3.

SAFETY AND SECURITY

Street crime in Madrid usually consists of purse snatchers and pick-pockets, most of whom work in pairs or groups. There are some areas where you should be more cautious. Plaza de Santa Ana and the bars around it is an area where the gypsies work. Bag snatching has been raised to an art form in and around Plaza del Sol, Plaza Mayor, and El Rastro. The area around the Chueca metro stop is known for drugs, and the most prevalent red light district is between the Gran Vía and Calle Montera.

If you are robbed or attacked, report the incident to the nearest police station (Policia Nacional Comisaria); you will need a police report to file any insurance claims back home. The Policia Nacional headquarters for Madrid is open twenty-four hours a day: Jefatura Superior de Policía, Calle del Fomento 24; tel: 91 541 71 60; metro: Santo Domingo, 2. There are other offices throughout the city.

TELEPHONE

The country code for Spain is 34; the telephone code for Madrid is 91. For directory inquiries, dial 003; for general information, directory assistance, dial 098. To get the time, dial 093, and to get the weather, dial 906 36 53 65. For more information about making calls in Spain, see "Telephone," page 30.

You can make international or local telephone calls from either of these two main *telefónica* offices: Paseo de los Recoletos 37-41; metro: Colón, 4; and Gran Vía 30; metro: Callao or Gran Vía, 1, 5. Both are open Mon–Sat 9:30 A.M.–midnight, Sun and holidays noon–midnight. Or, go to the Palacio de Comunicaciones, Plaza de Cibeles; metro: Banco de España, 2; hours: Mon–Fri 8 A.M.–midnight, Sun and holidays 8 A.M.–10 P.M.

TOURIST INFORMATION

In the summer there are information kiosks at Puerta del Sol and at the Prado Museum. Information officers in blue and yellow outfits are stationed at the Prado, the Palacio Real, and in the Plaza Mayor to answer questions. Summer hours are July and August, daily 10 A.M.–2 P.M., 4–8 P.M. For a complete weekly listing of what's happening in the city—from films, theater, the arts, and museums to a comprehensive section of restaurant advertising—buy the *Guía del Ocio* at any newsstand. It comes out every Friday, and though it is written in Spanish, it is easy to decipher.

There is also a tourist information line: Call 010, Mon–Fri 8:30 A.M.–9:30 P.M. Calls are handled in French and English as well as Spanish, and they answer questions about events promoted by the Madrid City Council.

The major tourist offices are:

Oficina Municipal de Turismo
Plaza Mayor 3
Tel: 91 366 54 77, 91 588 16 36
Metro: Sol, 1, 2, 3
Hours: Mon–Fri 10 A.M.–8 P.M., Sat until 2 P.M.

Torre de Madrid
C/ de la Princessa 1 (entrance on corner of Plaza de España)
Tel: 91 541 23 25
Metro: Plaza de España, 3, 10
Hours: Mon–Fri 9 A.M.–7 P.M., Sat until 1 P.M.

TRANSPORTATION

Madrid is an easy city to negotiate. There is an excellent metro system, extensive bus routes, and reasonably priced taxis, and except for the hot summer months, walking is very pleasant. On the other hand, avoid if at all possible renting a car in Madrid. Traffic is horrendous, street parking difficult, and parking lots expensive. A million cars jam the city streets daily—don't make it a million and one. If you are renting a car for trips around Madrid, pick it up on your way out of town.

Airport

Shuttle buses leave every fifteen minutes from outside the arrivals terminal, and they drop off/pick up in the city at Plaza de Colón (metro: Colón, 4). At Colón the bus terminal is underground beneath the plaza, and buses leave from here every quarter hour for the Barajas Airport. Depending on traffic, the 16km trip can take from a half hour to an hour. A one-way ticket is roughly 400ptas. Airport information is 91 393 60 00.

Bus

Madrid's bus system—Empresa Municipal de Transportes (EMT)—
has 170 routes. The main office is at Calle de Alcántara 24-26; tel: 91 580
19 80 or 91 401 99 00 (twenty-four hours); metro: Lista, 4. While the
bus allows you to see more as you travel, mastering the schedule and
routes could take more vacation time than you want to devote to it. If you
plan on using the bus, it is best to buy a combination *Bonobús* ticket (*bono
de diez viajes*), which allows you ten rides for around 700ptas. You can't
buy *Bonobús* tickets on the bus; they are sold at *estancos* (tobacco shops),
newsstands, and the EMT information booths at Puerta del Sol, Plaza de
Cibeles, Plaza de Callao, and other locations around the city. Route maps
are available from the tourist offices. Buses run from 6 A.M. to midnight,
and there are several all-night routes that leave from the Plaza de la
Cibeles and Puerta del Sol every half hour from 12:30 to 2 A.M., and
hourly from 2 to 6 A.M.

If you plan on spending more than a week in Madrid, consider buying
a monthly season ticket, *Abono Transportes.* Unlike the *Bonobús* ticket, this
is valid for both the metro and the bus. A one-month, unlimited ticket
for Zone A, which covers all of Madrid, costs around 4,500ptas, with
lower rates for those under twenty-one or over sixty-five. To purchase an
Abono Transportes, you need an identity card, available only from *estancos,*
and two passport-size photos. After the initial purchase, you can buy
tickets, *cupones,* to revalidate the original card at metro stations, EMT
kiosks, and *estancos.* The *Abono* is valid for a calendar month, not for thirty
days from the date of purchase.

Metro

The Madrid metro system is fast, clean, and easy to master. It runs
daily from 6 A.M. to 1:30 A.M. Each line is identified by a number and
color code. For best results, buy a multitrip ticket (*bono de diez viajes*) for
ten rides; it costs around 700ptas and can be purchased either from a
ticket booth inside the metro station or at one of the automatic machines.
If you plan on being in Madrid for more than a week, consider buying a
monthly *Abono Transportes* ticket, which is good on both the buses and the
metro (see "Bus," above, for a full description). For metro information,
try the office at Calle de Cavanilles 58; tel: 91 552 59 09; metro: Conde
de Casal, 6; hours: Mon–Fri 8:30 A.M.–2 P.M.

Taxis

Taxis are cheap in comparison to many other European cities, and
there are plenty of them—more than fifteen thousand roam the city
streets. Taxis are painted white with a red stripe on the front doors, and a
taxi from the airport to central Madrid should run about 2,700ptas,
depending on traffic, how much luggage you have, and any other supple-
mental charges, such as for Sunday and driving at night. To avoid being

ripped off, use taxis that are in the official ranks outside at the airport, and make sure the meter is at zero when you start. Avoid scam artists who approach you in person inside the airport terminal.

It is so easy to hail a cab that it is seldom necessary to call one. If you need to, here are some numbers of taxi services: 91 547 82 00, 91 447 51 80, 91 445 90 08. Remember, the cost of the trip starts from the point where the call was answered. If you want a receipt, ask for *un recibo, por favor*. If you think you have been cheated, make sure the receipt is fully filled out, including the driver's signature and the number of the taxi. Keep a copy of the receipt and send the original to the city taxi office, Sección de Auto Taxi y Vehículos de Alquiler, Ayuntamiento de Madrid, Calle de Vallehermoso 1, 28015, Madrid; tel: 91 477 07 14/15.

Trains

There are two main train stations in Madrid, Atocha, and Chamartín. You can buy train tickets at the American Express office, the individual train stations, the Barajas Airport arrivals hall, or the main RENFE office, Calle de Acalá 44; tel: 91 562 33 33; metro: Banco de España, 2; hours: Mon–Fri 9 A.M.–7 P.M., Sat until 1 P.M. For information, call 91 563 02 02 or 91 328 90 20.

WALKING TOURS

Every Saturday morning you can take advantage of a guided tour of Madrid's old city, or the Madrid of the Austrias, as it is officially named. The English-language tours leave from the municipal Tourist Office at Plaza Mayor 3 at 10 A.M.; tel: 91 588 16 36. If you want the tour conducted in Spanish, be there at noon. The price is 500ptas for adults, and 400ptas for students and seniors. The tour lasts about two hours and is an in-depth look at how Madrid was dominated by the Hapsburgs from the sixteenth to the eighteenth centuries. One of the most interesting aspects of the tour is the visit to Madrid's splendid Town Hall, which is otherwise not open to visitors. At the end of the tour, you can buy sweets handmade by nuns. You will never see the nuns, who are hidden behind a wooden door. Instead, they ask how many cookies or candies you want to buy, then you slide the money in through a little window, and they slide your purchase out.

Hotels in Madrid by Area

ANTÓN MARTÍN, LA LATINA, LAVAPIÉS, AND EL RASTRO

The areas south of Puerta del Sol and the Plaza Mayor and between Gran Vía de San Francisco and Calle de Atocha are roughly divided into La Latina, Lavapiés, and El Rastro. To the southeast, and close to the Centro del Arte Reina Sofía, is Antón Martín. The La Latina area contains the old Muslim quarter known as La Morería and the Mudéjar tower of the second-oldest church in Madrid, San Pedro El Viejo. Also here is the tree-shaded Plaza de la Paja, which was a major center in the city before Plaza Mayor was built. This graceful plaza is ringed with restored buildings and is a fine place sit and relax over a cool drink—away from Madrid's maddening traffic. During the reign of Queen Isabella, the Plaza de Lavapiés was the center of Madrid's Jewish community. El Rastro is the Sunday morning outdoor flea market, and here you can find everything from nuts and bolts to cheap clothing, expensive antiques (some of a dubious age), and great junk food—as well as pickpockets on the prowl, so be careful.

HOTELS

($) indicates a Big Splurge

HOSTAL BARRERA ★★ (41)
C/ de Atocha 96, 2°
15 rooms, 3 with shower or bath and toilet, some with shower only

By the entry, a collection of snapshots of previous guests tells you all you need to know: Lots of happy campers have stayed here, and you will do well to join them. This fifteen-room *hostal* offers impressive value and a convenient location within walking distance to both the Museo del Prado and the Centro de Arte Reina Sofía. Simple decorating touches pull the rooms together and give them a sense of style. In each one there are one or two framed travel photos taken by family members or friends during trips in Spain or abroad. As with most small hotels, the best rooms face out, even though that means an element of noise. One of these is No. 11, a bright single with a shower but no toilet (none of the singles have full private facilities). It has a fabric backdrop behind the bed with matching blue trim on the curtains and tiles. A round table with a cushioned chair adds a comfortable note. Number 10 is another single, but without a shower. The room has a shelf, good mirror, and a medicine chest over a sink. Number 7 is a nice blue-and-red twin-bedded room, and No. 6, in green, is slightly bigger with a bentwood coat rack to make up for the smaller closet; it also has lovely photos of a house in Dublin, Ireland, and of London Bridge. My least favorite rooms are No. 18, a corner room with too much noise, and No. 15, a dark, inside-facing double with bars on the windows. Note that if you pay in cash and don't need a receipt, and the tax will be included in your bill, not charged extra.

ENGLISH SPOKEN: Fluently

FACILITIES AND SERVICES: Lift

NEAREST TOURIST ATTRACTIONS: Museu del Prado, Centro de Arte Reina Sofía, and Museo Thyssen-Bornemisza, Botanical Gardens, Retiro Park

TELEPHONE
91 527 53 81
FAX
91 527 39 50
EMAIL
snowy@accesocero.es
METRO
Antón Martín, 1
CREDIT CARDS
MC, V
RATES
Single 2,200–3,200ptas, double 3,500–3,900ptas, triple 5,100–5,600ptas, plus 7 percent tax
BREAKFAST
Not served

HOTEL CORTEZO ★★★ (40, $)
C/ del Doctor Cortezo 3, near C/ de Atocha
90 rooms, all with shower or bath and toilet

The hotel is on a small street close to the famous Plaza Mayor and the Rastro flea market, which operates on Sunday mornings. The modern, color-coordinated rooms are equipped with all the necessities—from air-conditioning to a safe—and are typical of a worldwide chain

TELEPHONE
91 369 01 01; toll-free in the U.S., Best Western 800-528-1234
FAX
91 369 37 74
INTERNET
www.bestwestern.com

METRO
Tirso de Molina, 1
CREDIT CARDS
AE, DC, MC, V
RATES
Single 12,000ptas, double
15,000ptas, triple 19,000ptas,
suite 18,500ptas, plus
7 percent tax
BREAKFAST
Buffet 1,100ptas per person

in that they offer absolutely no elements of surprise. Number 111, a double, has peachy-pink walls, tile floors, and dark furniture. There is an armchair, a glass-topped writing desk, and a window that looks onto an interior courtyard. In the bathroom, I like the regulation-size tub, the mirrored sink space, and the stack of good towels. Room 114 is a twin-bedded room with a city view. It has the same colors and furniture, but the slightly larger bathroom has a window and stool so you can sit down if you want. My major complaint with this hotel is that the hall carpeting is way past its prime and needs to be replaced. However, since all the rooms have tile floors, you won't have to live with aging carpets, which with any luck will be replaced before you check in.

ENGLISH SPOKEN: Yes

FACILITIES AND SERVICES: Air-conditioning, bar, conference room, direct-dial phone, hair dryer available, laundry service, lift, minibar, parking (1,950ptas per day), restaurant, room service, room safe (100ptas per use), satellite TV

NEAREST TOURIST ATTRACTIONS: Rastro flea market, Plaza Mayor, Plaza de la Puerta del Sol

PENSIÓN MOLLO (no stars, 42)
C/ de Atocha 104, 4°
13 rooms, 3 with shower or bath and toilet

TELEPHONE
91 528 71 76
METRO
Antón Martín or Atocha, 1
CREDIT CARDS
None, cash only
RATES
Single 1,900ptas, double
3,500–3,600ptas, triple
5,300ptas, tax included
BREAKFAST
Not served

Aniceto and his wife, Victoria, have been offering Cheap Sleeps in Madrid for almost twenty years to budget-minded travelers willing to climb the seventy-five steps from the street to the fourth-floor door of the pension. The rooms are clean. Two doubles and one triple have private facilities, several have shower boxes, and all the others share three new bathrooms that have stall showers and tubs. Most of the rooms face the busy Calle de Atocha, and yes, that means they are noisy, but also larger and lighter. The alternative is to book a dark room with an interior view. Nothing is fancy here, including the prices, which are fair and a good value.

ENGLISH SPOKEN: Yes

FACILITIES AND SERVICES: None

NEAREST TOURIST ATTRACTIONS: Centro de Arte Reina Sofía, Museo del Prado, Museo Thyssen-Bornemisza, Botanical Gardens, Retiro Park

CHUECA, MALASAÑA, AND GRAN VÍA

Gran Vía is well named. It's Madrid's main thoroughfare, running from Plaza de la Cibeles to Plaza de España and dividing the old and new parts of the city. Grand buildings in a variety of architectural styles—from rococo to Art Deco and modern—line each side of the wide boulevard, which is also the commercial center of the city. It has more banks, hotels of all categories, shops, and people than you could ever count. The areas of Chueca and neighboring Malasaña offer a look into the lives of everyday people going about their business. The Museo Municipal, the Museo Romántico, and several lovely churches are also of interest here. After the sun sets the area is transformed into one of Madrid's liveliest nocturnal centers, with enough bars, cafés, discos, and restaurants to suit everyone's taste and pocketbook.

HOTELS

($) indicates a Big Splurge

HOSTAL ANDORRA ★★ (10)
Gran Vía 33, 7°
20 rooms, all with shower or bath and toilet

The Andorra is near the middle of Gran Vía, putting it as close to the Palacio Real and the Opera as to Puerta del Sol. The sitting room has three windows facing the busy avenue—along with a row of five contour chairs in front of a television set—but luckily the rooms face a

TELEPHONE
91 532 31 16
FAX
91 531 66 03
EMAIL
andorra@arrakis.es
METRO
Callao, 3, 5

CREDIT CARDS
AE, DC, MC, V
RATES
Single 4,800ptas, double
6,700ptas, triple 8,200ptas, tax
included
BREAKFAST
Contintental 350ptas per
person

side street, which is a real bonus when it comes to getting a good night's sleep. Provided you like the location, you will like the rooms, which have matching furnishings, the television positioned at eye level, and the serviceable private bathrooms. Number 709 is a large twin or triple with a balcony. However, the mirrored armoire is so close to the bed that it is difficult to get into it to access your clothes, and if the Murphy bed on the other wall is down, the room becomes a tight fit for three. Three people can live more comfortably in No. 715, which is on the interior side of the building; it has three twin beds that leave more space to negotiate the room.

ENGLISH SPOKEN: In varying degrees

FACILITIES AND SERVICES: Direct-dial phones, hair dryer, fans, lift, room safe (150ptas per use), TV

NEAREST TOURIST ATTRACTIONS: Shopping along Gran Vía, Opera, Palacio Real

HOSTAL BENAMAR ★ (3)
C/ de San Mateo 20, 2°
22 rooms, 1 with shower or bath and toilet

TELEPHONE
91 308 00 92
FAX
91 319 52 55
METRO
Tribunal, 1, 10
CREDIT CARDS
None, cash only
RATES
Single 2,300ptas, double
3,700ptas, triple 6,200ptas, tax
included
BREAKFAST
Not served

Owner José runs a clean, quiet backpacker's Cheap Sleep near the university district and Chueca. The rooms have recently been repainted, and all but the triple share four communal bathrooms. Most of the simple rooms have a balcony and hot and cold running water, but you can forget about such "frills" as bedside lights, comfortable seating, or decor of any sort. Still, it's cheap and clean, and José speaks English.

ENGLISH SPOKEN: Yes

FACILITIES AND SERVICES: None

NEAREST TOURIST ATTRACTIONS: Active nightlife, but must use public transportation for everything else

HOSTAL MARGARITA ★★ (5)
Gran Vía 50, 5°
8 rooms, 2 with shower or bath and toilet, 5 with shower and sink

TELEPHONE AND FAX
91 547 35 49
METRO
Callao, 3, 5
CREDIT CARDS
MC, V
RATES
Single 3,500–4,500ptas, double
5,500ptas, triple 7,200ptas, tax
included

José and Margarita are a friendly couple who have two sons living in the United States. If you want to see the perfect picture of a proud grandmother, just ask Margarita about her four granddaughters! Their *hostal* is a friendly place where guests are invited to relax in their old-fashioned living room and watch television, or to use a small refrigerator and microwave to prepare a meal, which you can eat at their kitchen table. For Cheap Sleepers, these kitchen priviledges could be the deciding factor in choosing this basic but clean eight-room *hostal*, where the plain little nests have tile floors, an armoire with drawers, and a bouquet of fake flowers. Some of the interior rooms are improved further with stained-glass windows (rather than opaque) and laminated headboards.

ENGLISH SPOKEN: Yes

FACILITIES AND SERVICES: Air-conditioning, lift, use of small refrigerator and microwave, free office safe

NEAREST TOURIST ATTRACTIONS: Gran Vía, Opera, Palacio Real

BREAKFAST
Not served

HOSTAL RESIDENCE LAURIA ★★(5)
Gran Vía 50, 4°
21 rooms, all with shower or bath and toilet

The Bruña family should be proud of their well-maintained two-star *hostal residencia*, which I found to be one of the best in its category on the Gran Vía. While the rooms are not overflowing with character, the pine furniture matches, there are bedside lights, and you can see out of the clear windows to the flats beyond. Everything is in good shape, the halls are bright, the bathrooms modern—it all adds up to a good Cheap Sleeping choice in Madrid.

ENGLISH SPOKEN: Yes

FACILITIES AND SERVICES: Direct-dial phone, lift, free office safe, TV

NEAREST TOURIST ATTRACTIONS: Twenty-minute walk to Plaza de la Puerta del Sol or the Palacio Real

TELEPHONE
91 541 91 82
FAX
91 541 91 88
METRO
Callao, 3, 5
CREDIT CARDS
MC, V
RATES
Single 4,200ptas, double 5,700ptas, triple 7,200ptas, plus 7 percent tax
BREAKFAST
Not served

HOSTAL RESIDENCIA ABRIL ★ (4)
C/ de Fuencarral 334, 4°, dcha
9 rooms, 4 with shower or bath and toilet, 2 with shower and sink

The rooms at the Abril are simple, spartan, spotless, and short on worldly comforts—but for a Cheap Sleep in Madrid, they are not a bad deal provided you can live in a room with opaque windows. If so, check into No. 2, a double with a wood-simulated lineoleum floor and pine furnishings; No. 3, a coordinated twin on the back; or No. 5, a cute blue single with a shower and basin in the room. The hall bathroom facilities are good, so peseta-pinchers can save even more by reserving a bathless abode. The Feli family lives here and runs the place with

TELEPHONE
91 531 53 38
METRO
Gran Vía, 1, 5
CLOSED
Aug 15–30
CREDIT CARDS
None, cash only
RATES
Single 2,000–3,200ptas, double 3,400–3,700ptas, triple 4,600–4,800ptas, tax included
BREAKFAST
Not served

the help of their pretty young daughter, Maria, who speaks English.

ENGLISH SPOKEN: Yes

FACILITIES AND SERVICES: Lift

NEAREST TOURIST ATTRACTIONS: Nightlife in Chueca and Malasaña

HOSTAL RESIDENCIA DELFINA (no stars, 14)
Gran Vía 12, 4°, dcha
14 rooms, all with shower or bath and toilet

TELEPHONE
91 522 64 23, 91 522 64 22

METRO
Gran Vía, 1, 5

CREDIT CARDS
None

RATES
Single 3,600ptas double 5,600ptas, triple 6,100ptas, tax included

BREAKFAST
Not served

The Delfina is a neat and tidy Gran Vía choice for those Cheap Sleep voyagers who want to stay on one of Madrid's most important and busy boulevards. Guests are ushered in through an iron-gated entry to a tiled reception area. The air-conditioned rooms have mirror-like polished floors and private bathrooms, many of which have their own window. Some might object to the half bathtubs, but at least you get your own and don't have to share it with anyone else. Furnishings are acceptable, but I wish the owner would remove the plastic draped over the tables in each room.

ENGLISH SPOKEN: Limited

FACILITIES AND SERVICES: Air-conditioning, lift, free office safe, TV

NEAREST TOURIST ATTRACTIONS: Shopping on Gran Vía, Museo Thyssen-Bornemisza, Museu del Prado

HOSTAL RESIDENCIA PRADA ★★ (7)
C/ de Hortaleza 19, 3°
20 rooms, all with shower or bath and toilet

TELEPHONE
91 521 20 04, 91 522 25 69

FAX
91 531 60 88

METRO
Gran Vía, 1, 5

CREDIT CARDS
MC, V

RATES
Single 3,900ptas, double 5,700ptas, triple 6,700ptas, tax included

BREAKFAST
Not served

Jaime and Marisa, a brother and sister team, pay attention to every detail and are tough taskmasters when it comes to keeping their exceptional *hostal* in tip-top condition. Rather than rely on anyone else to even approach their exacting standards, they do all the work themselves—from meeting and greeting their guests, to answering questions about what to see and do in Madrid, to making sure all the rooms and baths are in sparkling order. The third-floor *hostal residencia* has a large entryway with a gold-painted twelve-foot mirror that would not be out of place in the Spanish Royal Palace. Farther on, the comfortable sitting room is furnished with English Colonial pieces that Marisa personally selected. A mix of fresh and silk plants and flowers adds a welcoming touch. The twenty bedrooms are done in bamboo with matching spreads and curtains, have either hardwood or original tile floors, and have clear windows with a view. With the exception of No. 409, which hasn't much maneuvering space around the bed, all the rooms can be safely recommended. Each bathroom has a magifying mirror, shelves, hooks, good light, nice towels, and modern fixtures.

ENGLISH SPOKEN: Yes

FACILITIES AND SERVICES: Air-conditioning, direct-dial phone, lift, room safe (100ptas per use), TV

NEAREST TOURIST ATTRACTIONS: Nightlife in Chueca, walking distance to Plaza de la Puerta del Sol and central Madrid

HOSTAL SIL ★★ (1)
C/ de Fuencarral 95, 3°, dcha
20 rooms, 18 with shower or bath and toilet, 2 with shower and sink

The twenty-room Hostal Sil offers excellent value for money, provided you don't mind staying in an off-beat location that's a few metro stops away from action central. It is, however, handy for Malasaña, an old working-class district and one of the main nightlife areas of Madrid. In addition to air-conditioning and a satellite TV, each nice room has matching furniture, good wardrobe space, and in most, a functional bathroom. Number 304 has a decorative marble fireplace and two balconies: one off the room and the other off the bathroom. Families can check into No. 305, which has a sitting room and blue-tile bathroom.

ENGLISH SPOKEN: Yes

FACILITIES AND SERVICES: Air-conditioning (in-room thermostat), direct-dial phones, lift, some minibars (will charge if you put in your own food or drinks), satellite TV

NEAREST TOURIST ATTRACTION: Not much, must use public transportation

TELEPHONE
91 448 89 72, 91 593 09 93

FAX
91 447 48 29

METRO
Bilbao, 1, 4, or Tribunal, 1, 10

CREDIT CARDS
MC, V

RATES
Single 4,200ptas, double 6,200ptas, triple 7,500ptas, tax included

BREAKFAST
Not served

HOSTAL SONSOLES ★★ (6)
C/ de Fuencarral 18, 2°, dcha
40 rooms, all with shower or bath and toilet

An elevator brings you to the second-floor Sonsoles, a *hostal* with a slightly formal tone. Next to the reception desk are two sitting rooms with elaborate chandeliers and matching side lights. Green velvet sectionals, live plants, and an assortment of periodicals and bric-a-brac complete the comfortable picture. While the rooms are

TELEPHONE
91 532 75 23, 91 532 75 22

FAX
91 532 75 22

EMAIL
m.g.d@mx3.redestb.es

INTERNET
www.personal.redestb.es/m.g.d/

METRO
Gran Vía, 1, 5
CREDIT CARDS
MC, V
RATES
Single 3,900ptas, double
4,900ptas, triple 6,700ptas,
plus 7 percent tax
BREAKFAST
Not served

not particularly special, they are clean and coordinated, with desk space, at least one chair, and balconies overlooking the busy street. Their main drawback is a lack of bedside lights, but this is a common minus in almost every Cheap Sleep in this category in Madrid. If you are traveling solo, ask for No. 336, a white room with a tile floor and above-average furniture. The blue bathroom has an enclosed shower and tub, decent towels, and enough light to see what you are doing. Twosomes can check into No. 347, a twin-bedded room with an entryway, desk, two chairs, and a pink bathroom. Unfortunately, luggage space is limited.

ENGLISH SPOKEN: Very limited

FACILITIES AND SERVICES: Direct-dial phone, room safe (100ptas per use), satellite TV, piped-in room music

NEAREST TOURIST ATTRACTIONS: Nightlife around Chueca, about fifteen-minute walk to central Madrid

HOSTAL TRIANA ★★ (12)
C/ de la Salud 13, at Gran Vía
40 rooms, all with shower or bath and toilet

TELEPHONE
91 532 68 11, 91 532 68 12,
91 532 30 99
FAX
91 522 97 29
METRO
Gran Vía, 1, 5
CREDIT CARDS
MC, V
RATES
Single 4,400ptas, double
5,900ptas, triple 7,700ptas,
quad 8,700ptas, tax included
BREAKFAST
Not served

Victor Gonzalez has spent a half century running his popular *hostal* in central Madrid. Most of the rooms have twin beds, white walls, coordinated fabrics, and inlaid wood floors. Those along the front have balconies and are the premier picks. Others face inside walls or laundry lines and get occasional wafts of cooking smells. The baths are small but functional and have handheld showers over regulation tubs. On each floor there is a little sitting area. The family also owns a shoe store, and the lobby contains a shoe display, which might turn some people off—but let's face it, every little bit of advertising helps!

ENGLISH SPOKEN: Yes, and French

FACILITIES AND SERVICES: Air-conditioning in fourteen rooms (500ptas supplement in July and August), direct-dial phone, hair dryer available, laundry service, free office safe, TV

NEAREST TOURIST ATTRACTIONS: Shopping on Gran Vía, nightlift in Chueca, walk to Plaza de la Puerta del Sol

HOSTAL ZAMORAN ★ (6)
C/ de Fuencarral 18, 2°, izqda
14 rooms, 13 with shower or bath and toilet

My notes read: Clean as a whistle, firm beds, sweet owner, Rafaella, lives on site.

No. 2: Adorable in pink, lots of space, even a balcony and a bath with 3/4-tub and handheld shower. No. 3: Firm beds, a little less space, still pink. No. 4: Double bed, inside room, can't see out of opaque, pebbled windows, small bath with 1/2-tub. No. 9: Narrow window in bedroom, another in bath, nice wardrobe with drawer space. No. 10: Twin on back, white lacy shower curtain and blue flower theme on bathroom floor tiles . . . could eat off the floor!

This one-star *hostal* looks like a Cheap Sleep winner to me. I hope you agree.

ENGLISH SPOKEN: None

FACILITIES AND SERVICES: Lift, TV

NEAREST TOURIST ATTRACTIONS: Chueca nightlife, central Madrid

TELEPHONE
91 532 20 60, 91 522 33 56
METRO
Gran Vía, 1, 5
CREDIT CARDS
None, cash only
RATES
Single 2,400–3,700ptas, double 4,800ptas, triple 6,700ptas, tax included
BREAKFAST
Not served

HOTEL ANACO ★★★ (13)
C/ de las Tres Cruces 3, at Gran Vía
39 rooms, all with shower or bath and toilet

If you can get a room on the second floor, in low season, you will get a top-drawer Cheap Sleep in a key location that's a mere New York–minute away from most must-sees on a Madrid visitor's list. Why the second floor? Because in addition to being recently redone, it is completely nonsmoking. The third and sixth floors are scheduled for renovation, so be sure to check before you book your room. That is not to say that the rooms on these two floors are uninhabitable. They are serviceable, and those on the sixth floor have terraces, but the fifties' decor has seen its day. The redone rooms have a contemporary feel, with snazzy bathrooms featuring plenty of fluffy towels and stainless-steel basins set in mirror-backed marble sinks. The rooms have a good work space with a tensor light and a supportive office chair, hardwood floors, firm mattresses, and double-paned glass on the windows to muffle unwanted sounds. The hotel has three pricing periods: Low season is December through February, not including the ten days or so around Christmas and New Year's; midseason is July and August; and high season is March to June and September through November.

TELEPHONE
91 522 46 04
FAX
91 531 64 84
METRO
Gran Vía, 1, 5
CREDIT CARDS
AE, DC, MC, V
RATES
Single 8,000–9,000ptas, double 11,500ptas, triple 15,000ptas, extra bed 4,000ptas, plus 7 percent tax; lower rates in off-season
BREAKFAST
Continental 500ptas per person

ENGLISH SPOKEN: Yes

FACILITIES AND SERVICES: Air-conditioning, bar, direct-dial phones, some hair dryers, lift, parking (1,500ptas per day), nonsmoking floor, room safe (100ptas per use), restaurant, radio, satellite TV

NEAREST TOURIST ATTRACTIONS: Central Madrid

HOTEL ATLÁNTICO ★★★ (9, $)

Gran Vía 38

80 rooms, all with shower or bath and toilet

TELEPHONE
91 522 64 80, toll-free in U.S., Best Western 800-528-1234

FAX
91 531 02 10

EMAIL
h_atlantico@mad.servicom.es

METRO
Callao, 3, 5, or Gran Vía, 1, 5

CREDIT CARDS
AE, MC, V

RATES
Single 12,800ptas, double 16,800ptas, triple 21,200ptas, tax included

BREAKFAST
Buffet included; cost can be deducted if arranged when reserving through the hotel, not through the 800 number

The Hotel Atlántico occupies a key position on the Gran Vía, one of the city's lovely, wide boulevards that teems night and day with people and traffic. The recently redone hotel has all the whistles and bells people expect in an upscale, modern, big city hotel. The open, cream-colored lobby features a large tapestry hung on a polished brass rail and an attractive dining room, where the buffet breakfast is served. The light color scheme continues throughout the hallways and into the revamped, soundproofed bedrooms, which have coordinated floral fabrics on the curtains and bedspreads. Seating is on brass-framed camp chairs. For the most part, bathrooms are up-to-date with fixed shower nozzles over full-size tubs, excellent towels, and sufficient lighting.

ENGLISH SPOKEN: Yes

FACILITIES AND SERVICES: Air-conditioning, bar, direct-dial phone, hair dryer, minibar, room safe (some free, others 100ptas per use), satellite TV

NEAREST TOURIST ATTRACTIONS: Central Madrid

HOTEL MÓNACO ★ (8)

C/ de Barbieri 5

33 rooms, all with shower or bath and toilet

TELEPHONE
91 522 46 30

FAX
91 521 16 01

METRO
Gran Vía, 1, 5, or Chueca, 5

CREDIT CARDS
AE, MC, V

RATES
Single 8,000ptas, double 11,000ptas, tax included

BREAKFAST
Continental 550ptas per person

If you fancy yourself a latter-day Mae West and prefer lounging away the afternoons in satin nightgowns on elegently tattered furniture—or if you know and love the Hotel Esmeralda in Paris (see *Cheap Sleeps in Paris*)—the Hotel Mónaco may be just your kind of place. While its thirty-plus faded and jaded rooms are in desperate need of maintenance, let alone a major spring cleaning, no one can fault the abundance of colorful history attached to this former bordello. The building was originally a series of private apartments, but around 1920, a French architect bought it and turned it into a home for his lover. In less than a year, it was a brothel, and remained Madrid's most active until 1959, when it became the Hotel Mónaco. In the time since, no one has tried very hard to improve any aspect of the hotel, but the faux marble columns and murals of Greek gods and goddesses in the lobby are still intact, as are the exhausted pieces of leather furniture and the neon signs pointing to the cafeteria. The prices are relatively low, but rather than value, most of what you get is worn satin and mirrors and an atmosphere not far removed from the hotel's brothel days.

A brass, red-carpeted staircase suitable for a grand entrance leads to the rooms, which are hilariously done in decadent kitsch. You can't see out of the window in the dimly lit No. 343, but who needs to if you are occupying a room with a floor-to-ceiling mirror behind a sagging double bed? Number 237 has a view of a wall from both the room and the bathroom, which is so big that it has a stretch tub, two tables, and a separate toilet. The water drips and the green tiles are bilious. The bedroom features twin beds with back and side mirrors, and the tile floor sports a basket weave pattern. Number 123 is one of the most celebrated, and it's often used for photo shoots for fashion magazines and video backdrops for rock bands. It has a mirrored wall behind the pink satin and ruffle-covered bed, which also has a mirrored canopy above and two mirrored bedside tables flanking either side. The bathroom is something else—all in rose marble with arches over a stretch tub in need of resurfacing. All the brass fixtures are original, as are the antiquated porcelain table and the cut-out ceiling detail. In No. 125, you step up to the bed, which has mirrors on the opposite wall as well as on the headboard. A six-light chandelier gives off muted light. Number 126 is a twin-bedded room with no window, just more mirrors—a full wall (that needs reglazing) behind the bed and another over the marble-topped dresser. The big bathroom does have a window, along with two bare light bulbs dimly illuminating the aging sink. For a Louis XVI experience, reserve No. 127; its entire ceiling is draped in pink to look like a campaign tent. This should be enough of a sampling to give you an idea of what to expect—and to know if this unique Cheap Sleep in Madrid is for you.

ENGLISH SPOKEN: Yes

FACILITIES AND SERVICES: Air-conditioning in some rooms, bar, direct-dial phones, lift, TV

NEAREST TOURIST ATTRACTIONS: Central Madrid

HOTEL NUEVO GAOS ★★★ (11)
C/ de Mesonero Romanos 14, 2°, at Gran Vía
23 rooms, all with shower or bath and toilet

TELEPHONE AND FAX
91 532 71 06
METRO
Callao, 3, 5, or Gran Vía, 1, 5
CREDIT CARDS
AE, DC, MC, V
RATES
Single 6,000ptas, double
7,400–8,400ptas, triple
9,800ptas, quad 12,500ptas,
plus 7 percent tax
BREAKFAST
Not served

The rooms at Hotel Nuevo Gaos are much better than the lobby, which is filled ugly settees covered in a black bamboo pattern, but never mind—you are not sleeping here! Instead, you will be staying in an air-conditioned, nicely coordinated room with hand-painted detail on the door and on the interior woodwork. If possible, request a room with a balcony, perhaps No. 12, a two-room suite with twin beds in one and a sofa bed, leather chairs, and a pull-down desk in the other. Number 18 is a smaller twin, with two chairs and no balcony. Bathrooms are acceptable, provided you can live with the Madrid phenomenon of half- and three-quarter-size tubs with handheld showers above them.

ENGLISH SPOKEN: Yes

FACILITIES AND SERVICES: Air-conditioning, direct-dial phone, hair dryer, lift, parking (1,500per day), free office safe, room safe in half the rooms (100ptas per use), TV

NEAREST TOURIST ATTRACTIONS: Nightlife in Chueca, central Madrid

PALACIO REAL AND THE OPERA ____

Although relatively central, the area around the Palacio Real and the Opera goes unnoticed by most visitors to Madrid, who tend to pass through quickly on their way to the grand sites. The three-thousand-room Palacio Real (Royal Palace) serves as the ceremonial home of Spain's royal family, and is open to the public unless there is an important state function. It stands on the site of the old Alcázar built by the Muslims in the ninth century, and has been a royal residence since Felipe II moved his court to Madrid in 1561. The ceremonial changing of the Royal Guard occurs at noon on the first Wednesday of every month. Separating the Palacio Real from the Opera (the Teatro Real) is the lovely Plaza de Oriente where Franco once rallied the crowds. Facing the Royal Palace on the other side is Madrid's cathedral, which was opened after years of renovations in 1933 by Pope John Paul II.

HOTELS

Hostal Paz ★★	**129**
Hotel Opera ★★★ ($)	**129**

($) indicates a Big Splurge

HOSTAL PAZ ★★ (16)
C/ de la Flora 4, 1°, dcha
10 rooms, 6 with shower or bath and toilet

There are no frills or flounces here, but there are some mighty Cheap Sleeps to be had in these spartan rooms, where almost everything matches, including the sheets. The owner is a sweet *señora* who relies on her sons to help her with English-speaking guests. I like the fact that for this rock-bottom price you get an air-conditioned room that has satellite TV and a private bathroom if you want it. If your dirty travel clothing takes more room in your luggage than your wearable wardrobe, you can have your clothes washed at the hostel for the equivalent of $7 per kilo. To avoid noise, ask for an interior room, but be prepared for a window fitted with no-see shower-door glass and a view of a wall or your neighbor's line of drying laundry.

ENGLISH SPOKEN: Only if the owner's sons are there

FACILITIES AND SERVICES: Air-conditioning, laundry service, lift, satellite TV

NEAREST TOURIST ATTRACTIONS: Opera and Palacio Real, ten minutes to Puerta del Sol

TELEPHONE AND FAX
91 547 30 47

METRO
Opera, 2, 5

CREDIT CARDS
MC, V

RATES
Single 2,700ptas, double 4,500ptas, triple 6,200ptas, plus 7 percent tax

BREAKFAST
Not served

HOTEL OPERA ★★★ (15, $)
Cuesta de Santo Domingo 2, at the Fuente al Teatro Real
79 rooms, all with shower or bath and toilet

If you like traditional decor and peace and quiet in a full-service hotel, book a room at the lovely Hotel Opera, which is one of the best three-star picks in Madrid. From here you can easily walk to the Royal Palace and Opera, stroll to the Plaza Mayor, and in under fifteen minutes be standing at the Puerta del Sol, the very heart of Madrid. The hotel has recently been redone in tones of gold and royal blues and has seventy-nine rooms, all of which face out and some of which have balconies overlooking old Madrid. I think No. 804, with a panoramic view of the Royal Palace and the Opera, is one of the best of these. The well-appointed room has twin beds, a desk and chair, and a new bathroom with enough space for all

TELEPHONE
91 541 28 00

FAX
91 541 69 23

EMAIL
hotelopera@siniz.net

INTERNET
www.softly.es/turismo/sercotel

METRO
Opera, 2, 5

CREDIT CARDS
AE, DC, MC, V

RATES
Single 10,500–11,800ptas,
double 14,800ptas, triple
19,000ptas, extra bed
2,500ptas, baby bed 400ptas;
25 percent discount for children
under 12 sharing parents' room,
lower weekend rates; all rates
plus 7 percent tax

BREAKFAST
Buffet 1,200ptas per person

your toiletries, plus those the hotel offers you. All rooms ending in the number ten can comfortably sleep three and have big bathrooms with good sink space. If you are traveling alone, consider one of the three rooms lettered A, B, or D. These are unusual top-floor rooms nestled under the eaves of the mansard roof with windows that open out. The bathrooms admittedly are too small for a full tub, but the showers are perfectly adquate. Room C, for two, is similar to these three singles, and has a view from its roof-top window of the Opera Square. The hotel also runs El Café de la Opera, where dinner is served by waiters who are also accomplished singers and who perform Spanish lyric opera to piano accompaniment during your meal.

ENGLISH SPOKEN: Yes

FACILITIES AND SERVICES: Air-conditioning, bar, conference room, direct-dial phone, hair dryer, laundry service, lift, minibar, restaurant, free room safe, radio, satellite TV, some Jacuzzis

NEAREST TOURIST ATTRACTIONS: Opera, Palacio Real, Plaza Mayor, fifteen minutes to Puerta del Sol

PLAZA DE LA PUERTA DEL SOL _____

Every visitor to Madrid passes through the Plaza de la Puerta del Sol. It is called *puerta* (or gate) because it was the main gate out of fifteenth-century Madrid. Today it serves as the city's main transportation hub, and as it has been since the sixteenth century, it's a popular gathering place for rallies and New Year's Eve celebrations. Near the statue of the Bourbon king Carlos III is the city's symbol: the statue of a bear smelling a *madroño,* or strawberry tree. This statue is a favorite meeting place for locals and is known as the center of the city; like Notre Dame in Paris, it is the point from which all distances are measured in Spain. To see this spot, look for a stone slab that says Kilometre Zero on the pavement in front of the clock tower. Also here is the main branch of El Corte Inglés, a giant department store with everything you could ever need or want.

HOTELS

Hotel Carlos V ★★★ ($)	132
Hotel Europa ★	133
Hotel Paris ★★	134

OTHER OPTIONS
Residence Hotels
| Edificio Principe II ★★ | 153 |

($) indicates a Big Splurge

HOSTAL RESIDENCIA ESMERALDA ★★ (20)
C/ de la Victoria 1, 2°, at C/ de San Jerónimo
19 rooms, all with shower or bath and toilet

Almost every room faces out in this snappy Cheap Sleep, where the pretty rooms have dark wood floors and are furnished in rustic, Spanish-style furniture. Each color-coordinated space has a mirrored wardrobe, an assortment of pictures hanging on the white stucco walls, air-conditioning, and a private bathroom. Matilda, the on-site manager, speaks some English, and she will even do your laundry for you. At the Esmeralda, if you pay in cash and don't need a written receipt, they will include the 7 percent IVA in the rate, rather than charge it extra. Over a four- or five-day stay, this could add up to some real savings.

ENGLISH SPOKEN: Yes

FACILITIES AND SERVICES: Air-conditioning, direct-dial phone, laundry service, lift, free office safe, satellite TV

NEAREST TOURIST ATTRACTIONS: Central Madrid, walking distance to the Museo Thyssen-Bornemisza and Museo del Prado

TELEPHONE
91 521 00 77, 91 521 07 58
FAX
91 521 07 58
METRO
Sol, 1, 2, 3
CREDIT CARDS
MC, V
RATES
Single 4,500ptas, double 5,800ptas, triple 7,700ptas, quad 8,700ptas, plus 7 percent tax
BREAKFAST
Not served

HOSTAL RESIDENCIA RIESCO ★★ (24)
C/ del Correo 2, 3°, at Puerta del Sol
30 rooms, all with shower or bath and toilet

Next to the Comunidad de Madrid and a few minutes' walk from Plaza Mayor, this old-fashioned *hostal residencia* offers budget travelers private facilities with every room. In the welcoming sitting room, everything seems to be oversized, including the three-foot-tall porcelain German shepherd, the television screen, and the antique painting of the Plaza de la Puerta del Sol. For three decades, the matriarch of the family has been running the place with a firm hand and continues to do so: She expects her guests to be neat and tidy, abstaining from room picnics and washing and drying large loads of

TELEPHONE
91 522 26 92, 91 532 90 88
FAX
91 532 90 88
METRO
Sol, 1, 2, 3
CREDIT CARDS
None, cash only
RATES
Single 3,900ptas, double 5,700ptas, tax included
BREAKFAST
Not served

hand laundry. Rooms tend to be larger than most, and the spreads match the curtains more often than not. One of the best is No. 304, a sunny room with a balcony, two double beds, and a dated bath with blue tiles and one shelf.

ENGLISH SPOKEN: Yes, and French

FACILITIES AND SERVICES: Direct-dial phone, lift

NEAREST TOURIST ATTRACTIONS: Walking distance to Plaza Mayor, Plaza de la Puerta del Sol, Museo Thyssen-Bornemisza, and Museo del Prado

HOSTAL RESIDENCIA VERACRUZ II ★★ (20)
C/ de la Victoria 1, 3°, at C/ de San Jerónimo
21 rooms, all with shower or bath and toilet

TELEPHONE
91 522 76 35
FAX
91 522 67 49
METRO
Sol, 1, 2, 3
CREDIT CARDS
MC, V
RATES
Single 4,200ptas, double 5,900ptas, triple 7,500ptas, plus 7 percent tax
BREAKFAST
Not served

Thank goodness there is a lift, otherwise the three-story climb up the graceful, polished wooden stairway might prove too daunting to attempt. Once you're here, the Veracruz provides clean, perfectly adequate rooms with new baths in a great location. If you are a Cheap Sleeper looking for some place around the heart of tourist Madrid, the simple, spotless rooms at the Veracruz II should fill the bill quite nicely. Speaking of the bill, as with many small *hostales*, if you are willing to pay in cash and leave without a receipt, they will include the 7 percent IVA in the rate.

ENGLISH SPOKEN: None

FACILITIES AND SERVICES: Air-conditioned, direct-dial phone, lift, free room safe, satellite TV

NEAREST TOURIST ATTRACTIONS: Walking distance to everything in central Madrid, including Museu Thyssen-Bornemisza and the Prado

HOTEL CARLOS V ★★★ (17, $)
C/ del Maestro Victoria 5
67 rooms, all with shower or bath and toilet

TELEPHONE
91 531 41 00, toll-free in U.S., Best Western 800-528-1234
FAX
91 531 37 61
EMAIL
hotel.carlosv@tsai.es
INTERNET
www.hotelsearch.com/madrid/carlosV
METRO
Sol, 1, 2, 3
CREDIT CARDS
AE, DC, MC, V

The smart Hotel Carlos V occupies a choice spot on a pedestrianized street behind the Descalzas Reales Monestary. Also within a stone's throw is Madrid's monolithic department store, El Corte Inglés. The classic hotel has a traditional atmosphere, both in the attractive second-floor lounge area and in the lovely coral-colored breakfast room, which is accented with brass lights. The rooms are done in universal "hotel modern" with enough space to move in and live comfortably, whether you are checking in for business or pleasure . . . or both. An added feature for some may be the black-out drapes, which are standard in every room. My favorite rooms are the five with terraces, four of which have a double bed and one with twins. Number 507, the twin-bedded room, has a table and chairs on the terrace—where you can enjoy breakfast or an early evening drink—and the room has a desk area, built-in wardrobe, bedside lights, and a beautiful gray-tiled bath with a tub and enclosed shower. Room No. 116 would be fine for a family because it has two double beds plus a day bed. It also has a little balcony overlooking the street.

ENGLISH SPOKEN: Yes

FACILITIES AND SERVICES: Air-conditioned, bar, direct-dial phone, hair dryer, laundry service, lift, minibar, parking (1,175 per day), room safe (200ptas per day), satellite TV

NEAREST TOURIST ATTRACTIONS: Easy walking distance to Plaza de la Puerta del Sol, Plaza Mayor, all of central Madrid

RATES
Single 11,600ptas, double 14,700–17,600ptas, triple 19,800ptas, plus 7 percent tax

BREAKFAST
Included, cannot be deducted

HOTEL EUROPA ★ (18)
C/ del Carmen 4, at Puerta del Sol
80 rooms, all with shower or bath and toilet

The Europa's definitely dated and eclectic aura reminds me of a granny's parlor, filled with collections that have been lovingly gathered over a long lifetime. The salon is loaded with an infinite variety of just plain stuff, including four Chinese urns, a glass curio case loaded to the max, a red velvet sofa with antimacassars on the arms, a TV set, an old Spanish Olivetti typewriter, and an assortment of real, silk, and plastic plants and flowers. The gaudy paintings and dried flower arrangements continue in the halls, leading one to feel that it is all a little overdone, but who wouldn't be amused by the animal skin lurking under a large dining table or the oversized pumpkin and watermelon sitting on top of it? The rooms, thankfully, do not mirror the public areas. In fact, if anything, you could call them spartan. Everything matches in No. 216, which is a quiet choice with a bare wood floor, twin beds, and a pretty view onto a plant-filled interior patio. The large, very clean bathroom has loads of space, good towels, and light. I think this is one of the best rooms in the house. Number 214 has a balcony overlooking the pedestrian walkway below. The problem here is that there is only one chair, which is one less than the two of you will need, unless one of you uses the bed to sit on.

TELEPHONE
91 521 29 00

FAX
91 521 46 96

EMAIL
hoteleuropa@genio.infor.es

INTERNET
www.hoteleuropa.net

METRO
Sol, 1, 2, 3

CREDIT CARDS
AE, MC, V

RATES
Single 6,200ptas, double 8,400ptas, triple 11,500ptas, quad 13,500ptas, plus 7 percent tax

BREAKFAST
Continental 600ptas per person

ENGLISH SPOKEN: Yes

FACILITIES AND SERVICES: Bar, direct-dial phones, fan, hair dryer, laundry service, lift, parking (1,400ptas per day), restaurant, room service, room safe (200ptas per day), satellite TV

NEAREST TOURIST ATTRACTIONS: Heart of central Madrid

HOTEL PARIS ★★ (19)
C/ de Alcalá 2
120 rooms, all with shower or bath and toilet

TELEPHONE
91 521 64 91
FAX
91 521 64 96
METRO
Sol, 1, 2, 3
CREDIT CARDS
AE, DC, MC, V
RATES
Single 9,500ptas, double 12,500ptas, triple 15,000ptas, tax included
BREAKFAST
Continental included

The Hotel Paris occupies a privileged position on the Plaza de la Puerta del Sol, the one place every visitor to Madrid passes through. Not only is the Puerta del Sol a meeting point for three metro lines and all the major bus routes, but taxis regularly troll the area, and you are minutes away on foot from a shaded seat on the Plaza Mayor, the El Corte Inglés department store, and more than a dozen recommended Cheap Eats (see *Cheap Eats in Spain*). The hotel enjoys a loyal following who appreciate the midrange prices, the comfortable and pleasant surroundings, and the agreeable multilingual staff. The lobby has four red sofas arranged with French-style chairs to create easy conversational groupings. The wide hallways have similar small seating areas.

Some of the rooms are better than others. The best choices are those that are air-conditioned and do not face the street; however, those on the street have double-glazed windows that do buffer some of the noise. Number 519 is a very quiet, air-conditioned twin. Because it has more space than some of the others, you can spread out and settle in with ease. I even like its older-style bathroom with a metal hat rack used to store the towels. If you are here during the winter when air-conditioning is not an issue, consider front-facing Room 306, a yellow-colored twin that has a working desk, good closet and drawer space, an armchair for reading, and a luggage rack. The bright new bath has enough counter area for your toiletries, but the hotel provides nothing but the soap and the towels.

ENGLISH SPOKEN: Yes

FACILITIES AND SERVICES: Air-conditioning in some rooms, bar, conference room, direct-dial phone, laundry service, lift, restaurant, room safe (100ptas per use), satellite TV

NEAREST TOURIST ATTRACTIONS: Everything in central Madrid

PLAZA DE SANTA ANA AND HUERTAS

The Plaza de Santa Ana is a small, nondescript square that is one of the premier centers of Madrid nightlife. It is anchored at one end by the Reina Victoria hotel—which was Hemingway's favorite and now is preferred by many matadors—and at the opposite end by the the oldest playhouse in Madrid, the Teatro Español, whose facade is decorated with the busts of many famous Spanish playwrights. The real drawing cards are the numerous bars, cafés, restaurants, and nightclubs around the square (see *Cheap Eats in Spain* for a list of recommendations), but it's also populated by a contingent of gypsies, so watch your wallet. Huertas is a street that runs east of the Plaza de Santa Ana. By day it appears like countless other streets, filled with shops and restaurants patronized by neighborhood locals. However, when the sun sets, the night owls come here for the endless bar scene.

HOTELS

($) indicates a Big Splurge

HOSTAL AGUILAR ★★ (22)
C/ de San Jerónimo 32, 2°
48 rooms, all with shower or bath and toilet

The big, barnlike *hostal* stretches out over two floors in an old building that sits midway between the Museo Thyssen-Bornemisza and the Plaza de la Puerta del Sol. The large, open rooms are furnished in a plain, easy-care

TELEPHONE
91 429 59 26, 91 429 36 61
FAX
91 429 26 61
METRO
Sol, 1, 2, 3, or Sevilla, 2

CREDIT CARDS
MC, V

RATES
Single 4,000ptas, double 6,100ptas, triple 7,900ptas, quad 9,800ptas, extra bed 2,600ptas, tax included

BREAKFAST
Not served

dormitory style that is a snap to keep clean. Because of the abundance of space in the rooms, they are ideal picks for families or friends wishing to all share the same room. On that note, there are only four double beds in the *hostal,* all others are singles. Bathrooms are equally impressive, and some even have a bidet, a rare fixture in this price range.

ENGLISH SPOKEN: Yes

FACILITIES AND SERVICES: Air-conditioning, direct-dial phones, lift, free office safe, satellite TV

NEAREST TOURIST ATTRACTIONS: Central Madrid, Museo Thyssen-Bornemisza, Museo del Prado, Botanical Gardens, Retiro Park

HOSTAL ARMESTO ★★ (35)
C/ de San Agustín 6, 1°, dcha, at C/ de Cervantes
6 rooms, all with shower or bath and toilet

TELEPHONE
91 429 09 40, 91 429 90 31

METRO
Antón Martín, 1

CREDIT CARDS
None, cash only

RATES
Single 5,100ptas, double 6,200ptas, triple 7,700 ptas, tax included

BREAKFAST
Not served

What a great little Cheap Sleep Maria and Emilio run! They work very hard, are proud of their *hostal,* and are committed to making your stay friendly and very pleasant. The six double rooms, each with a private bathroom, are fresh and bright, display matching fabrics and colors, and are well furnished with a comfortable chair, chest of drawers, and a place to put your luggage. All the rooms are well maintained, so you will not have to suffer knicked or marred walls, bedspreads sporting holes, or stains lurking on the floors.

ENGLISH SPOKEN: Quite limited

FACILITIES AND SERVICES: Fans, free office safe, TV

NEAREST TOURIST ATTRACTIONS: Museo Thyssen-Bornemisza, Museo del Prado, Retiro Park

HOSTAL ASTORIA ★★ (23)
C/ de San Jerónimo 30, 5°
26 rooms, all with shower or bath and toilet

TELEPHONE
91 429 11 88

FAX
91 429 20 23

EMAIL
hostalastoria@hotmail.com

METRO
Sol, 1, 2, 3, or Sevilla, 2

CREDIT CARDS
AE, MC, V

RATES
Single 4,800ptas, double 6,400–7,900ptas, triple 8,500ptas, plus 7 percent tax

The twenty-six rooms, each with a private bath, are on the fifth floor, and yes, there is a lift from the street. No one could ever call these rooms anything but functionally compact, yet they are some of the very few in Madrid in this Cheap Sleeping category that have modems as standard issue. If you don't mind some noise, ask for one of the eight with a view, seven of which are doubles, the other a single. There are four rooms similar to No. 50, a tight triple that faces the street and has precious little moving-about space.

ENGLISH SPOKEN: Yes

FACILITIES AND SERVICES: Air-conditioning, hair dryer, lift, modems in all rooms, room safe (100ptas per use), TV

NEAREST TOURIST ATTRACTIONS: Museo Thyssen-Bornemisza, Museo del Prado, Botanical Gardens, central Madrid

BREAKFAST
Not served

HOSTAL CASTRO ★ (34)
C/ del León 13, 1°, at Lope de Vega
12 rooms, 10 with shower or bath and toilet

The owner of Hostal Castro is very nice and eager to please, but her English is quite limited. However, if you speak any Spanish or French, this is a good Cheap Sleeping bet in Madrid. A container of holy water, a framed painting of the Last Supper, and other religious items create a pious theme to the small entry and reception area. In the rest of the twelve-room *hostal,* fake plants abound—even in the communal hall bathrooms—but they add a welcome touch of color to this cozy, clean place. All the simple yet sweet rooms have bare tile floors, differing color schemes, and either a bowl of potpourri or a little bouquet of flowers in each one. Rose-pattern curtains frame a sunny window in No. 7, a reasonably large room with a balcony, crisp white walls, and a pink satiny spread on the double bed. Pink is also lavishly used in No. 12, where even the bathroom fixtures, shower curtain, and lacy overcurtain are pink. If pink isn't your color, No. 3, a double on the street, is done in blue, and so is the little bathroom adjoining it. However, since the bathroom needs paint, its color may have changed by the time of your arrival. Rooms 2 and 11 are done in green, including pea-green bathroom fixtures.

ENGLISH SPOKEN: Limited English, more French

FACILITIES AND SERVICES: None

NEAREST TOURIST ATTRACTIONS: Museu del Prado, Museu Thyssen-Bornemisza, and Centro de Arte Reina Sofía, Botanical Gardens, Retiro Park

TELEPHONE
91 429 51 47

METRO
Antón Martín, 1

CLOSED
Aug

CREDIT CARDS
None

RATES
Single 2,700ptas, double 4,700ptas, tax included

BREAKFAST
Not served

HOSTAL JAÉN (no stars, 32)
C/ de Cervantes 5, 3°, dcha
7 rooms, all with shower, 1 also with toilet

The Crespo family's *hostal* on a relatively quiet street in this tourist-friendly sector of Madrid is cute, cheerful, cheap, and well put together. You can walk to the big

TELEPHONE AND FAX
91 429 48 58

METRO
Antón Martín, 1

CLOSED
Aug
CREDIT CARDS
None
RATES
Single 3,100–4,100ptas, double
4,400–4,600ptas, tax included
BREAKFAST
Not served

three museums, or you could choose not to leave the nearby Plaza de Santa Ana all day: Come here for your morning coffee and pastry, stay for a good-value lunch, while away the afternoon sipping fresh lagers at the square's four famous beer parlors, enjoy a dinner of tapas bar–hopping, and continue into the wee hours as the bar action gets into full swing.

For best results at the Jaén, request one of the five rooms that have a balcony. I like No. 2, which has a pink quilt pattern on the bed and its own shower and sink in the room. The owners are proud of No. 3, in which they have used the same pretty green fabric as a backdrop behind the beds, on the spreads, and again on the curtains, proving once again that you don't need a big budget to decorate attractively. This room is also the only one with a private shower and toilet, albeit quite small. The rooms to absolutely avoid are Nos. 8 and 10; they are so airless and claustrophobic you will think you are living in a closet. In No. 8, the sole window looks onto the reception area. Worse yet, No. 10 has no window at all, only a vent over the door. In any of the other rooms, your stay should be a happy one.

ENGLISH SPOKEN: Yes

FACILITIES AND SERVICES: Fans in rooms, lift, free office safe, TV

NEAREST TOURIST ATTRACTIONS: Museo Thyssen-Bornemisza, Museo del Prado, Botanical Gardens, Retiro Park

HOSTAL PERSAL ★★ (33)
Plaza del Angel 12, at C/ de las Huertas
77 rooms, all with shower or bath and toilet

TELEPHONE
91 369 46 63
FAX
91 369 19 52
EMAIL
hostal.persal@mad.servicom.es
METRO
Sol, 1, 2, 3
CREDIT CARDS
AE, MC, V
RATES
Single 5,400ptas, double
7,900ptas, triple 10,700ptas,
quad 13,500ptas, tax included
BREAKFAST
Continental included

The main bullfighting season for Madrid runs from mid-May to mid-June. Many famous bullfighters hang their capes at Hemingway's favorite Madrid hotel, the nearby Regina Victoria, which faces the Plaza de Santa Ana. Their traveling entourage stays around the corner at the Hostal Persal, which as you can imagine is a much Cheaper Sleep. If you are here during the "season," you will see the assistants leaving the hotel in full regalia . . . so have your cameras ready.

The Persal has been run by the same dedicated family for years. Today it is under the helm of Angel and Pepe, two polite and charming brothers who are always on hand to see that everything runs smoothly. The well-kept, functional rooms evoke the late fifties and early sixties—when chrome and leatherette were in vogue and the popular colors were brick and green with gold highlights. As the Plaza de Santa Ana is one of the main swinging hubs of Madrid's restaurant and bar scene, you might want to ask for one of the inside rooms when booking; they overlook a sunny interior courtyard that is filled with green plants in the spring and summer. Number 209 is one of these, but be careful, the distance from the foot of the bed to the wall is limited. If you can stand some noise, ask for No. 114, a big double with a large closet and balcony; its older-style bath has a three-tiered shelf for all those extra beauty supplies we women think we need. Families are given No. 101, a two-room, two-balcony suite that faces out.

ENGLISH SPOKEN: Yes

FACILITIES AND SERVICES: Air-conditioning, bar, direct-dial phone, fans, hair dryer available, lift, free room safe, satellite TV

NEAREST TOURIST ATTRACTIONS: Easy walk to Plaza de la Puerta del Sol, about ten minutes to Plaza Mayor, Museo Thyssen-Bornemisza, Museo del Prado, and the Botanical Gardens

HOSTAL RESIDENCIA CARRERA ★★ (23)
C/ de San Jerónimo 30, 3°
10 rooms, all with shower or bath and toilet

There are two other Cheap Sleeps in this building (see the Hostal Astoria, page 136, and the Hostal Victoria III, page 142), and together they prove that you don't need to spend big bucks to get a good, clean, centrally located Cheap Sleep in Madrid. The Carrera has been owned and operated for ten years by a very gentle soul, Francisco, whose French is better than his English. His ten rooms have white stucco walls and bare, polished hardwood floors. Double-glazed windows on the front help muffle the traffic noise. The furniture is modern, the room safe is free, and the tiled bathrooms are shiny and clean—it all adds up to an ideal Cheap Sleep.

ENGLISH SPOKEN: Limited, better French

FACILITIES AND SERVICES: Air-conditioning, direct-dial phone, lift, free room safe, piped-in room music, TV

NEAREST TOURIST ATTRACTIONS: Museo Thyssen-Bornemisza, Museo del Prado, Botanical Gardens, central Madrid

TELEPHONE
91 429 68 08, 91 369 13 25

METRO
Sol, 1, 2, 3, or Sevilla, 2

CREDIT CARDS
MC, V

RATES
Single 4,600ptas, double 6,100ptas, triple 8,000ptas, quad 12,000ptas, plus 7 percent tax

BREAKFAST
Not served

HOSTAL RESIDENCIA GONZALO ★★ (36)
C/ de Cervantes 34, 3°
12 rooms, all with shower or bath and toilet

TELEPHONE
91 429 27 14
FAX
91 420 20 07
METRO
Antón Martín, 1
CREDIT CARDS
DC, MC, V
RATES
Single 4,700ptas, double
5,700ptas, triple 7,200ptas,
plus 7 percent tax
BREAKFAST
Not served

Two of Madrid's most important museums, the Thyssen-Bornemisza and the Prado, are a short walk away from this family-run *hostal* on the third floor of a typical Madrid multiple-use building. All the rooms have been redone and everything in them is brand, spanking new: the beds, the mattresses, the built-in wardrobes, the desks, the chairs (two in each room), and the bathrooms. Even the doorknobs are new. Several rooms are big enough to comfortably sleep three, notably No. 2, with a double and a twin bed plus a sunny balcony, and No. 8, which has an inside view. Rooms 4 and 6 are designed for two and have big bathrooms with normal-size tubs. The reception area is just as nice as the rest of the *hostal,* and it's here that you will meet other guests and get to know the family and their two sons, Antonio and Javier, who have lived here all their lives.

ENGLISH SPOKEN: Yes

FACILITIES AND SERVICES: Direct-dial phone, lift, TV

NEAREST TOURIST ATTRACTIONS: Museo Thysssen-Bornemisza, Museo del Prado, Botanical Gardens

HOSTAL RESIDENCIA MATUTE ★★ (39)
Plaza de Matute 11, 1°, at C/ de las Huertas
25 rooms, all with shower, 15 also with toilet

TELEPHONE AND FAX
91 429 55 85
METRO
Antón Martín, 1
CREDIT CARDS
MC, V
RATES
Single 3,000–3,500ptas, double
4,200–5,300ptas, triple 6,300–
7,000ptas, tax included
BREAKFAST
Not served

Owner Alberto Gutierrez was born in Cuba and lived for many years in New Orleans before deciding to return to his family's roots and settle in Madrid. Alberto, who speaks fluent English, is a friendly host who is always on hand to kibitz with his guests and to make sure things run well. In the sitting room, a large portrait of his mother watches over a sprinkling of antiques, four baskets of fake flowers, and the obligatory television set. The location puts visitors in a prime position smack in the heart of Plaza de Santa Ana's bustling restaurant and bar scene. That also means that in the front-facing rooms street noise often continues well past bedtime. The well-maintained, clean rooms have no real decorating theme, but the colors somehow work, and in general the rooms are exceptional for their price range. Every room has its own basin and shower; more than half have a toilet as well. Most of them have a comfortable chair, hooks in the bathroom, a luggage rack, and enough space to ward off feeling cramped and closed-in. Traveling trios can check into No. 15, which has three twin beds, two comfortable chairs, a window and balcony on the street, and private facilities. Numbers 7 and 14 are both inside doubles with matching furniture and private bathrooms, but No. 7 has a three-quarter-size tub and a pull-chain toilet. Breakfast is not served, but there are enough bars within a five-minute radius to provide early morning sustenance for weeks.

ENGLISH SPOKEN: Yes

FACILITIES AND SERVICES: Direct-dial phone, lift, free office safe, TV

NEAREST TOURIST ATTRACTIONS: Museo Thyssen-Bornemisza, Museo del Prado, Botanical Gardens, Plaza Mayor, and Plaza de la Puerta del Sol

HOSTAL RESIDENCIA REGIONAL ★★ (29)
C/ del Príncipe 18, 3°
12 rooms, 6 with shower or bath and toilet

For the last quarter century, Isidero Caballero has been offering modest rooms in his third-floor *hostal* for dedicated Cheap Sleepers. The only amenity is the original cage elevator with beveled-glass doors that carries you up to the third floor. The reception area has a sofa and two cigar-colored leatherette chairs. The elegant building is old, and so are the twelve rooms, but despite their age, they are clean. Otherwise, expect some creaks and cracks and furnishings that are a mixture of semi-antiques, early garage sale, and late K-Mart. However, if you always look to the bottom line, and always want the numbers to be very small, this is a reliable Cheap Sleep in a nice corner of Madrid.

ENGLISH SPOKEN: Limited

FACILITIES AND SERVICES: Lift

NEAREST TOURIST ATTRACTIONS: Plaza de la Puerta del Sol, Museo Thyssen-Bornemisza, Museo del Prado, Botanical Gardens

TELEPHONE
91 522 33 73

METRO
Sol, 1, 2, 3

CREDIT CARDS
None, cash only

RATES
Single 2,600–3,600ptas, double 3,500–4,500ptas, triple 4,600–5,600ptas, tax included

BREAKFAST
Not served

HOSTAL RESIDENCIA SAN ANTONIO ★ (34)
C/ del León 13, 2°, at Lope de Vega
12 rooms, all with shower or bath and toilet

Air-conditioned rooms with a color television set won't come much cleaner or cheaper than the ones at the Hostal Residencia San Antonio. If you ask for No. 5, with its geranium-lined balcony, you will have twin beds made up with monogrammed linens that match the ruffly, green-print quilted bedspreads. Lacy sheers cover

TELEPHONE
91 429 51 37

METRO
Antón Martín, 1

CREDIT CARDS
None

RATES
Single 3,100ptas, double 4,900ptas, plus 7 percent tax

the window and are bordered by green drapes, and the white stucco room is large enough to accommodate a writing table and two chairs. The bath with a shelf and a light over it is very small, but it's all yours. Number 9 is a single on the street with a narrow window, a balcony, and a bathroom that's just fine. In addition, if you pay cash and and can do without a written receipt, they will not charge the 7 percent IVA.

ENGLISH SPOKEN: Limited, but they do speak French

FACILITIES AND SERVICES: Air-conditioning, TV

NEAREST TOURIST ATTRACTIONS: Plaza de Santa Ana, Museo Thyssen-Bornemisza, Museo del Prado, Botanical Gardens

HOSTAL VICTORIA III ★★ (23)
C/ de San Jerónimo 30, 4°
12 rooms, all with shower or bath and toilet

The rooms aren't big, but they are some of the best choices in the building. What are you going to get for your Cheap Sleeping peseta? Fresh, clean rooms with unadorned furniture, hardwood floors, and nice but small bathrooms and a few complimentary toiletries. Most rooms have a workspace, some have brass beds, and all have a picture painted directly on the wall with a frame imaginatively placed around it. There is a small bar in the reception area where you can enjoy a cool drink while sitting on turquoise leatherette sofas. The operation is run by a pleasant man who, despite the fact that he doesn't speak much English, certainly does his best to meet the needs of his multinational guests—who know a good deal when they find it.

ENGLISH SPOKEN: Barely, but German

FACILITIES AND SERVICES: Air-conditioning, bar, direct-dial phones, lift, free room safe, room music, satellite TV

NEAREST TOURIST ATTRACTIONS: Plaza de la Puerta del Sol, Museo del Prado, Botanical Gardens, and Museo Thyssen-Bornemisza

HOSTAL VILLA MAÑEZ ★★ (35)
C/ de San Agustín 6, 2°, dcha, at C/ de Cervantes
8 rooms, all with shower or bath and toilet

If you want to roll out of bed and (almost) into the Prado or the Thyssen-Bornemisza, the Botanical Gardens, or Madrid's huge Retiro Park, this is a safe, clean choice that will also enhance your cardiovascular system.

There is no lift to the second-floor site, forcing you to hoof it up and down the stairs throughout your stay. What is the payoff? Eight basic rooms, mostly done in pink—including the walls and shower curtains, the utilitarian furniture, and your own bathroom, with towels that need some fabric softener. No, it isn't fabulous, but if everything else in the area is booked, it's a port in a storm.

ENGLISH SPOKEN: Yes

FACILITIES AND SERVICES: TV

NEAREST TOURIST ATTRACTIONS: Museo del Prado, Museo Thyssen-Bornemisza, Retiro Park

RATES
Single 5,000ptas, double 6,200ptas, triple 7,700ptas, tax included

BREAKFAST
Not served

HOTEL INGLÉS ★★★ (25, $)
C/ de Echegaray 8
58 rooms, all with shower or bath and toilet

The hotel is old but well kept, with only a few wrinkles showing here and there, thanks to a series of face-lifts. The big drawback for many will be the lack of air-conditioning, but if you are here in the late fall through early spring, that won't matter at all. Those caveats aside, the Hotel Inglés offers guests not only well-appointed, spacious rooms but the chance to work out or practice judo or karate in the fully equipped gym. Motorists will especially appreciate the reasonably priced, secure car parking, which is very hard to come by in this part of Madrid. White marble halls lead to the rooms, which are unexciting from a decorating standpoint but have the three-star must-haves: hair dryer, room safe, and satellite TV. Several suites, such as the two-room No. 313, are especially recommended for those who need more living space. Number 313 features an entry and a windowless double bedroom—with its own TV and luggage and desk space—that overlooks a large sitting room with three comfortable chairs and a small balcony. The black-tile bathroom has a tray of toiletries and an enclosed shower and bathtub. Number 304 has two twin-bedded rooms designed for family stays. It has an interior outlook, making it more condusive to a good night's sleep.

ENGLISH SPOKEN: Yes

FACILITIES AND SERVICES: Bar, direct-dial phone, gym for karate and regular workouts (1,000ptas per day), hair dryer, laundry services, lift, parking (1,400ptas per day), room safe (100ptas per use), satellite TV

TELEPHONE
91 429 65 51

FAX
91 420 24 23

METRO
Sol, 1, 2, 3, or Sevilla, 2

CREDIT CARDS
AE, DC, MC, V

RATES
Single 9,000–10,500ptas, double 12,500–20,000ptas, triple 16,500ptas, quad 20,000ptas, plus 7 percent tax

BREAKFAST
Continental 600ptas per person

NEAREST TOURIST ATTRACTIONS: Plaza de Santa Ana, Museo Thyssen-Bornemisza, Museo del Prado, Botanical Gardens

HOTEL SANTANDER ★★ (21)
C/ de Echegaray 1, corner of C/ de San Jerónimo
35 rooms, all with shower or bath and toilet

TELEPHONE
91 429 95 51, 91 429 66 44, 91 429 46 44, 91 429 56 44

FAX
91 369 10 78

METRO
Sol, 1, 2, 3, or Sevilla, 2

CREDIT CARDS
MC, V

RATES
Single 7,500ptas, double 8,500ptas, suite 9,500ptas, tax included

BREAKFAST
Not served

Let's just say it's different. The Hotel Santander is the sort of eclectic, nostalgic, overdone place guests either absolutely adore or positively cannot stand. I think there are some real virtues to staying at this Cheap Sleep primely positioned between two of Madrid's major museums and the center of the city, Plaza de la Puerta del Sol. The small entry has ersatz Art Nouveau statues and some plants, but if the German shepherd dog, Piper, is on duty, there will hardly be enough room for both of you in the miniature lobby, which is jammed with four ornate French chairs squeezed among two huge floor-standing ashtrays, a floor lamp, a coffee table, a television set, a shelf with assorted brochures, and the beginning of the marble stairway. Posted by the reception desk are the house rules: No eating in the rooms, no washing either, and only three people in the lift at one time. These are enforced by the reception crew, firmly headed by Lillian, who rules her queendom with an iron hand.

I certainly agree with everyone who wants to stay in No. 325, a two-room corner suite that has brass beds, a large bathroom with a stretch tub, and a comfortable sitting room with windows letting in the morning light. There are other nice rooms. Number 211 is a small, quiet double on the back, and No. 217 is a large twin on the street with red bedspreads and drapes, interesting ceiling detail, and an inlaid wood floor. I also like the comfortable chair and old bentwood hat and coat rack that holds whatever won't fit into the armoire. The bathroom is large, the bathtub long enough, and the towels thick enough. So there it is. If you like it plain and simple, this is not your Cheap Sleep in Madrid. But if you are old-fashioned and nostalgic, it very well could be.

ENGLISH SPOKEN: Yes, and French

FACILITIES AND SERVICES: Direct-dial phone, hair dryer available, laundry service, free office safe, TV

NEAREST TOURIST ATTRACTIONS: Plaza de la Puerta del Sol, Museo Thyssen-Bornemisza, easy walking distance to Museo del Prado and Botanical Gardens

PLAZA MAYOR

The imperial Plaza Mayor was constructed in the seventeenth century under the reign of Felipe II, and it served as a market and as a gathering place for state occasions, executions, plays, and bullfights. It was not completed until the reign of Felipe III, whose bronze equestrian statue sits in the middle of the square. Through the years a series of fires destroyed the square and nearly all its buildings. Only one original building remains—the seventeenth-century Spanish Baroque building with its painted facade. Today the buildings house luxury apartments and offices, and the plaza itself is a magnet for tourists, who sit in the many outdoor cafés and restaurants (and usually pay way too much for a meal). On Sunday there is an active stamp market, at Christmas the square is filled with stalls selling food and religious articles, and during the rest of the year, dance bands play, artists hold court, and people come and go just as they have for centuries.

HOTELS

HOSTAL COMERCIAL ★ (27)
C/ de Esparteros 12, 2°
15 rooms, 5 with shower or bath and toilet

There are several *hostales* in this building, but I think this is one of the best, thanks in a large part to the owner, Paco, a multimedia artist who seems to be able to create almost anything he sets his mind to. Aside from completely renovating the *hostal,* laying all the tile floors, and adding such artistic touches as faux finished moldings, he has found time to create wood sculptures, make stained-glass windows, and design a wooden chandelier that hangs in the TV area of the sitting room. Other nice additions are his collection of healthy green plants and a colorful fish tank. What about the rooms? All are pleasantly habitable; some have little marble bathrooms, others share acceptable hall facilities; and all but one have their own balcony.

ENGLISH SPOKEN: Limited

TELEPHONE
91 522 66 30

METRO
Sol, 1, 2, 3

CREDIT CARDS
None, cash only

RATES
Single 1,900–3,100ptas, double 3,300–5,200ptas, triple 6,100ptas, tax included

BREAKFAST
Not served

FACILITIES AND SERVICES: TV in some rooms

NEAREST TOURIST ATTRACTIONS: Plaza Mayor, Puerta del Sol, all of central Madrid

HOSTAL LA MACARENA ★★ (30)
C/ de la Cava de San Miguel 8
25 rooms, all with shower or bath and toilet

TELEPHONE
91 365 92 21, 91 366 61 11

FAX
91 364 27 57

METRO
Sol, 1, 2, 3

CREDIT CARDS
MC, V

RATES
Single 5,700ptas, double 7,700ptas, triple 9,700ptas, quad 12,500ptas, tax included

BREAKFAST
Not served

The Hostal la Macarena received my Cheap Sleeping stamp of approval the minute I walked through the door of the first room and saw the simple yet well-thought-out, color-coordinated decor and arrangement. In addition, fifteen rooms have balconies, some of which are enclosed and become an extension of the room you can use 365 days a year. Number 204 has a nice bathroom and enclosed balcony, as well as a lovely view of one of the archways leading to Madrid's famous Plaza Mayor. Another room with an enclosed balcony is No. 214, which has a polished wooden floor and can be booked as a triple, but I would suggest it only as a double. For a calmer choice, ask for No. 217 on the back; it has a bigger room and bathroom and a window you can see through, but no balcony. Another quiet choice is No. 211, which has a balcony overlooking a pedestrian street and a bathroom with a tub and shower. Finally, I like the inviting sitting area, which opens onto three balconies; the attractive hallways and their wonderful collection of sepia prints of old Spain; and above all, the pleasant reception by the staff in this excellent family-owned Cheap Sleep in Madrid.

ENGLISH SPOKEN: Yes

FACILITIES AND SERVICES: Direct-dial phones, lift, free office safe, piped-in room music, satellite TV, video

NEAREST TOURIST ATTRACTIONS: At the edge of Plaza Mayor, center of Madrid

HOSTAL MONTALVO ★★ (28)
C/ de Zaragoza 6, 3°
31 rooms, all with shower or bath and toilet

TELEPHONE
91 365 59 10

FAX
91 364 52 60

EMAIL
tijcalhostal@anit.es

METRO
Sol, 1, 2, 3

CREDIT CARDS
AE, DC, MC, V

Gabriel, the young owner, is a real go-getter, never missing an opportunity. For example, he doesn't serve breakfast at the *hostal*; instead he gives a discount at a Plaza Mayor café where he has an interest. There are no minibars, but for the asking you can have soft drinks, champagne, whiskey, coffee, or tea twenty-four hours a day. He also makes sure that there is always someone on the desk who speaks English. The rooms, which are located down meandering halls, will never be endorsed by Martha Stewart, but for the most part they are sunny and serviceable for the short haul: The maintenance is good, colors aren't jarring, and there is usually a framed poster or print, a chair, and some sort of writing space. There are several corner rooms with two windows and balconies, and bathrooms have shelves, mirrors, good towels, and sufficient light, though some have those half-tubs that are just fine for a shower but require pretzel twists if you try to take a bath.

ENGLISH SPOKEN: Yes

FACILITIES AND SERVICES: Direct-dial phones, laundry service, lift to the *hostal* (but not between the *hostal*'s two floors), TV

NEAREST TOURIST ATTRACTIONS: Almost on Plaza Mayor, everything in central Madrid

RATES
Single 4,300ptas, double 5,400ptas, triple 8,100ptas, quad 9,200ptas, tax included

BREAKFAST
Not served

HOSTAL RESIDENCIA NUESTRA SEÑORA DE LA PALOMA ★ (27)
C/ de Esparteros 12, 3°
18 rooms, 5 with shower or bath and toilet

You can't reserve by fax, pay with a credit card, reach the third-floor hostal by lift, or converse very well with the desk staff in English, but when you look at those Cheap Sleeping prices . . . who cares? If you speak a little French or Spanish and are fit enough to hike up the stairway, consider this exceptional Cheap Sleep well located between Puerta del Sol and Plaza Mayor. Let me assure you that the rooms and hall facilities are antiseptically clean, quiet, and outfitted with decent towels and ironed sheets on the beds. Sunshine streams through the windows. If you want to splash out and spend a bit more, consider Room 15, a sunny double with a desk and chair and a tiny private bathroom, or Room 17, a twin double with a window in both the bedroom and the bathroom.

ENGLISH SPOKEN: Very limited, but they do speak French

FACILITIES AND SERVICES: Free office safe

NEAREST TOURIST ATTRACTIONS: Between Plaza Mayor and Plaza de la Puerta del Sol, central Madrid

TELEPHONE
91 532 21 72

METRO
Sol, 1, 2, 3

CREDIT CARDS
None

RATES
Single 1,800ptas, double 4,000ptas, tax included

BREAKFAST
Not served

HOTEL PLAZA MAYOR ★★ (31)
C/ de Atocha 2
20 rooms, all with shower or bath and toilet

The Hotel Plaza Mayor is well sited between the Plaza Mayor—and its popular outdoor cafés—and the

TELEPHONE
91 360 06 06

FAX
91 360 06 10

EMAIL
h-plazamayor@ctv.es

METRO
Sol, 1, 2, 3

CREDIT CARDS
AE, MC, V

RATES
Single 6,000ptas, double 8,600–12,000ptas, triple 12,500ptas, plus 7 percent tax; lower rates in the off-season

BREAKFAST
Not served

Plaza de la Puerta del Sol, the heart, soul, and transportation hub of the city. The rooms demonstrate how a little thought and attention to decorating detail can turn a small, ordinary space into a bright, cheerful home away from home. Number 503, on the corner of the hotel, is done in blue and has three large windows flooding the room with sunlight. The brass bed is coordinated with the glass-topped metal table and chair, and the gorgeous bathroom rivals those in many four-star picks. Number 303, in yellow, is equally nice, and so is No. 302, a pleasing double with an enclosed stall shower in the bathroom. The small lobby has an oriental rug and matching stair runner. While you are here, be sure to notice the 1930 photo of Plaza Mayor that hangs to the left of the reception desk. If you are interested in old photos of Madrid, ask to see those that the owner sells for around 500ptas each.

ENGLISH SPOKEN: Yes

FACILITIES AND SERVICES: Air-conditioning, direct-dial phone, lift, room safe (200ptas per day), TV

NEAREST TOURIST ATTRACTIONS: Between Puerta del Sol and Plaza Mayor, all of central Madrid

PRADO

The magnificent Museo del Prado contains one of the greatest art collections in the world. It is housed in a neoclassical building designed in 1785 by Juan de Villanueva. Despite the museum's importance, it is limited in size, and there is only space enough to display a fraction of the masterpieces in the Spanish royal art collection. By the way, if you plan on visiting Madrid's Big Three art museums, it makes sense to buy the Paseo del Arte ticket, which is valid for a year and allows one visit to each museum for substantial savings (for complete details, see "Museum Discounts," page 111). Close to the Prado Museum is the three-hundred-acre Retiro Park, which was built in 1630 when it formed the principal gardens of the Royal Palace of the Buen Retiro. One of the best times to visit it today is on Sunday mornings when it is the haven of many Madrileño families, who enjoy rowing on the lake, watching puppet shows and other street artists, buying from hawking vendors, walking their dogs, or just enjoying the lovely gardens and the fifteen thousand trees that make up the city's most popular green space.

HOSTAL RESIDENCIA SUD-AMERICANA
(no stars, 37)
Paseo del Prado 12, 6°, izda
8 rooms, none with shower or bath and toilet

The only other place to sleep as close to the Prado Museum is the Ritz Hotel, where the opulent rooms start around $300, not including tax, tips, and breakfast. More budget-minded travelers can check into this honest-to-goodness Cheap Sleep offering bottom-of-the-barrel prices. Everything about the place is vintage, including the lack of private plumbing and the swatches of oil cloth draped over some of the beat-up tables. Even though everything is old or old-fashioned, it is neat as a pin, and it's obvious those worn floors have been swabbed down daily for decades. Most of the whitewashed rooms overlook an interior court, but there is light, and let's face it—they are quiet. If you land in a nest facing the Prado, bring a pair of heavy-duty, industrial-strength ear plugs, unless you enjoy lying awake counting motorbikes backfiring and horns honking.

ENGLISH SPOKEN: No, but the owner's son does
FACILITIES AND SERVICES: Lift
NEAREST TOURIST ATTRACTIONS: Across the street from the Museo del Prado, Botanical Gardens, Museo Thyssen-Bornemisza, Centro de Arte Reina Sofía, Retiro Park

TELEPHONE
91 429 25 64
METRO
Banco de España, 2
CLOSED
Aug
CREDIT CARDS
None
RATES
Single 2,800ptas, double 5,300ptas, triple 6,400ptas, tax included
BREAKFAST
Not served

SALAMANCA _____

Salamanca is considered Madrid's premier designer shopping district and one of its best apartment areas. It also contains two interesting, delightful smaller museums: the Museo Lázaro Galdiano and Museo Sorolla. The Museo Lázaro Galdiano is a private collection of fifteen thousand paintings and objects d'art in the four-story mansion and gardens of financier José Lázaro Galdiano, who amassed the eclectic collection. The Museu Sorolla is the former home and painting workshop of the Valencian artist Joaquín Sorolla, who is recognized as Spain's foremost Impressionist painter.

HOTELS

Hostal Residencia Galiano ★★★ ($)   **150**

($) indicates a Big Splurge

HOSTAL RESIDENCIA GALIANO ★★★ (2, $)

C/ de Alcalá Galiano 6

29 rooms, all with shower or bath and toilet

TELEPHONE
91 319 20 00
FAX
91 319 99 44
METRO
Colón, 4
CREDIT CARDS
MC, V
RATES
Single 11,200–12,600ptas, double 15,800ptas, triple 19,700ptas, plus 7 percent tax
BREAKFAST
Continental 1,000ptas per person, served in your room or in the sitting room

The Hostal Residencia Galiano is the former palace of the Marqués de Perija and Conde de Antares, who still maintain living quarters on the top floor. Some of their art and antiques decorate the two sitting areas beyond the reception desk. Be sure to admire the carved, inlaid chest . . . and open its door for a delightful surprise. Also on display is an etched clock hanging over two brown velvet sofas, a lovely tapestry, a massive armoire, and an old trunk made into a glass-top table.

As you can imagine, the *hostal residencia* has a loyal following who return again and again for the Old World air fostered by the traditional, spacious rooms, which are nicely appointed with a comfortable armchair, writing desk, assorted prints, and a second telephone in the bathroom. They all have plenty of closet and drawer space to allow you to unpack and settle in. The baths are a bit dated, but they do have shelf space, hooks, and a basket of toiletries. The neighborhood is one of the nicest in Madrid and borders the most elegant shopping streets in the city.

ENGLISH SPOKEN: Usually in the morning, but limited otherwise

FACILITIES AND SERVICES: Air-conditioning, direct-dial phones, laundry service, lift, minibar, parking (1,500ptas per day), office safe (200ptas per day), satellite TV

NEAREST TOURIST ATTRACTIONS: Shopping, otherwise must use public transportation

Other Options

Sometimes a hotel does not adequately fit your travel needs. If you are staying a longer time and want the convenience of your own kitchen and more space, consider an apartment in a residence hotel. For students and the young at heart, camping and youth hostels offer other options. While there are no apartment rental agencies that are specific to Madrid, both El Sol Vacation Villas and Villas International can book you an apartment in the city; please see their listings in "Apartment Rental Agencies," page 89, in the Barcelona section.

Camping

Camping under the stars does have its advantages, certainly if you are looking for one of the Cheapest Sleeps *near* Madrid. However, note the word *near*. While you might be saving some money by pitching a tent, keep in mind that it will be far, far from all the sights, sounds, and bright lights of Madrid. A full list of campsites in and around Madrid is available from tourist offices.

CAMPING OSUÑA
Avenida de Logroño s/n

If you can stand the incessant noise from the planes landing and taking off from the airport, the prices are as cheap as they come. The campground is open all year, and it's the only one accessible to Madrid by public transporation. There are also some rooms available if you want to stay here but didn't bring any camping gear (call for prices).

TELEPHONE: 91 741 05 10
METRO: Canillejas, 5, then bus 105 or 115
CREDIT CARDS: None, cash only
RATES: 700ptas per person, 700ptas for tent or caravan, 700ptas for electricity, tax included

ENGLISH SPOKEN: Yes

FACILITIES AND SERVICES: Bar, restaurant, convenience store, playground

NEAREST TOURIST ATTRACTIONS: None

CARAVANING EL ESCORIAL
Carretera de Guadarrama a El Escorial

The luxurious campground is about an hour outside of Madrid, north of El Escorial. It has four swimming pools; basketball and tennis courts; a restaurant, bar, and cafeteria; and a launderette, supermarket, and disco.

TELEPHONE: 91 890 24 12

METRO: None, 15km from Madrid

CREDIT CARDS: MC, V

RATES: One car, one caravan, or tent and electricity: 2,100ptas plus 680ptas per person, children under ten 650ptas, tax included

ENGLISH SPOKEN: Yes

FACILITIES AND SERVICES: Bar, cafeteria, restaurant, disco, convenience store, launderette, playground, four swimming pools

NEAREST TOURIST ATTRACTIONS: None

Residence Hotels

APARTAMENTOS LOS JERONIMOS ★★★ (38)
C/ de Moreto 9
25 apartments, all with shower or bath and toilet

TELEPHONE
91 420 02 11, 91 420 05 70

FAX
91 429 44 58

METRO
Atocha, 1

CREDIT CARDS
AE, MC, V

RATES
One-bedroom apartment (1–2 people) from 23,000ptas, 2-bedroom apartment (3 people) from 28,500ptas, 2-bedroom apartment (4 people) from 34,000ptas, extra bed 4,000ptas; all rates plus 7 percent tax; lower rates for longer stays

For temporary apartment living in Madrid, I do not know how you could top the conveniences and comfort offered by the Apartamentos Los Jeronimos. First there is the location in one of the most prestigious neighborhoods in Madrid. You are three minutes from the huge Retiro Park, and you would have to camp in the Botanical Gardens beside the Prado Museum, or check into the Ritz Hotel, to get any closer to the Goyas and El Grecos hanging there. From a day-to-day living standpoint, the neighborhood has four or five cafés and bars, two great bakeries, and a small convenience store that nevertheless houses an amazing treasure trove of everything you would need to put a gourmet meal on the table. If you don't feel like cooking, there is a restaurant and bar in conjunction with the apartments, and for something more upscale, one of Madrid's finest restaurants is two doors away.

As for the apartments and the amenities they offer, I can honestly say they are some of the best I have ever experienced. Everything is color coordinated, with comfortable sofas and chairs, good lighting, excellent mattresses, glorious closet space, and beautiful bathrooms. Kitchens are well stocked, the Monday-to-Saturday maid service is professional and precise, and the list of extras amazing. Some of the units have a fireplace, others have their own small, private swimming pool and solarium. Most of the apartments have a lovely, large terrace with an umbrella-shaded table and chairs where you can watch the sunset over the roof of the Prado. Management is superb; they are always ready to help their guests in whatever way possible to ensure a successful stay. All in all, this is a great choice, and I give it my highest recommendation.

ENGLISH SPOKEN: Yes

FACILITIES AND SERVICES: Air-conditioning (with in-room thermostats), bar, direct-dial phone, hair dryer, fitted kitchens, laundry service, lift, maid service (Mon–Sat), restaurant, room service, free room safe, swimming pool and solarium in some units, satellite TV

NEAREST TOURIST ATTRACTIONS: The Prado, Retiro Park, easy walk to Plaza de Santa Ana

EDIFICIO PRINCIPE II ★★ (26)
C/ del Príncipe 11, 1°
36 apartments, all with shower or bath and toilet

The apartments are new, modern, and simply outfitted with easy-care, plain furniture and bright rose- and salmon-colored fabrics. They range in size from studios to units that comfortably house six. Space is not a problem—in fact, you won't know what to do with it all. All the bathrooms are new, closet space for all your clothes and luggage is more than ample, and kitchens are adequate with Corning smooth-surface stove tops and large refrigerators. The only problem I found in the kitchens was the lack of adequate pans, but I am sure management has added more by now. The location is very good. You are close to a huge El Corte Inglés department store, which has one entire floor devoted to food shopping. If you don't feel like cooking, there are scores of wonderful Cheap Eats nearby (see *Cheap Eats in Spain*). For more

BREAKFAST
Not served

TELEPHONE
91 429 44 70

FAX
91 429 42 49

METRO
Sol, 1, 2, 3

CREDIT CARDS
AE, DC, MC, V

RATES
Studio (1–2 people) from 9,000ptas, apartments (2–6 people) from 12,000–20,000ptas, plus 7 percent tax; lower rates for stays over 30 days

BREAKFAST
Not served

cultural pursuits, you can walk to both the Thyssen-Bornemisza and Prado Museums.

ENGLISH SPOKEN: Yes

FACILITIES AND SERVICES: Air-conditioning, direct-dial phones, fitted kitchens, laundry service, lift, free office safe, satellite TV

NEAREST TOURIST ATTRACTIONS: Central Madrid, Museo Thyssen-Bornemisza, Museo del Prado

Youth Hostels

There are two Hostelling International youth hostels in Madrid. The demand for beds far exceeds the supply, so if you know your dates, it pays to reserve ahead. Official hostel cards are required, there is a maximum three-night consecutive stay, and you can stay no more six nights total in a two-month period. Plan on being in before 1:30 A.M. when the curfew is enforced, and the doors are locked until 8 A.M. the next morning. See the "Students and Teachers" section under "Discounts," page 19, for the contact information in the United States.

To book a bed while in Madrid, contact Red Española de Albergues Juveniles, Calle José Ortega y Gasset 71; tel: 91 347 77 00; fax: 91 401 81 60; Internet: www.mtas.es/injuve/reaj98.htm. The Hostelling International booking center in Madrid for onward reservations is TIVE Office, Calle Fernando el Católico 88; tel: 91 543 74 12; fax: 91 544 00 62.

ALBERGUE JUVENIL CASA DE CAMPO
Casa de Campo
132 beds, none with private facilities

The hostel is in the middle of Madrid's largest park, the Casa de Campo. Rooms house from two to six, and each bathoom is shared by only two rooms. The biggest drawback is that the area is not safe at all after dark.

TELEPHONE: 91 463 56 99

FAX: 91 464 46 85

METRO: Lago, 10

CREDIT CARDS: None

RATES: Over 26 years, 1,500ptas per person; under 26 years, 1,000ptas per person, tax included

BREAKFAST: Included

ENGLISH SPOKEN: Yes

FACILITIES AND SERVICES: Bar, cafeteria, rooms for disabled, garden, laundry

NEAREST TOURIST ATTRACTIONS: None, must use public transportation

ALBERGUE JUVENIL SANTA CRUZ DE MARCENADO
C/ Santa Cruz de Marcenado 28
72 beds, none with private facilities

The modern hostel has beds in rooms that sleep four to eight people. It is about a thirty-minute walk to the center of Madrid.

TELEPHONE: 91 547 45 32

FAX: 91 548 11 96

METRO: Argüelles, 4

CREDIT CARDS: V

RATES: Over 26 years, 1,600ptas per person; under 26 years, 1,000ptas per person, tax included

BREAKFAST: Included

ENGLISH SPOKEN: Yes

FACILITIES AND SERVICES: Garden, lift, wheelchair access

NEAREST TOURIST ATTRACTIONS: None, must use public transportation

SEVILLE

Seville lights up for a feast day as a face lights up with a smile.
—*Arthur Symons*, Cities, *1903*

When you mention Spain, many of the images that come to mind—the colorful flamenco dancers, bullfights, whitewashed houses in the land of Carmen, Don Juan, and Figaro—have been inspired by Andalucía and are personified by its capital, Seville. The city is a melting pot of cultures rich with history and grandeur, overflowing with ancient, magnificent works of art, and anchored by its two majestic monuments: the Christian cathedral and the Muslim Alcázar. To visit Seville is to travel through time and experience the beauty of Roman culture, Arabian sensitivity, Jewish mystery, and Christian splendor. To lose yourself in her winding streets lined with fragrant orange trees, to sit in her taverns echoing with soulful flamenco, to join the festival throngs during *Semana Santa* and *Feria de Abril*, or to simply stroll her parks and feed the snow white pigeons, who light on your head, shoulders, and arms in an excited flutter, is to experience the ethereal magic of Seville.

The city is justly famous for its *fiestas*. The two most famous are weeklong festivals that follow one another: Holy Week, or *Semana Santa*, is a sixteenth-century religious festival that takes place between Palm Sunday and Easter Sunday, and two weeks later is April Fair, or *Feria de Abril*, which is the biggest, most colorful celebration in Spain. No two dates on the national calendar are as quintessentially Spanish or as eagerly attended. *Semana Santa* consists of amazing processions of masked penitents and carnival-style floats by day, and at night, Sevillanos take to the streets for singing, eating, and drinking. During *Feria de Abril*, all work is pushed aside and everyone—from toddlers to octogenarians—dons colorful regional dress and participates in the citywide, weeklong bash of round-the-clock partying, bullfights, parades, and fireworks. These two events are worth a special trip, but be prepared for higher prices and advance preparations, as early as a year ahead or more. During this time, every bed within a twenty-mile radius will be booked, and accommodations can cost 100 percent more than the normal rate. *Feria de Abril* coincides with Seville's bullfighting season (the second most important after Madrid), and it draws the best bullfighters in the country to the Maestranza bullring, which is known as one of the most beautiful and prestigious *plazas de toros* in Spain.

Seville was the host of the 1992 Expo, which celebrated the five hundredth anniversary of Christopher Columbus's voyage from Seville to colonize the New World. This event reinvigorated the city and created a dramatic burst of renewed tourist interest, which in part resulted in an acute shortage of comfortable hotel rooms in the low-to-mid price range.

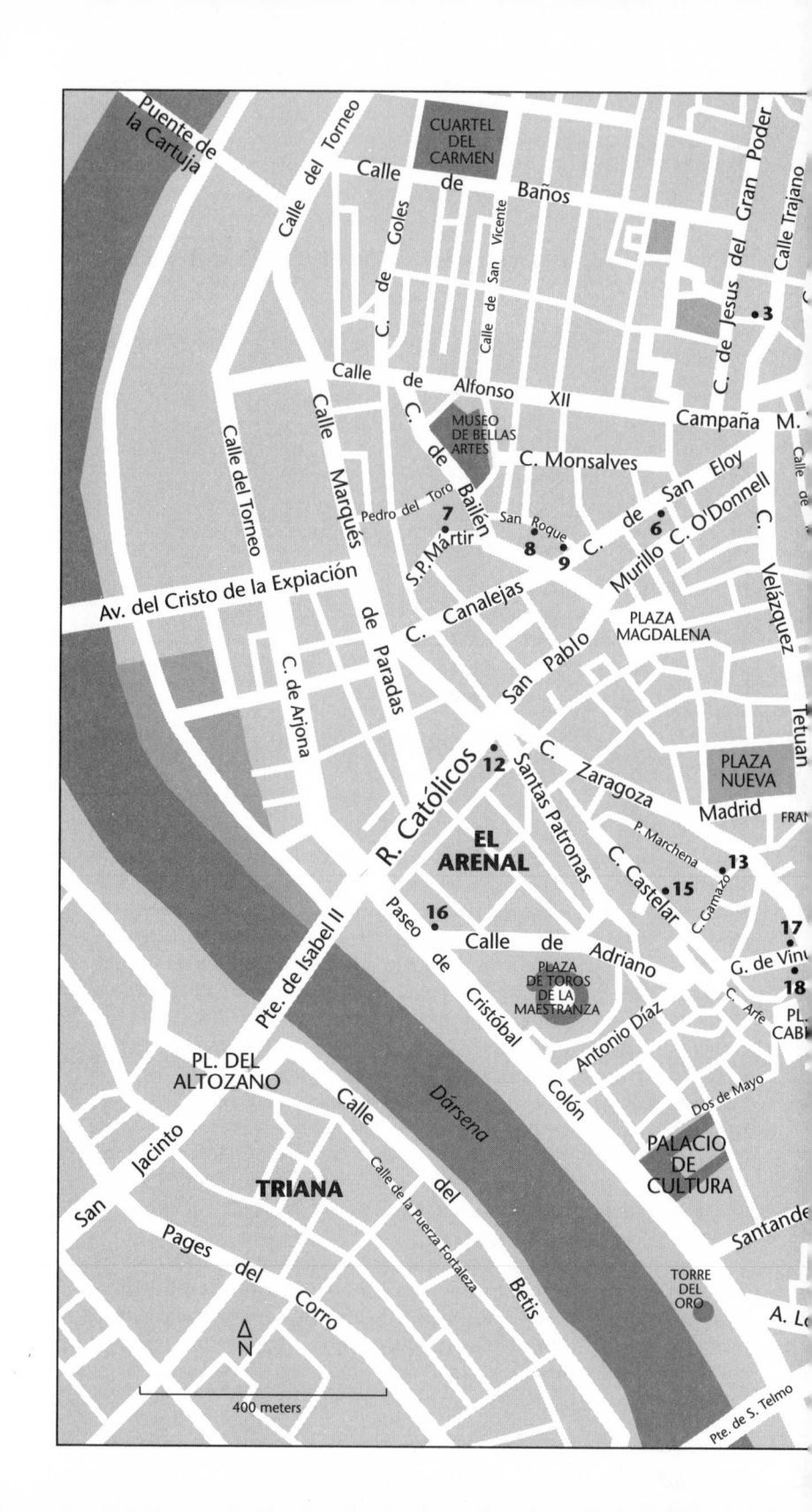

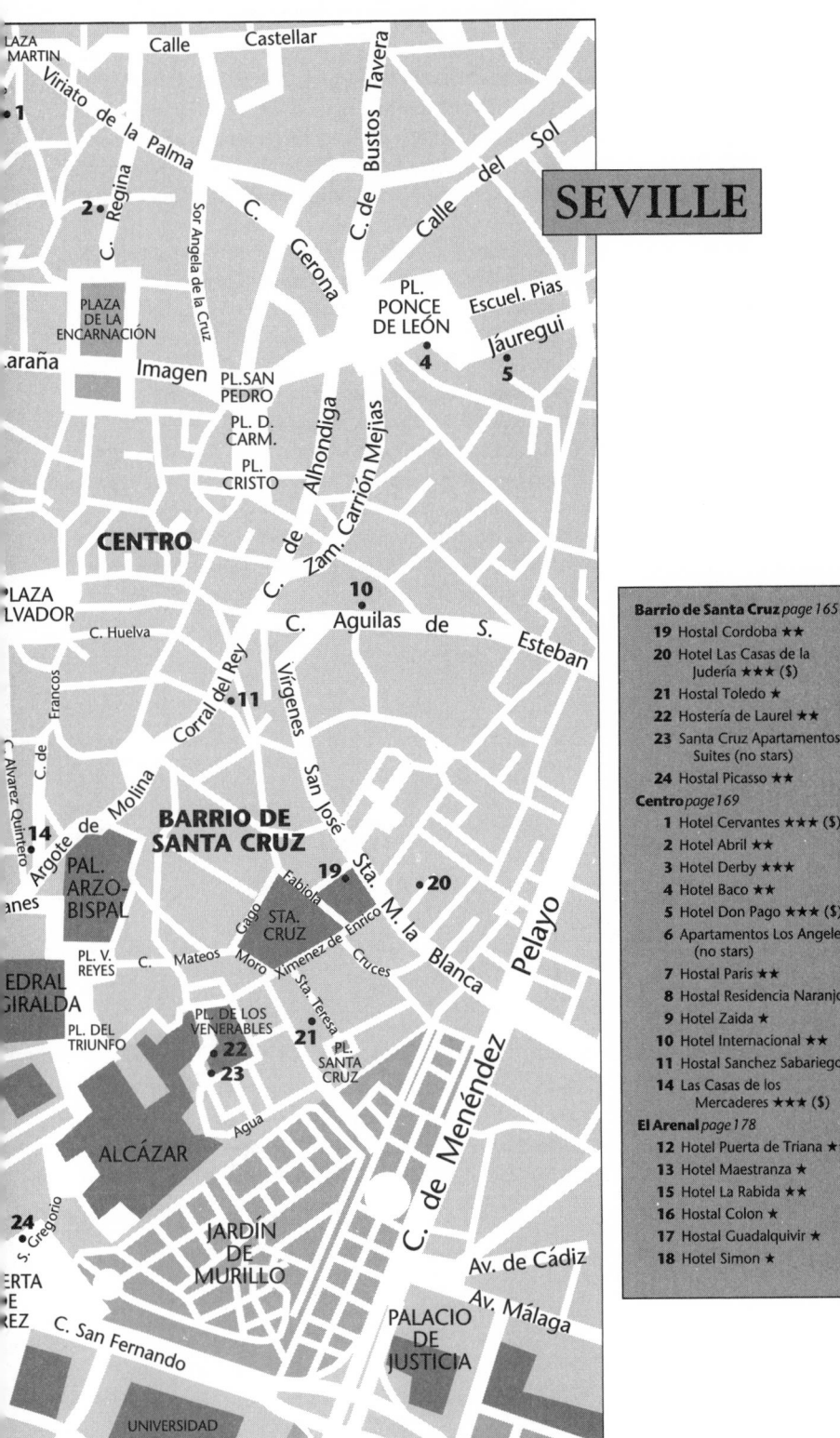

SEVILLE

This continues today, making Seville one of the worst hotel bottlenecks in the country, especially during high season. During these times it is important to arrive with confirmed, written reservations guaranteeing your room and price. On the other hand, during the off-season and during the scorching heat in the summer, hotel prices are often dramatically discounted.

One of the most delightful things to do in Seville is to ride in a horsedrawn carriage to the Plaza de España, a dramatic building next to María Luisa Park that was built in 1929 for the Latin American Exhibition and today houses government offices. Each of Spain's fifty-one provinces are represented on the benches, alcoves, and pillars with beautiful caramic *azulejo* tiles depicting important historical events, maps, or scenes from each locale. Also along the circle that surrounds the plaza are statues of important characters in Spanish history. This is a favorite spot to spend a lazy afternoon—rowing on the minicanals or sitting under a shade tree and watching the crowds wander by. Toward the end of the park are several museums with archaeological and popular arts collections. At the opposite end of the city is the Museo de Bellas Artes, which has paintings by Murillo and is the city's most important art museum.

General Information

ADDRESSES

Addresses in Spain are written differently than those in the States. For a description of how to decipher Seville addresses and of their many abbreviations, please see the "Addresses" section, page 33, under "How to Use *Cheap Sleeps in Spain.*" However, many establishments in Seville don't have street numbers, so always make sure you know the full name of the place you're looking for. Even if you are only going to be in Seville a few days, it pays to buy a detailed street map, and even then finding a good map of the Barrio de Santa Cruz is nearly impossible. You can almost be assured of getting lost in its maze of narrow streets. But since the area is small with colorful photo ops at every turn, relax and enjoy your confusion. When in doubt, just follow the crowd.

BUSINESS HOURS

You can go to the bank Monday to Friday from 9 A.M. to 2 P.M. and until noon on Saturday. Shops are open Monday to Friday from 9:30 or 10 A.M. to 1:30 P.M., and again from 4:30 to 8:30 P.M. Many small shops close Saturday afternoon. Department stores are open continuously from 10 A.M. to 8 P.M.

CLIMATE

Best weather is from May to mid-June and from Septembr through October, with March through April considered high season. In the summer it is not at all unusual to have weeks on end of temperatures soaring above 100°F. Some of the best restaurants are closed in the summer, and many locals leave the city. The winter can be damp and rainy.

CONSULATES

The U.S. consulate is at Paseo de las Delicias 7; tel: 95 423 18 85; hours: Mon–Fri 10 A.M.–1 P.M., 2–4:40 P.M.

The British consulate is at Plaza Nueva 8; tel: 95 422 88 75; hours: Mon–Fri 8 A.M.–3 P.M.

DISABLED TRAVELERS

In Seville, the Oficina de Turismo para Personas Descapacitadas can give you information on how to negiotate the city if you have a disability. They are at Calle Patricio Sáenz 7; tel: 95 438 66 45.

EMERGENCY NUMBERS

For information on where to go to seek medical treatment in a nonemergency situation, see "Medical Problems," below.

Ambulance	95 442 55 65
Medical emergency	061, 091
Pharmacies (24 hours)	010
Police	091 (national), 092 (local)

HOLIDAYS AND FESTIVALS

Other than national holidays, the two most important holiday periods are Holy Week, *Semana Santa,* and two weeks later, April Fair, or *Feria de Abril. Semana Santa* is a religious celebration that centers around elaborate religious processions, and *Feria de Abril* is a weeklong party that takes place at El Real de la Feria in Los Remedios, west of the Guadalquivir River. During these events, vast crowds triple the size of the city and increase prices by at least double, but they are spectacles you must see to believe. For dates and general information, contact the Office of Tourism in Seville; tel: 95 422 14 04.

Parade for the Three Kings	*Cabalgata de los Reyes Magos*	January 5
Maundy Thursday	*Jueves Santo*	Day before Good Friday
Holy Week	*Semana Santa*	Palm Sunday to
April Fair	*Feria de Abril*	Last week of April
	Corpus Christi	Usually June
Feast of St. John the Baptist	*Día de San Juan Bautista*	June 24
	Velá de Santiago	July 24–26 (on the west side of the river)
National flamenco festival	*Bienal de Flamenco*	September (in even-numbered years)
Feast of the Immaculate Conception	*La Imaculada Concepción*	December 8

LOST PROPERTY

If you lose something while in Seville, go to the Plaza de la Gavidia police station, which is near Plaza de la Victoria; tel: 95 422 88 40.

MEDICAL PROBLEMS

The best thing to do in an emergency is to go to the *urgencias,* or casualty department, of any major hospital (see "Emergency Numbers," above, for immediate care). The main general hospital is Hospital Virgen de Rocío, Avenida Manuel Siurot s/n; tel: 95 424 81 81. It's about two miles south of the Parque de María Luisa. English-speaking doctors are on duty at the Hospital Universidad, Avenida Dr. Fedriani s/n; tel: 95 455 74 00 or 95 437 84 00.

MONEY

There are many banks and ATMs in central Seville where the rates are far more advantageous than at any tourist exchange office. El Corte Inglés department stores have favorable exchange rates, low commissions, and are open all day long, but not on Sunday.

The American Express Foreign Exchange Service is next to the Hotel Inglaterra on Plaza Nueva 7; tel: 95 421 16 17 or 95 421 30 04; hours: Mon–Fri 9:30 A.M.–1:30 P.M., 4:30–7:30 P.M.

POST OFFICE

The main post office is at Avenida de la Constitución 32; tel: 95 421 95 85; hours: Mon–Fri 8:30 A.M.–8:30 P.M., Sat 9 A.M.–2 P.M. The *Lista de Correos-poste restante* office for general delivery is open Mon–Fri 9 A.M.– 8 P.M., Sat 9 A.M.–1 P.M.

The *poste restante* (general delivery) address in Seville is:
The recipient's name
c/o Poste Restante
Seville, Spain

SAFETY AND SECURITY

The same safety advice applies in Seville as for the rest of Spain: Violent crime is rare, but pickpockets, purse snatchers, and auto thieves are in great supply, so exercise caution in tourist areas, in crowds, and especially at night.

The main station for the municipal police is at Pabellón de Brasil, Paseo de la Delicias 15, south of the Parque de María Luisa; tel: 95 461 54 40. The national police are at Plaza Concordia, s/n. Dial 091 in an emergency.

TELEPHONE

The telephone code for Seville is 95, and the main *telefónica* office is at Calle Sierpes 11. For further information about making international calls and calling within Spain, see "Telephone," page 30.

TOURIST INFORMATION

The main tourist office is at Avenida de la Constitución 21; tel: 94 422 14 04; hours: Mon–Fri 9 A.M.–7 P.M., Sat 10 A.M.–2 P.M. Others are located at Paseo de las Delicias 9; tel: 95 423 44 65; hours: Mon–Fri 8:30 A.M.–6:30 P.M.; and on Calle de Arjona (near the Punte de Isabel II bridge); tel: 95 421 36 30; hours: Mon–Fri 9 A.M.–8 P.M. and Sat–Sun until noon.

Transvías operates daily, one-hour city tours on double-decker buses from 10 A.M. to 7 P.M. Buses leave from Paseo de Cristóbal Colón opposite the bullring (Maestranza), which is north of the Torre del Oro. The tour is hardly dynamic, as you never get off the bus, but it is a good way to get a quick overview before launching out yourself. The telephone number is

95 450 20 99. There are also several one-hour river cruises that can be picked up from the embarcadero by the Torre del Oro.

TRANSPORTATION

There is no metro in Seville, and in the time it takes you to figure out the bus routes, chances are you could walk to wherever you are going. Seville is a city that is best seen on foot, and the main sites are within reasonable walking distance from the hotels listed in this book. One of the most delightful ways to see the city is to hire one of the horsedrawn carriages that wait for customers by the cathedral. Trips can last as long as you like, and rates are affordable, especially if there are four in your party.

For airport information, call 95 451 06 77 or 95 451 61 11.

Bus

The central bus station is at Calle José María Osborne 11; tel: 95 441 71 11; hours: Mon–Sat 10 A.M.–8 P.M. You can get bus route information from the station, from tourist offices, or from information booths at major stops. From the Santa Justa train station, take No. 27 to Plaza de la Encarnación in the center of the city. From the airport, take the hourly bus operated by Amarillos to the city center at the Puerta de Jerex at the top of Avenida Roma.

Taxi

Taxis are cheap, and they are the best way to get around at night. All cabs are metered. Tele Taxi: 95 462 22 22; Radio Taxi: 95 458 00 00.

Train

The RENFE information and reservation office is at Calle Zaragoza 31, off Plaza Nueva; tel: 95 441 41 11, 94 441 47 00; hours: Mon–Fri 9 A.M.–1 P.M. and 4–7 P.M.

The Santa Justa Train Station is about two kilometers from the city center on Avenida de Kansas City; tel: 95 454 02 02.

Hotels in Seville by Area

Seville doesn't have an ambience. It is ambience.
—*James A. Michener*

BARRIO DE SANTA CRUZ ————————

The Barrio de Santa Cruz, formerly the medieval Jewish quarter of Seville, is a picturesque neighborhood of whitewashed houses with wrought-iron balconies and flower-filled courtyards. In the Plaza de Santa Cruz is a lovely wrought-iron cross that was made in 1692.

The Giralda Tower, once a minaret on the city's mosque and now attached to the cathedral, is one of Seville's most treasured and impressive landmarks. Built of brick in 1184 to 1195, the ninety-three-meter tower is the tallest in Spain, and it's crowned by a bronze weather vane, which is known as *El Giraldillo*. The dazzling view from the top is worth the climb up the wide interior ramp, which is actually fairly easy.

The Gothic cathedral was completed in 1507 and is the third largest church in the world, after St. Peter's in Vatican City and St. Paul's in London. Its Sacristía Mayor houses the Tomb of Columbus and paintings by Murillo and other Spanish masters.

Los Reales Alcázares—which is known simply as the Alcázar (or fortress)—is one of the oldest royal residences in Europe, and it's the oldest in the Spanish Crown. It dates from 913, when it was built as a fortified Muslim palace, and later was expanded many times under the reigns of various monarchs. The magnificent Moorish palace is surrounded by gardens and tiled courtyards filled with the pungent, sweet scent of orange trees. The Alcázar is the most important example of civil architecture in Seville.

————

HOTELS

OTHER OPTIONS
Residence Hotels
Santa Cruz Apartamentos-Suites (no stars)   **185**

($) indicates a Big Splurge

HOSTAL CORDOBA ★★ (19)

TELEPHONE
95 421 53 35
CLOSED
Dec 1–Feb 2
CREDIT CARDS
None
RATES
Single 3,600ptas, double
6,100ptas, tax included
BREAKFAST
Not served

C/ Farnesio 12, at C/ Fabiola
12 rooms, 7 with shower or bath and toilet

For over twenty years, the Almagro family has been welcoming guests to their clean, well-priced *hostal* in the Barrio de Santa Cruz. It is a pretty place, just what you would expect to see in Seville, with a colorful tiled court-yard entry and a beautiful collection of ferns, which are lovingly tended by the father. Also helping at the front desk is Ana, his pretty young daughter, who has polished her English by conversing with their many repeat guests.

Not all the rooms have private bathrooms, but don't let that worry you—the hall facilities are spotless. The white-painted rooms are furnished in simple pine and have wrought-iron grills over the windows, a common sight in Seville. I think this is one of the city's better two-star picks, not only because of its prime location, but because the Cheap Sleeping price includes air-conditioning, an absolute necessity during the summer.

ENGLISH SPOKEN: Yes

FACILITIES AND SERVICES: Air-conditioning

NEAREST TOURIST ATTRACTIONS: Barrio de Santa Cruz, cathedral, Alcázar

HOSTAL PICASSO ★★ (24)

TELEPHONE AND FAX
95 421 08 64
EMAIL
hpicasso@arrakis.es
CREDIT CARDS
MC, V
RATES
Doubles 7,600–6,700ptas,
extra bed 3,100ptas, plus
7 percent tax
BREAKFAST
Not served

C/ de San Gregorio 1
30 rooms, 8 with shower or bath and toilet

It's new, imaginatively decorated, priced right, in a super location, and everyone is friendly. What more could you want? Well, for one thing, a few more square feet in each room, which in some cases are so small they are little more than enlarged closets masquerading as sleeping space. The *hostal*'s adobe-tiled entry is cleverly done in blue-and-white half-tiled walls with shocking glow-winkie green sponge-painted walls above that are covered with copper pans and decorative plates. It looks great. And all of the floors overlook an attractive interior patio filled with healthy green plants. However, great-ness ends and miniscule begins once you cross the thresh-old of your room. While I give them high marks for their bright colors, patio views, and smart print fabrics, these are tiny—as in itsy-bitsy—spaces. There's just no getting around it. None of them has room for a table or chair, never mind a closet (unless you count the exposed pole, where you could hang a few things). In the summer, don't even think of reserving a room without air-conditioning, or you will swelter. With these warnings in mind, you could still be a happy Cheap Sleeper at the Picasso—so long as you are traveling *very* lightly.

Note: There are no specifically single rooms, but of course you can book a double for single usage.

ENGLISH SPOKEN: Yes

FACILITIES AND SERVICES: Air-conditioning in some rooms

NEAREST TOURIST ATTRACTIONS: Barrio de Santa Cruz, cathedral, Alcázar

HOSTAL TOLEDO ★ (21)
C/ Santa Teresa 15
9 rooms, all with shower or bath and toilet

TELEPHONE
95 421 53 35

CLOSED
Dec 1–Feb 2

CREDIT CARDS
None

RATES
Single 3,600ptas, double 6,100ptas, tax included

BREAKFAST
Not served

The Barrio de Santa Cruz is the oldest and most desirable part of Seville, but unfortunately, decent, budget-priced hotels are in very short supply. Thus, to be a Cheap Sleeper here, you will have to lower a few expectations. If you don't mind less-than-ideal accommodations that are still authentically Seville, you may have a satisfying stay at this Cheap Sleeping pad. The place has potential . . . oh boy, would I love to get my hands on this one and redo it from top to bottom. Since that isn't going to happen any time soon, you will have to take the place "as is." The owner, an older woman, will greet you from her perch in the front courtyard while motioning for her companion to let you in, and he will show you the rooms. All the open hallways overlook an interior courtyard . . . very Seville. Along the halls are a few pieces of old furniture that naturally need refinishing and a collection of dusty fake flowers . . . too often, very Seville. The rooms are clean and, for the most part, generous in size. Number 2, a twin with high ceilings, a tile floor, and a balcony, has matching furniture, a desk, and a two-drawer armoire. A gold, satiny material covers the beds and is used as curtains. In the bathroom there is a shower, but no curtain. Number 4 is similar: the same sort of furniture, a balcony, and a curtainless shower. A frilly white spread covers the double bed and pink curtains frame the window that faces a wall. See what I mean?

It all boils down to how much you can live without if you want the Barrio de Santa Cruz to be your temporary address in Seville.

ENGLISH SPOKEN: Limited

FACILITIES AND SERVICES: None

NEAREST TOURIST ATTRACTIONS: Barrio de Santa Cruz, cathedral, Alcázar

HOSTERÍA DE LAUREL ★★ (22)
Plaza de los Venerables 5
22 rooms, all with shower or bath and toilet

TELEPHONE
95 422 02 95, 95 421 07 59
FAX
95 421 04 05
EMAIL
host-laurel@eintec.es
INTERNET
www.eintec.es/host-laurel/
CREDIT CARDS
AE, DC, MC, V
RATES
Single 9,000ptas, double 12,500ptas, triple 15,000ptas, quad 17,000ptas; children under 10 are free; half-pension 2,800ptas per person, per day; full pension 5,000ptas per person, per day; all prices plus 7 percent tax
BREAKFAST
650ptas per person

We all know about Don Juan, the famous Spanish lover, but did you know that around 1844 the romantic writer Don Jose Zorrilla was inspired by the atmosphere of this inn when he created his most famous character, Don Juan Tenorio? You won't be surprised when you see the inn, which occupies a central location in this famous old quarter of Seville. In addition to a wonderful tiled bar festooned with hanging hams and braids of garlic, there is a pretty formal dining room and an alluring patio with every table filled for lunch and afternoon drinks. The twenty-two rooms, most of which open onto an interior atrium/courtyard, are some of the best in the area. All are nicely yet simply executed with matching furniture and enough space for a luggage rack and a chair. Marble tiled bathrooms offer good towels, hooks, and a small shelf to hold a basket of complimentary toiletries. Management and staff are helpful and competent.

ENGLISH SPOKEN: Yes

FACILITIES AND SERVICES: Air-conditioning, direct-dial phones, hair dryer, lift, restaurant, TV

NEAREST TOURIST ATTRACTIONS: Center of Barrio de Santa Cruz, easy walk to the cathedral, Alcázar, and Murillo Gardens

HOTEL LAS CASAS DE LA JUDERÍA ★★★ (20, $)
Plaza de Santa Maria la Blanca s/n, Callejón de Dos Hermanas 7
87 rooms, all with shower or bath and toilet

TELEPHONE
95 441 51 50
FAX
95 442 21 70
EMAIL
juderia@300m.es
INTERNET
www.ibernet.net/lascasas
CREDIT CARDS
AE, DC, MC, V

Hidden on a small street off Santa Maria la Blanca is one of Seville's loveliest hotels—and definitely the best three-star in town. The hotel is part of a group called *Casas y Palacios de España*, which has two other properties in Seville, including Las Casas de los Mercaderes (see page 177). Their other location, Las Casas del Rey de Baeza, is, unfortunately for Cheap Sleepers, a four-star hotel and priced accordingly.

The minute you walk into the lovely, plant-lined courtyard of Las Casas de la Judería, you know you will have a memorable stay. The rooms are built around two main courtyards that have big, open verandas with groupings of padded wicker sofas and armchairs—inspiring leisurely late afternoons devoted to reading or relaxing with a cool drink before venturing out for dinner. All the individually decorated rooms display restrained elegance and have beautiful furnishings and the utmost in comforts. Number 29, a standard double with its own terrace, is done in mauve and tan, with complementary prints covering two comfortable chairs, the bedspread, and draperies. There is a small secretary desk, a double closet where you can hang your things and feel at home, and a white-tiled bathroom fitted with thick towels, complimentary toiletries, and its own window. For something a little more spacious, reserve No. 30, a suite with an entryway large enough for two chairs and a table. The lovely twin-bedded room has a sofa bed and chair and, to one side, a work space with an Oriental rug on the dark wood floor. The feeling of spacious comfort is further enhanced by the walk-in closet, the small balcony with a roof-top view, and the tile bathroom with beautiful brass fittings and its own window for ventilation. The hotel is well located on the edge of the Barrio de Santa Cruz. An easy, interesting walk gets you to the cathedral, the magnificent Alcázar, and many restaurants listed in *Cheap Eats in Spain*.

ENGLISH SPOKEN: Yes

FACILITIES AND SERVICES: Air-conditioning, bar, conference room, direct-dial phone, hair dryer, lift for Rooms 18–57 (no lift for Rooms 1–17), laundry service, minibar, parking (2,000ptas per day), free room safe, satellite TV

NEAREST TOURIST ATTRACTIONS: Edge of Barrio de Santa Cruz, walking distance to the cathedral and Alcázar

RATES
Single 10,500ptas, double for single usage 14,000ptas, double 26,500–30,000ptas, suite 40,000ptas; lower rates in off-season; all rates plus 7 percent tax

BREAKFAST
Buffet 1,400ptas per person

CENTRO

The center of Seville, with its twisting streets and small plazas, extends north of the cathedral. The pedestrian, awning-shaded Calle de Sierpes and its adjoining streets comprise the main shopping district, and its boutiques, clothing shops, and cafés are always buzzing with people. At the bottom end of Calle de Sierpes, near the Plaza de San Francisco, is the Royal Prison where Cervantes created one of the most enduring characters of the literary world: Don Quixote de la Mancha. The Plaza de San Francisco has been Seville's main public square since the sixteenth century, when it was the site of Inquisition burnings and criminal executions. Today it is where dignitaries sit in comfort to watch the *Semana Santa* processions.

The Museo de Bellas Artes, on the western edge of the central district, was a convent until it became an art museum in 1839, and today it is considered one of the most important in Spain. Among other treasures, the museum has a roomful of Murillos, the famous Sevillan painter who is also buried in the Barrio de Santa Cruz.

Depending on where you stay in the Centro, you won't be more than a twenty-minute walk from the cathedral, Alcázar, and Barrio de Santa Cruz.

HOTELS

OTHER OPTIONS
Residence Hotels

($) indicates a Big Splurge

HOSTAL PARIS ★★ (7)
C/ San Pedro Mártir 14
15 rooms, all with shower or bath and toilet

TELEPHONE
95 422 98 61

FAX
95 421 96 45

CREDIT CARDS
AE, DC, MC, V

RATES
Single 3,700ptas, double 6,200ptas, plus 7 percent tax

You won't have many real creature comforts at the Hostal Paris, but it is clean, new, and well maintained. Like many small *hostales* in Seville, it has three levels with rooms overlooking an interior courtyard. The best rooms at Hostal Paris are on the second and third levels. The rooms on the first level open onto the courtyard, but are dark and depressing because little light can seep through the safety-bar-covered windows. The rooms are furnished in basic pine with knee-hole desks and bright red or deep aqua spreads and curtains. The bathrooms, a few of which have a window, have three-quarter-size tubs with a handheld shower and sliver of soap.

ENGLISH SPOKEN: Limited

FACILITIES AND SERVICES: Air-conditioning, direct-dial phone, parking can be arranged in a public lot (1,500ptas per day), free office safe, TV

NEAREST TOURIST ATTRACTIONS: Museo de Bellas Artes, shopping, twenty-minute walk to the cathedral and the Alcázar

BREAKFAST
Not served

HOSTAL RESIDENCIA NARANJO ★★ (8)
C/ San Roque 11
27 rooms, all with shower or bath and toilet

The Naranjo is slightly off the usual tourist path, so if everything else is full, you will probably stand a chance of finding a room here—and that's not at all bad, so long as you don't mind an over-the-top, ornate decorating scheme throughout the reception and sitting areas. Greek statues flanking the front door set the tone. In the entryway and lobby, gilt and velvet are mixed with faux arches and stained-glass windows, all of which strive for a feeling of opulence that never quite gets off the ground. Kitsch is alive and well in the salon, which has deep burgandy drapes hanging across an entire wall. Along another are black sofas and chairs positioned for watching television, and mixed in is a gold four-foot-high vase, tile-accented walls, and a collection of oversize mirrors and pictures.

Thank goodness the rooms, which are universally acceptable, don't follow this theme. Number 102, a typical room facing the street, has a pine armoire with a matching headboard and bedside tables. The television is mounted on the ceiling, forcing you to watch it while lying on the double bed, which is covered in a pink satin bedspread. The small bathroom is sufficient for a short stay. There are lights over the mirror and a half bathtub, which means no stretching out in a bubble bath—just the usual Spanish routine of standing with the handheld shower.

ENGLISH SPOKEN: Yes

FACILITIES AND SERVICES: Air-conditioned, direct-dial phone, free room safe, radio, TV

TELEPHONE
95 422 58 40, 95 421 09 91

FAX
95 421 69 43

CREDIT CARDS
MC, V

RATES
Single 3,600ptas, double 5,200ptas, triple 7,300ptas, quad 8,000ptas, plus 7 percent tax

BREAKFAST
Not served

NEAREST TOURIST ATTRACTIONS: Museo de Bellas Artes, shopping, twenty-minute walk to the cathedral and the Alcázar

HOSTAL SANCHEZ SABARIEGO ★ (11)
Corral del Rey 23
13 rooms, 10 with shower or bath and toilet

TELEPHONE
95 421 44 70
CREDIT CARDS
None
RATES
Single 3,200ptas, double 7,300ptas, triple 8,200–9,200ptas, tax included; lower rates in off-season
BREAKFAST
Not served

The Hostal Sanchez Sabariego has no lift, no air-conditioning, no TV, and takes no credit cards. Why does it still succeed? Because the Sanchez family, who have been here for decades, offer Cheap Sleeps in the center of Seville and because of their friendly, outgoing manner with all their guests. The colorful courtyard is typical, filled with a two-tiered fountain, bright tiles, and heavy Spanish wood furniture. Upstairs is another sitting area, loaded with family knickknacks, and on the roof, a large collection of geraniums. The rooms open onto wide walkways circling the courtyard, and they are a mixed bag, some much more appealing than others. One or two have a black air-conditioning hose stretched across one wall, which certainly does little to improve room aesthetics. Another, the so-called Principal Room, has a matching antique armoire and twin beds, which are blessed by a religious shrine hung over them. The wooden chandelier in the ceiling has no lights; instead they have installed a florescent light over the door and another between the beds. This lighting "improvement" means you can see what you are reading in bed, but again, it doesn't add to the ambience of the room. Number 105 is a big room with its private toilet just outside the door. No, the *hostal* isn't really as grim as it sounds; actually it's quite okay when you consider the price, off-season discounts, location, and all the other interesting, like-minded Cheap Sleepers you probably will meet during your stay.

ENGLISH SPOKEN: Yes, and it is excellent
FACILITIES AND SERVICES: None
NEAREST TOURIST ATTRACTIONS: Cathedral, edge of Barrio de Santa Cruz

HOTEL ABRIL ★★ (2)
C/ de Jerónimo Hernández 20, at C/ Regina
20 rooms, all with shower or bath and toilet

TELEPHONE
95 422 90 46
FAX
95 456 39 38

For a quiet, central location in Seville for a price that will not send your pocketbook into orbit, I think this attractive twenty-room hotel makes perfect Cheap Sleeping sense. All the rooms have the same good-quality matching furniture, box spring mattresses, pleasing floral prints, both on the curtains and on the top section of the bedspreads. The small but modern baths have a good selection of towels. When reserving ask for Rooms 301 or 302, both suites that sell for the same price as a double. Each of these nice rooms has an entry area with a desk and built-in closet. In addition to the twin beds are a sofa bed and a bathroom with its own window. Space here is not enormous, but it will certainly do. The only rooms I would avoid are Nos. 106 and 206 because in each the only window looks into an inside hall. However, they would be quiet.

ENGLISH SPOKEN: Yes

FACILITIES AND SERVICES: Air-conditioned, bar, direct-dial phone, hair dryer, lift, free office safe, satellite TV

NEAREST TOURIST ATTRACTIONS: Center of Seville, almost everything within a twenty-minute walk

CREDIT CARDS
AE, DC, MC, V

RATES
Single 6,200ptas, double 8,700ptas, triple 10,500ptas, plus 7 percent tax

BREAKFAST
500ptas per person

HOTEL BACO ★★ (4)
Plaza Ponce de León 15
25 rooms, all with shower or bath and toilet

Connoisseurs of cod flock to the famous Restaurante El Bacalao (see *Cheap Eats in Spain*), and the two-star hotel cognoscenti pack their adjoining Hotel Baco. What started as a restaurant on the Plaza Ponce de Léon specializing in cod—prepared in every way known to civilized humanity—has grown into a mini-empire consisting of the restaurant, the hotel, and a fabulous deli/market that offers a huge selection of wines, gourmet foods from all over Spain, and of course, cod sold in every guise imaginable.

The hotel is a standout in its class. Its fresh, clean Sevillian style confidently bridges the past with the present, starting with the beautiful tiled stairway leading from the small reception desk to the twenty-five well-done rooms. Number 102, in gold and sienna tones, is an excellent double with a huge four-door wardrobe and two small balconies that face the street. The bathroom has a regulation tub with a shower guard. For a quieter choice, request No. 109, which has an interior view, twin beds, and the same nice bathroom. Deciding where to eat won't be a problem: You can dine in the formal restaurant, have great tapas sitting at the bar, or go to the deli and create a picnic for later.

ENGLISH SPOKEN: Yes

TELEPHONE
95 456 50 50

FAX
95 456 34 54

CREDIT CARDS
AE, EC, MC, V

RATES
Single 7,500ptas, double 10,500ptas; extra bed is 10 percent of room rate; all rates plus 7 percent tax

BREAKFAST
Continental 600ptas per person

FACILITIES AND SERVICES: Air-conditioning, direct-dial phone, hair dryer, lift, minibar, parking (2,000ptas per day), restaurant, free room safe, satellite TV, trouser press

NEAREST TOURIST ATTRACTIONS: Near Convent of Santa Catalina, about a thirty-minute walk to most tourist destinations

HOTEL CERVANTES ★★★ (1, $)
C/ de Cervantes 10
48 rooms, all with shower or bath and toilet

TELEPHONE
95 490 02 80, 95 490 04 08
FAX
95 490 05 36
CREDIT CARDS
AE, DC, MC, V
RATES
Single 11,000ptas, double 15,500ptas, extra bed 4,000ptas, plus 7 percent tax
BREAKFAST
Buffet 1,100ptas per person

True, Hotel Cervantes is a little off the usual tourist trail, but for many, this is its appeal and charm. And yet it's still only a thirty-minute walk to the Barrio de Santa Cruz, where you can hire a horse-drawn carriage and leisurely ride to the Plaza de España, the waterfront, and the lovely Parque de María Luisa.

The three-floor hotel opens onto a stained-glass-covered patio filled with flowering plants and accented with a small fountain. The rooms are uniformly done in clear yellow, orange, blue, or green and framed prints by Picasso, Miró, and August Macke. The laminated furnishings include luggage racks. The white-tile baths offer a shelf, a few toiletries, and if space permits, a stool to sit on. The best rooms are Nos. 110 and 210, two large rooms overlooking the patio, and those ending in numbers 2 through 5. A buffet breakfast is served in a modern room with pink-tablecloth-covered tables and black lacquer chairs.

ENGLISH SPOKEN: Yes

FACILITIES AND SERVICES: Air-conditioning, bar, direct-dial phone, hair dryer available, lift, laundry service, minibar, free safe in some rooms, TV

NEAREST TOURIST ATTRACTIONS: Shopping, about a thirty-minute walk to most tourist sites

HOTEL DERBY ★★★ (3)
Plaza del Duque s/n, at C/ Trajano
75 rooms, all with shower or bath and toilet

TELEPHONE
95 456 10 88
FAX
95 421 33 91
CREDIT CARDS
AE, DC, MC, V
RATES
Single 9,000ptas, double 12,500ptas, triple 15,000ptas, plus 7 percent tax

Close your eyes and think Motel 6—or any other budget chain hotel in any major, midcity location—and you have the Hotel Derby in Seville. It is popular with package tours to Spain because it offers predictable rooms in a nondescript atmosphere that appeals to those travelers who want no surprises whatsoever. Why am I telling you about it? For several reasons. First, it is right across the plaza from El Corte Inglés, Spain's major department store, which sells everything from apples to zippers. It is also a fairly straight walk to the cathedral, the Alcázar, and the old part of the city. Third, the multilingual staff speaks English. And finally, the rooms and bathrooms are in good repair and come with the necessities many Spanish hotels lack: bedside lights, luggage racks, a small desk, an armchair, and sink space in the bathroom. Not only that, most have some sort of view. On the fourth floor, a restaurant and large sitting room open onto a wraparound terrace with a direct view of El Corte Inglés and the other commercial buildings in the neighborhood.

ENGLISH SPOKEN: Yes

FACILITIES AND SERVICES: Air-conditioning, bar, direct-dial phone, laundry service, lift, minibar, parking (1,500ptas per night), restaurant, free office safe, radio, TV, pay-per-view video

NEAREST TOURIST ATTRACTIONS: Shopping, twenty-minute walk to cathedral, Alcázar, Barrio de Santa Cruz

BREAKFAST
Continental 900ptas per person

HOTEL DON PAGO ★★★ (5, $)
Plaza Padre Jerónimo de Córdoba 4, off Plaza Ponce de León
220 rooms, all with shower or bath and toilet

The Hotel Don Pago offers all the comforts of a large city hotel with good off-season rates and even better weekend deals. These Cheap Sleeping prices are not routinely quoted; you must ask for them. The off-season months run from November through February and include July and sometimes August; weekend deals are every Saturday and Sunday throughout the year with the exception of April and May. One child under twelve occupying his or her parents' room is free, and any additional children receive a 50 percent reduction. The advantages don't stop here. If you arrive by train, you are five minutes away, and it is under fifteen from the airport. The rooftop swimming pool is a big drawing card when temperatures soar during the summer months. Other pluses include the buffet lunch and dinner served in the restaurant and the convenience of ordering a sandwich or light snack anytime from the bar.

The hotel has over two hundred cookie-cutter, surprise-free rooms, each with a small bath, and all done in unimaginative *hotel moderne*. Rooms on the fifth floor with a view on the square are the best. Try No. 510, a

TELEPHONE
95 422 49 31

FAX
95 422 28 24

CREDIT CARDS
AE, DC, MC, V

RATES
Single 11,000–12,200ptas, double 15,000ptas, triple 19,200ptas, plus 7 percent tax; rates lower in the off-season and on most weekends; one child under 12 staying in parents' room is free, half-price for additional children

BREAKFAST
Buffet breakfast 1,100ptas, buffet lunch or dinner 2,500ptas; all prices per person, plus 7 percent tax

large twin with a white louvered backdrop behind the bed, a barrel chair, luggage rack, double closet, and bath with good sink space and its own telephone. If you can't get a fifth-floor room, you can always venture up to the roof terrace, which has a view of the cathedral and most of Seville.

ENGLISH SPOKEN: Yes

FACILITIES AND SERVICES: Air-conditioning, bar, conference room, direct-dial phone, hair dryer, laundry service, lift, parking (1,500ptas per day), restaurant, room safe (200ptas per day), radio, swimming pool, satellite TV

NEAREST TOURIST ATTRACTIONS: Edge of center, about a thirty-minute walk to the cathedral

HOTEL INTERNACIONAL ★★ (10)
C/ Aguilas 17
24 rooms, all with shower or bath and toilet

TELEPHONE AND FAX
95 421 32 07
CREDIT CARDS
AE, DC, MC, V
RATES
Single 7,500ptas, double 9,500ptas, triple 12,500ptas, quad 15,500ptas, plus 7 percent tax
BREAKFAST
Not served

The Internacional offers large rooms for Cheap Sleepers and is built around a tiled courtyard filled with green plants. Opening off this courtyard is a large ground-floor family room with four twin beds, each with its own reading light. Closet space is ample, and so is the jumbo bathroom with a combination tub and shower, but there is only one towel to go with the three hooks. Still as large in No. 2, but this double has an opaque glass window on the inside and three knicks in the bathroom tub enamel. Better choices are Nos. 6 or 114. Number 114 is a double overlooking the main hotel courtyard, though its two windows are opaque, and the bathroom has a three-quarter-size tub. Number 6, a double or triple, has beige bedspreads and a large blue bathroom—and you can see out of the window.

ENGLISH SPOKEN: Yes

FACILITIES AND SERVICES: Air-conditioning, direct-dial phone, parking can be arranged (1,000ptas per day), free office safe, TV

NEAREST TOURIST ATTRACTIONS: About a twenty-minute walk to Barrio de Santa Cruz and the cathedral

HOTEL ZAIDA ★ (9)
C/ de San Roque 26
27 rooms, all with shower or bath and toilet

TELEPHONE
95 421 11 38, 95 421 36 12
FAX
95 421 88 10
CREDIT CARDS
AE, DC, MC, V

A sun shade over the top keeps the heat out of the two Moorish marble courtyards that make up the reception and lounge areas of the first-rate Hotel Zaida. Decorative arches, three-hundred-year-old columns, and patterned tile covering half the white walls highlight these public areas. The rooms offer good beds in a price category where sagging mattresses are the norm; you'll also find matching colors, built-in wardrobes, bedside tables, a small desk and chair, and a bathroom with a bright light over the sink. In some you can step out onto a balcony. Management is very pleasant; for groups of fifteen or more, they will prepare meals.

ENGLISH SPOKEN: Yes

FACILITIES AND SERVICES: Air-conditioning, lift, free office safe, radio, TV

NEAREST TOURIST ATTRACTIONS: Museo de Bellas Artes, shopping, twenty-minute walk to the cathedral and Alcázar

RATES
Single 4,500ptas, double 6,500ptas, triple 8,000ptas, plus 7 percent tax

BREAKFAST
Not served for individuals, but they will for groups of 15 or more

LAS CASAS DE LOS MERCADERES ★★★ (14, $)
C/ de Alvarez Quintero 9-13
47 rooms, all with shower or bath and toilet

Any hotel under the auspices of the *Casas y Palacios de España* will be captivating, and Las Casas de los Mercaderes is certainly no exception. For their other equally beautiful three-star hotel in Seville, see Las Casas de la Judería, page 168.

The location puts guests in the center of Seville, within easy walking distance of just about everything. The handsome reception and lobby areas are open and airy, enhanced by wicker armchairs, potted palms, and masses of fresh flowers. If you want a view, ask for rooms that end in numbers 1 through 6. All others face the interior patio, which means less noise but no balcony. The rooms are enriched with coordinated fabrics that successfully mix and match patterns, stripes and florals, in sunny colors. Mirrored wardrobes add a sense of space, but I do wonder why there is no chair by the desk. Bathrooms have shelves, hooks, and a full tub with shower. The breakfast buffet is laid out every morning in a second-floor, street-facing dining room that continues the wicker theme of the lobby.

ENGLISH SPOKEN: Yes

FACILITIES AND SERVICES: Air-conditioning, bar, direct-dial phones, hair dryer, lift, minibar, parking (2,000ptas per day), free room safe, satellite TV

NEAREST TOURIST ATTRACTIONS: Center of the city, shopping, Barrio de Santa Cruz, cathedral, Alcázar

TELEPHONE
95 422 58 58

FAX
95 422 98 84

CREDIT CARDS
AE, DC, MC, V

RATES
Single 10,500–13,700ptas, double 17,100 ptas, extra person 5,500ptas, plus 7 percent tax

BREAKFAST
Buffet 1,350ptas per person

EL ARENAL

El Arenal, a seafaring quarter in the seventeenth century, is defined by the twelve-sided Torre del Oro, a thirteenth-century Muslim watchtower on the banks of the Río Guadalquivir. Originally covered in gold *azulejo* tiles (thus its name), the Torre del Oro contains the Museo Marítimo, which has an interesting display of drawings of the port of Seville. Also of interest in this quarter is the seventeenth-century Hospital de la Caridad, which still operates as a charity hospital. The art in its chapel contains a number of priceless paintings, including several by Murillo—though most of the chapel's Murillos were stolen by Napoleon. On the river just north of the Torre del Oro is one of the oldest, and most important, bullrings in Spain, La Maestranza. Seville is the second most important bullfighting center in the country, after Madrid, and the bullring contains a museum about the sport (hours: Mon–Sat 10 A.M.– 1 P.M.).

HOTELS

Hostal Colon ★	**178**
Hostal Guadalquivir ★	**179**
Hotel La Rabida ★★	**179**
Hotel Maestranza ★	**180**
Hotel Puerta de Triana ★★	**181**
Hotel Simon ★	**182**

HOSTAL COLON ★ (16)
Paseo de Cristóbal Colón 3
12 rooms, 7 with shower only

TELEPHONE
95 442 37 84

CREDIT CARDS
None

RATES
Single 3,700ptas, double 6,700ptas, triple 8,500ptas

BREAKFAST
Not served

Clean and cheap it is—with dynamite views of the Río Guadalquivir—but comfortable . . . well, that undoubtedly will depend on your level of tolerence for climbing stairs and whether you can live without heat in the winter or air-conditioning in the summer. However, if you can time your visit between March and May or late September to November, when heating and air-conditioning are not mandatory, don't hesitate to check right in to this Cheap Sleep, which sits over a famous fish restaurant on a major street fronting the banks of the river. Seven of the big, brightly coordinated rooms have showers, all have hot and cold running water, but none have a private toilet. I didn't notice any chairs either, but in most rooms there is a wardrobe and a table. At these prices, who can complain? Still, I would avoid No. 1, a single on the back that is right next to the public toilet, and No. 3, with its only window so high you need a ladder to see out of it. This room is also devoid of closet space, lacks a table and chair, and is lighted by one bare bulb in the ceiling. While the other ten rooms won't be featured in *Travel & Leisure,* they are adequate for Cheap Sleepers on a tight budget.

ENGLISH SPOKEN: None

FACILITIES AND SERVICES: None

NEAREST TOURIST ATTRACTIONS: Río Guadalquivir, Barrio de Santa Cruz, cathedral, Alcázar

HOSTAL GUADALQUIVIR ★ (17)
C/ García de Vinuesa 21
7 rooms, all with shower or bath and toilet

When I was first told about this hotel, I thought: No singles, no lift, and no English . . . no way. Then I finally went to check it out, and it was much better than I ever imagined. Even the three main drawbacks aren't all bad: For translations, you can call Pedro, who runs the reception desk at the sister hotel (Hotel Maestranza, page 180); occupying a double gives you more space; and the three flights of stairs provide an aerobic workout for free. Every level has a small sitting area, starting with the reception area, which is furnished in wicker and has a collection of blue-and-white Seville plates on the walls. The rooms have matching furniture of a recent vintage, bright bedspreads, tile floors, and clean bathrooms with half-tubs and a shower above. Finally, the location is central and filled with loads of Cheap Eats for every taste and budget.

ENGLISH SPOKEN: None

FACILITIES AND SERVICES: Air-conditioning, free office safe, radio

NEAREST TOURIST ATTRACTIONS: Cathedral, Alcázar, Barrio de Santa Cruz

TELEPHONE
95 421 77 60

CREDIT CARDS
None

RATES
Double 6,500ptas, triple 9,350ptas, tax included

BREAKFAST
None

HOTEL LA RABIDA ★★ (15)
C/ Castelar 24
100 rooms, all with shower or bath and toilet

The Hotel La Rabida has weathered gracefully over the years, and it continues to offer a taste of Seville at affordable prices. Its priviledged position allows guests to easily walk to the cathedral and the Alcázar and stroll

TELEPHONE
95 422 09 60

FAX
95 422 43 75

CREDIT CARDS
AE, DC, MC, V

RATES
Single 6,500ptas, double
9,500ptas, triple 11,700ptas,
plus 7 percent tax
BREAKFAST
Continental 550ptas per person

through the charming old section of the city. Soft, overstuffed wicker settees and chairs fill the attractive Andalucían interior courtyard, which is dominated by a stained-glass ceiling and graceful Moorish arches. Guests can order a drink or dine in a plant-filled outdoor patio, which has a bubbling fountain with four ceramic frogs perched on it, or move into the more formal tiled dining room. The guest rooms are rather plain, but they have all the necessities to ensure a comfortable stay. Bathrooms are dated, but well maintained and clean. All in all, it is a very good Cheap Sleep in Seville.

ENGLISH SPOKEN: Yes

FACILITIES AND SERVICES: Air-conditioning, bar, direct-dial phone, hair dryer, lift, parking (1,500ptas per day), restaurant, free office safe, radio, satellite TV

NEAREST TOURIST ATTRACTIONS: Cathedral, Alcázar, Barrio de Santa Cruz, Río Guadalquivir

HOTEL MAESTRANZA ★ (13)
C/ Gamazo 12
18 rooms, all with shower or bath and toilet

TELEPHONE
95 422 67 66, 95 456 10 70
FAX
95 421 44 04
INTERNET
www.andalunet.com/
maestranza
CREDIT CARDS
MC, V
RATES
Single 6,000ptas, double
9,500ptas, triple 13,700ptas,
suite 18,500ptas, tax included;
rates lower in the off-season
BREAKFAST
Not served

The winner in the Cheap Sleeping one-star sweepstakes in Seville is the smartly refitted Hotel Maestranza. Just look at all its extras and conveniences, which you seldom see in a one-star, and which too many two- and even three-star Seville hotels sorely lack: direct-dial phone, room safe, satellite TV, parking, and lift. Then there are the rates: Already affordable, they become even more so in the off-season, when discounts are given. Another real plus is the reception manager, Pedro, whose English is as polished as is his enthusiasm for Seville, which he enjoys promoting with a determined passion.

The top-notch rooms have streamlined built-ins, including a working space and functionable wardrobe, firm beds, and modern bathrooms. Number 301, with a peek at the top spire of the cathedral and a huge bathroom, can be a double or triple; for maximum comfort, book it as a double. Number 104, overlooking the street, has a built-in corner desk, double wardrobes, and cocoa cotton spreads on the twin beds. Rooms 204, 205, and 206 are light and sunny rooms with views of La Giralda and tip of the cathedral. Word is going to spread quickly about this super Cheap Sleep value, so the minute you know your Seville dates, get in touch with Pedro and make reservations.

ENGLISH SPOKEN: Yes

FACILITIES AND SERVICES: Air-conditioning, direct-dial phone, hair dryer available, lift, nearby parking (1,500ptas per day), room safe (200ptas per day), radio, satellite TV

NEAREST TOURIST ATTRACTIONS: Cathedral, Río Guadalquivir, Alcázar, Barrio de Santa Cruz

HOTEL PUERTA DE TRIANA ★★ (12)
C/ Reyes Católicos 5
62 rooms, all with shower or bath and toilet

Good value and good taste await you at this choice two-star Cheap Sleeping pick, which is within walking distance of everything from the Río Guadalquivir to the bullring to shopping in the Barrio de Santa Cruz. The marble reception area has several comfortable seating areas defined by overstuffed sofas and French Provençal chairs positioned around Oriental throw rugs. A first-class selection of paintings and prints enrich the atmosphere both here and along the upstairs hallways. Additional seating surrounds the atrium fountain and leads to a mirrored breakfast area with bench-style banquettes covered in green-and-yellow tartan.

The rooms display a similar understated, coordinated look. Bathrooms are modern, well lighted, and equally appealing. All the singles are quiet interior rooms that overlook the inside patio. One of my favorite twin-bedded doubles is No. 304, with a mirrored eight-drawer wardrobe along the entry. The main part of the peach-colored room is up two steps, where the light blue–covered beds are flanked by bedside lights. Completing the arrangement is a working desk, comfortable chair, luggage rack, and a tree-shaded balcony. The pleasing staff is well schooled in client satisfaction and never seems too rushed to answer questions or be of service.

ENGLISH SPOKEN: Yes

FACILITIES AND SERVICES: Air-conditioning, direct-dial phones, hair dryer, lift, free office safe, satellite TV

NEAREST TOURIST ATTRACTIONS: Río Guadalquivir, cathedral, Alcázar, Barrio de Santa Cruz

TELEPHONE
95 421 5404

FAX
95 421 5401

CREDIT CARDS
AE, DC, MC, V

RATES
Single 8,000ptas, double 11,500ptas, triple 13,500ptas, plus 7 percent tax

BREAKFAST
Continental included, cannot be deducted

HOTEL SIMON ★ (18)

C/ García de Vinuesa 19

29 rooms, all with shower or bath and toilet

TELEPHONE
95 422 66 60, 95 422 66 15

FAX
95 456 22 41

INTERNET
www.sol.com/hotel-simon

CREDIT CARDS
AE, DC, MC, V

RATES
Single 8,250ptas, double 12,700–16,500ptas, plus 7 percent tax

BREAKFAST
Continental 550ptas per person

The Hotel Simon was built in the eighteenth century as a private mansion, and it remains today a resplendent reminder of Seville's romantic architecture. Ornate white wrought-iron gates frame the doorway, which leads to a beautiful tiled interior patio filled with ferns and other green plants. Antiques scattered here and there lend character and a sense of authenticity. It is easy to imagine a noble family dining in what is now the breakfast room. The ornate brown-and-white-tile room is lavishly accented with marble pillars and arches, a marble fireplace, and two marble-topped mirrored buffets.

The rooms don't pretend to be modern, and that accounts for their charm and desirability. Number 203 is a very pretty twin with matching old-fashioned floral prints on the curtains, bedspreads, table skirts, headboards, and chairs. The modern white bath has a magnifying mirror, basket of soaps, and a three-quarter-tub and shower. Next door, No. 204 is a suite with a daybed, desk, and two chairs in the passageway, which leads to a huge room large enough to accommodate a fifteen-foot triple-mirrored armoire. The theme here is maroon, and the gray and black tile floor has been restored. There are glass-topped bedside tables, a comfortable chair, a luggage rack, and a glassed-in balcony that can be enjoyed year-round. Room 215 retains its original tile floor and diminutive white-tile balcony. This double has no drawer space, but there are three shelves in the closet. There is also a table and an antique, portable dressing mirror. The hotel is conveniently located, within easy walking distance to all the major sites.

ENGLISH SPOKEN: Yes

FACILITIES AND SERVICES: Air-conditioning, direct-dial phone, hair dryer, free office safe

NEAREST TOURIST ATTRACTIONS: Cathedral, Alcázar, Barrio de Santa Cruz, Río Guadalquivir

Other Options

Camping

CAMPING SEVILLA
Carreterra Madrid Cadiz

This campsite is close to the airport, about six miles from the center of Seville. That is both good and bad. The good news is that if you don't have a car, you can get here on the airport bus. The bad news is that there will be noise from the planes . . . and lots of it. The campground is open year-round and has a swimming pool.

TELEPHONE: 95 451 43 79

CREDIT CARDS: None

RATES: 500ptas per person, plus 500ptas for a car or tent, plus 7 percent tax

ENGLISH SPOKEN: Limited

CLUB DE CAMPO
Dos Hermanas, a town outside Seville

This pretty campground with a restaurant and pool is located about twelve kilometers from the center of Seville. There are buses leaving every half hour from the main bus station in Seville.

TELEPHONE: 95 472 0205

CREDIT CARDS: MC, V

RATES: 600ptas per person, 600ptas per tent, 400ptas for car, plus 7 percent tax

ENGLISH SPOKEN: Limited

Residence Hotels

APARTAMENTOS LOS ANGELES (no stars, 6)

TELEPHONE
95 422 80 49

CREDIT CARDS
None

RATES
Single 8,000ptas, double 13,500ptas, triple 16,000ptas, plus 7 percent tax; rates lower in the off-season

BREAKFAST
Not served

C/ de San Eloy 37

6 apartments, all with shower or bath and toilet and kitchens

The building originally was a student hostel and has been turned into six apartments. They are managed and maintained by a hardworking woman who looks as though she has not had a vacation since she opened the place in 1992. She definitely prefers two or more people to occupy her units, and she does not offer any long-term rates, though she does recognize low-season rates from November through March. The apartments are right in the heart of Seville's shopping area, which makes it easy to buy groceries and other necessities to set up short-term housekeeping.

Not all of the apartments are the same, or equally nice. In fact, No. 2 is positively claustrophobic. You can't see much more than the tip of the cathedral, and the futon that doubles for a sofa is placed in the kitchen. Apartment 2B is better. It has a sliding glass door that opens onto an inside courtyard. The kitchen, which has a large refrigerator, has enough space to cook and serve a meal, and it's separated from the bedroom by a Japanese screen. However, work space borders on nonexistent, unless you count the coffee table, which also doubles as the dining table. Things improve in 2A, which has a small corner kitchen and two balconies. There is a futon/sofa in the sitting area, and proper twin beds in the bedroom. Bathrooms in all flats are serviceable.

ENGLISH SPOKEN: Very limited

FACILITIES AND SERVICES: Air-conditioning, equipped kitchens, lift, some free room safes, TV

NEAREST TOURIST ATTRACTIONS: Shopping, fifteen-minute walk to the cathedral, Alcázar, Barrio de Santa Cruz

SANTA CRUZ APARTAMENTOS-SUITES (no stars, 23)
Plaza de los Venerables s/n
13 apartments, with shower or bath and toilet and kitchens

If you are lucky enough to be staying in Seville for a week or more, do yourself an enormous favor and check into one of these stunning apartments in the very heart of the Barrio de Santa Cruz, the most beautiful and romantic part of Seville. This part of the city is filled with narrow, twisted pedestrian-only streets and lanes, lovely old homes, wrought-iron gates, and hidden patios hung with lush plants and colorful bougainvillea vines.

The individually conceived apartments match the top-drawer location. I simply don't know how you could top the American-style kitchens, all of which have a washing machine, and the newer ones also have a dryer. The large bathrooms have big tubs, lots of light, and plenty of sink space. Nothing is left to chance in the brightly colored living areas, which sucessfully combine functionally modern furnishings with a smattering of old-world Spanish antiques. Each apartment also has a large work space, in case you need to set up a mini-office and plug in a laptop and printer. The apartments are owned by Ramón del Pazo, who manages them with the help of his graciously charming daughter, Marta. They also operate the restaurant next to their apartments.

ENGLISH SPOKEN: Yes

FACILITIES AND SERVICES: Air-conditioning, bar, direct-dial phone, hair dryer, restaurant, radio, satellite TV, washer in all units, newer units also with dryer

NEAREST TOURIST ATTRACTIONS: Barrio de Santa Cruz, cathedral, Alcázar

TELEPHONE
95 422 35 83, 95 456 12 78

FAX
95 456 38 06

EMAIL
giraldillo@andalucia.net

INTERNET
www.sitrantor.es//asanta-cruz

CREDIT CARDS
DC, MC, V

RATES
Doubles 13,500, plus 7 percent tax; discounts in low season and for long stays

BREAKFAST
Not served

Shopping: Cheap Chic

Shopping in Spain is always a pleasurable pastime because the country's strong, vibrant mix of cultures is alive and well in each region's markets and shops. Even though large shopping malls and European chain stores are gaining ground, there are still many small, family-run shops that for generations have been producing magnificent ceramics and tiles, leather goods, silver jewelry, flamenco costumes, and *mantones* and *mantillas,* Spain's traditional lace and embroidered shawls. The country is also famous for Lladró porcelain figurines, handmade guitars, Mallorcan pearls, and espadrilles—or perhaps you'd like to go home with your very own ornately designed bullfighting apparel? While on your trip to Spain, it is not hard to find one-of-a-kind pieces destined to become family heirlooms. In addition, don't forget to visit the outdoor food markets, which offer wonderful opportunities to try local specialties, such as sausages, hams, olive oils, a wide variety of cheeses, and sherry wine vinegars, or to pick up a few aromatic spices, such as saffron threads, coriander, and cumin.

Business hours respect the siesta, and provide many opportunities for leisurely window-shopping combined with relaxing breaks for coffee or tea in the morning, and a glass of sherry and a few tapas in the early evening. Most stores are open from 9:30 A.M. to 1:30 or 2 P.M. and from 5 to 8 or 8:30 P.M. On Saturday many smaller stores close in the afternoon, and during the summer, afternoon hours are often much shorter, and they vary from shop to shop. Department stores are open Monday to Saturday nonstop from 10 A.M. to 9 P.M. Sunday shopping has not yet caught on, except for a few weeks before Christmas, and four other Sundays throughout the year. Above all, wherever you are, enjoy wandering and discovering on your own . . . that is the best part of shopping in Spain.

CHEAP CHIC IN SPAIN SHOPPING TIPS

1. Clothing in Spain is expensive; discount shopping has not reached the heights of retail therapy it has in the States. To get the lowest prices, you will have to take advantage of the sales, which are held in January, February, July, and August.

2. If you see something that you love, can afford, and can get home . . . buy it. You will never be sorry.

3. Pack an empty, soft, folding bag in your luggage so you can bring your purchases home with you. Even if you have to pay an airline overweight or extra bag charge, it will be worth every last cent. Having the store pack and ship your purchases can be expensive, and doing the packing and shipping yourself takes up valuable

vacation time. In addition, postal rates are high, and getting your packages past all the bureaucratic red tape will bring on many Maalox moments (see "Shipping" below).

4. Pay for your purchases with a credit card. This eliminates the need of walking around with large sums of cash. It also gives you a record of your purchases should they be lost or damaged.

5. With the exception of El Corte Inglés, which offers good exchange rates, never change money in a store (see "Money Matters," page 21).

6. When buying in a flea market, cash is king and a little haggling is expected. Otherwise, bargaining is not part of Cheap Chic shopping etiquette.

7. In most cities in Spain, there is an art to standing in line. In small shops and in food markets, people may not look like they are standing in line, but they are well aware of when it is their turn. When you arrive, ask ¿Quién es la última? which means "Who is last?" Whoever is last will answer by saying Yo, which means I am, and that you are the next in line after that person.

8. You can expect to be waited on until you have decided on your purchase. This means that sometimes, in busy smaller establishments, you may have to wait a very long time to be served.

9. Buy carefully; returning purchases is difficult. In larger stores you might be able to do it, but you will have to settle for store credit. Forget about getting your money back.

10. Always take the time to fill out the forms to get your tax refund (if you qualify). See "Tax Refund" below for complete details.

11. Don't pay more duty than you absolutely have to. You and every member of your family regardless of age can bring back $400 worth of duty-free purchases—so make sure everyone in your family declares his or her maximum allowance. For more customs information, see "Customs" below.

SHIPPING

If you are sending purchases home, keep these recommendations in mind. Receipts should be obtained from the store indicating the merchandise bought and the exact amount paid, with the IVA (value-added tax) listed separately on the same invoice. These receipts should also show how much has been paid for packing, shipping, and insurance. Shipping costs usually include the expenses only as far as a port or airport in the United States. There can be additional charges for customs, port handling, and forwarding to the final address. If you have insured your package, the store should give you the name and address of the insurance company. If, when you receive the package, it is damaged in any way, do not open it until you have notified the insurer and it has been inspected, and you have photographed the package in its damaged condition. The company must send an inspector to evaluate the damages, but beware, the inspector's fee must be paid by you and their fee can amount to more than the price you paid for the merchandise. If you think you are going to need shipping, it would be a good idea to do some homework before you go abroad so you know what you are in for. For starters, check out DHL at www.dhl.com. The company specializes in individual air freight shipments from 230 countries back to the United States.

TAX REFUND

All non-European residents are entitled to a tax refund in Spain so long as the purchase of goods exceeds 15,000ptas in the same store. In department stores it can be cumulative (not exceeding a three-month period of time), but in some smaller shops, they want you to spend your money on the same day. This tax is known as the VAT elsewhere in Europe; in Spain it is refered to as IVA (pronounced *eeva*). Depending on the nature of your purchase, the rebate ranges from 7 to 16 percent, with luxury goods cashing in at 33 percent. All Cheap Chic shoppers should take note, do the paperwork, and reap the refunds. Here is how the deal works:

1. Ask for the tax refund forms. . . . They are seldom volunteered.

2. Complete three copies of the IVA form the store gives you. The vendor must also provide you with a completed invoice that includes the price of each item, the amount of IVA paid, the ID number of the vender, and your passport number.

3. Ask to have your refund credited to a credit card. You don't need the hassle of trying to cash a check in Spanish pesetas at home, or paying the commission to do so.

4. The goods must be taken out of Spain within three months of purchase. When leaving Spain, show these forms, along with your purchases, to the Spanish customs agent at the border. If you are at the airport, once you have cleared passport control, go to a special booth for these transactions just before the entrance to the international area. Then get the papers stamped, and deposit them in a mailbox in the envelope the store will provide for you, or go to the bank in the airport for the reimbursement.

CUSTOMS

Every U.S. citizen, even an infant, who has been out of the United States for forty-eight hours or more is entitled to bring back, once every thirty days, $400 worth of duty-free merchandise acquired abroad. You are legally required to include every purchase you bring home—from toothpaste and hairbrushes to diamonds and castanets. Families can pool their duty-free purchases, so savvy Cheap Chic shoppers can use what their spouse and children do not. After reaching the $400 limit, there is a 10 percent charge on the next $1,000 and after that the amount varies according to the item. Some quantity limits apply to liquor and tobacco.

When clearing customs: *Play it safe. Declare everything.* Have your receipts ready and make sure they coincide with what you filled out on the landing card. These custom officials and their sharp-sniffing dogs have seen and heard it all, and they can spot a cheater at a glance. Above all, don't try to beat the system, don't smuggle, and for heaven's sake, don't do or carry drugs. People who look like hippies, aging or otherwise, get routinely stopped and undergo exhaustive searches by customs officials in many countries, not just the United States. So do ladies in fur coats and sunglasses, Gucci bags slung over gold-bedecked wrists. Remember: Be nice and be honest, and you will have no problems.

Purchases worth $100 or less can be mailed back to anyone in the States as an unsolicited gift and are considered duty-free. Best of all, they do *not* count toward your $400 limit. You can send as many of these unsolicited gifts as you wish. Duty will also be waived on packages you send to yourself that do not exceed $200 in total value. If your items exceed the $200 limit, you will pay duty on the entire amount, not just the amount over the base $200.

If you travel with expensive cameras, fancy watches, or valuable jewelry, it is a good idea to register them with customs before you leave U.S. soil or you could be questioned about them and even end up paying duty on them. Believe it or not, this has happened more than you can imagine.

For more information on the United States Customs rules and regulations, send for the free brochures *Know Before You Go* and *International Mail Imports*. Write to the U. S. Customs Service, Box 7407, Washington, DC, 20044; or visit their website at www.customs.gov.

SIZE CONVERSION CHART

WOMEN
Dresses

U.S.	8	10	12	14	16	
Continental	38	40	42	44	46	

Blouses and Sweaters

U.S.	10	12	14	16	18	
Continental	38	40	42	44	46	

Shoes

U.S.	4	5	6	7	8	9
Continental	36	37	38	39	41	42

MEN
Suits

U.S.	36	38	40	42	44	46
Continental	46	48	50	52	54	56

Shirts

U.S.	14	14.5	15	15.5	16	16.5
Continental	36	37	38	39	41	42

Shoes

U.S.	7	8	9	10	11	12
Continental	41	42	43	44	46	47

Cheap Chic Shopping in Barcelona

Barcelonan women are known for their Parisian sense of style and devotion to quality materials. The regal Art Nouveau neighborhood of L'Eixample is *the* area in the city they patronize for fine shopping in all categories. The two main shopping streets here are the Passeig de Gràcia and the wide Rambla de Catalunya. The city has been a textile center for centuries, but that has not had any effect on the astronomical cost of clothing; shoes, however, are a good buy. The city is also known for its art galleries, which are concentrated in the Barri Gòtic and on Calle de Montcada near the Picasso Museum. The following selection of Cheap Chic stores does not necessarily reflect the cheapest shopping options; rather it is a subjective list of a wide sampling of shopping possibilities to get you started on your own yellow brick road of Cheap Chic finds in Barcelona.

The number in parentheses to the right of each business name is the Cheap Chic map key number for the Barcelona city map.

SHOPPING STREETS

Passeig de Gràcia and Rambla de Catalunya south of Avinguda Diagonal in L'Eixample are the premier streets for boutique browsing and window shopping. In the Barri Gòtic, stroll along Carrer del Pi, Carrer de Portaferrissa, and Carrer de Santa Anna. I especially like Carrer de Petritxol (off Plaça del Pi); both sides are lined with art galleries, artists supplies, and contemporary handmade jewelry boutiques, and it has my favorite bakery and pastry shop, Xocoa (see *Cheap Eats in Spain*).

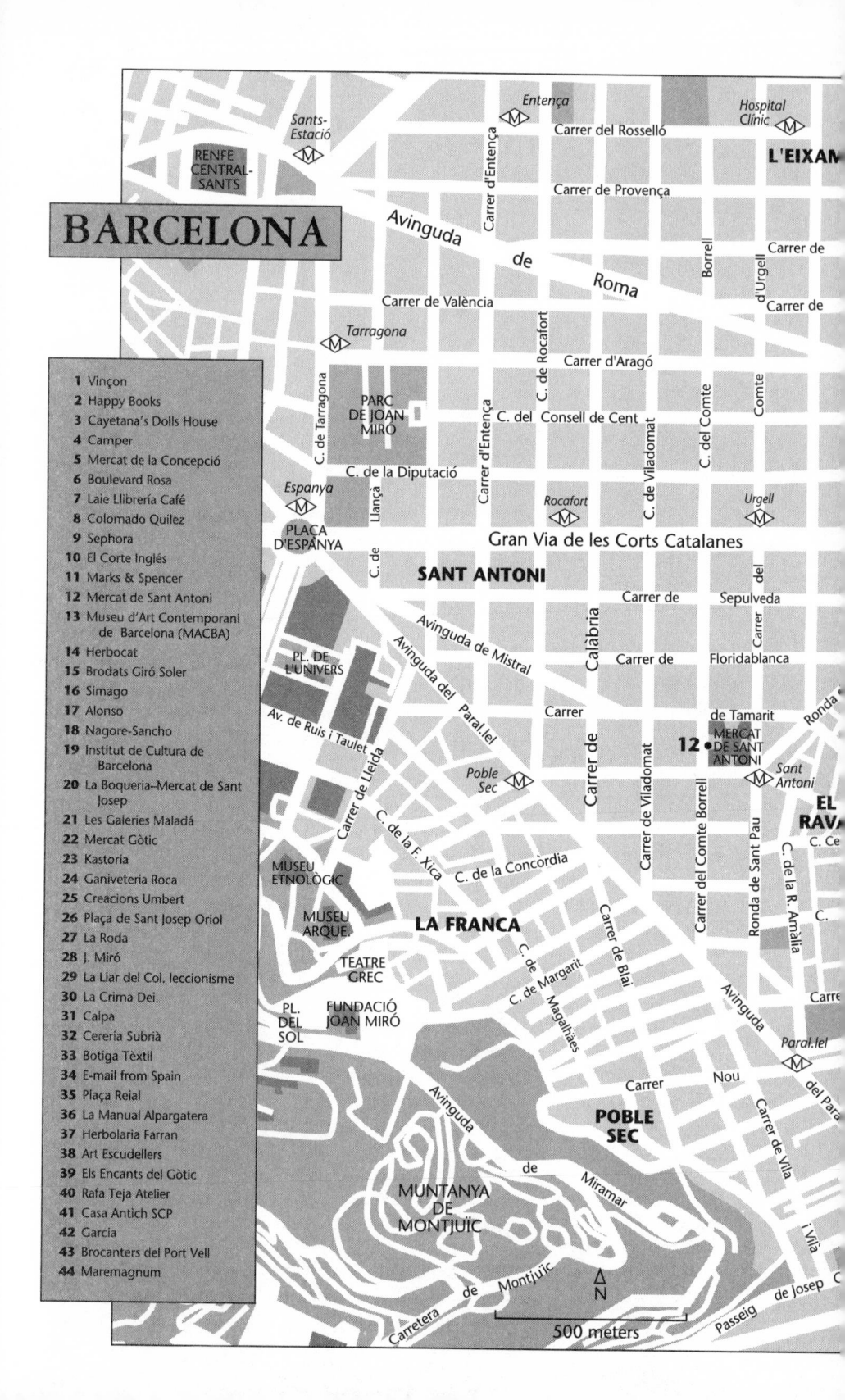

BARCELONA

1 Vinçon
2 Happy Books
3 Cayetana's Dolls House
4 Camper
5 Mercat de la Concepció
6 Boulevard Rosa
7 Laie Llibrería Café
8 Colomado Quilez
9 Sephora
10 El Corte Inglés
11 Marks & Spencer
12 Mercat de Sant Antoni
13 Museu d'Art Contemporani de Barcelona (MACBA)
14 Herbocat
15 Brodats Giró Soler
16 Simago
17 Alonso
18 Nagore-Sancho
19 Institut de Cultura de Barcelona
20 La Boqueria–Mercat de Sant Josep
21 Les Galeries Maladá
22 Mercat Gòtic
23 Kastoria
24 Ganiveteria Roca
25 Creacions Umbert
26 Plaça de Sant Josep Oriol
27 La Roda
28 J. Miró
29 La Liar del Col. leccionisme
30 La Crima Dei
31 Calpa
32 Cereria Subrià
33 Botiga Tèxtil
34 E-mail from Spain
35 Plaça Reial
36 La Manual Alpargatera
37 Herbolaria Farran
38 Art Escudellers
39 Els Encants del Gòtic
40 Rafa Teja Atelier
41 Casa Antich SCP
42 García
43 Brocanters del Port Vell
44 Maremagnum

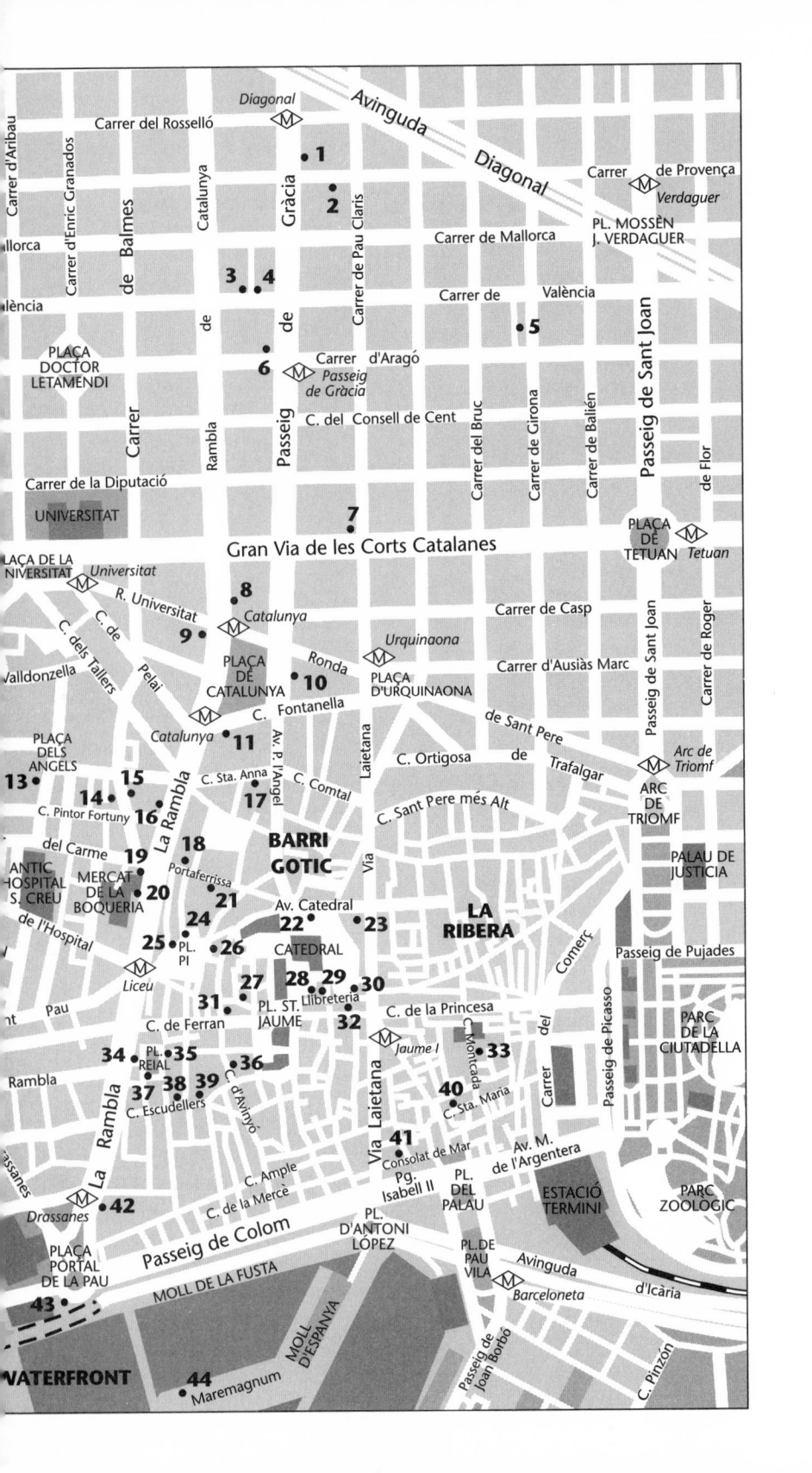

Bookshops

LAIE LLIBRERÍA CAFÉ (7)
C/ de Pau Claris 85

TELEPHONE: 93 318 17 39
FAX: 93 412 02 05
EMAIL: cafe@laiellibreria.com
INTERNET: www.gulliver.es/laie.htp
METRO: Urquinaona, 1, 4
CREDIT CARDS: AE, DC, MC, V
HOURS: Mon–Sat 10 A.M.–9 P.M.

ENGLISH SPOKEN: Yes

This international arts bookshop and café has many English titles. The café has an excellent lunch buffet with many vegetarian dishes (see *Cheap Eats in Spain*).

HAPPY BOOKS (2)
C/ de Provença 286

TELEPHONE: 93 487 30 01
FAX: 93 487 76 31
METRO: Diagonal, 3, 5
CREDIT CARDS: AE, MC, V
HOURS: Mon–Sat 9:30 A.M.–9 P.M.

ENGLISH SPOKEN: Yes

Here is Barcelona's answer to the bookstore/café as a place to hang out. In addition to a wide range of books, which are mostly in Spanish, look for videos, music, and maps.

INSTITUT DE CULTURA DE BARCELONA (19)
Palau de la Virreina, Rambla de Sant Josep 99

TELEPHONE: 93 301 77 75
FAX: 93 301 61 00
METRO: Liceu, 3
CREDIT CARDS: AE, MC, V
HOURS: Tues–Sat 10 A.M.–8:30 P.M.

ENGLISH SPOKEN: Yes

The bookshop in the city information center has an excellent selection of books on Barcelona plus a wonderful choice of interesting and artistic gifts, which range in price and theme from Picasso-inspired erasers to handscreened silk scarves and modern jewelry. If you are a music lover, don't miss Casa Beethoven next door, which is a treasure trove of music scores.

Candles

CERERIA SUBRIÀ (32)
Baixada de la Llibreteria 7

    TELEPHONE: 93 315 26 06
    METRO: Jaume I, 4
    CREDIT CARDS: AE, DC, MC, V
    HOURS: Mon–Fri 9 A.M.–1:30 P.M., 4–7:40 P.M., Sat 9 A.M.–1:30 P.M.
    ENGLISH SPOKEN: Yes

The oldest retail shop in Barcelona (opened in 1761) is now a candle shop. Even if you are not in the market for candles, which are all made on site, stop by to see the impressive original interior, which features statues of two women holding torchlights at the foot of the curved stairs.

Ceramics and Tiles

ART ESCUDELLERS (38)
C/ dels Escudellers 23–25

    TELEPHONE: 93 412 68 01
    FAX: 93 412 15 01
    METRO: Liceu, 3
    CREDIT CARDS: AE, DC, MC, V
    HOURS: Daily 11 A.M.–11 P.M.
    ENGLISH SPOKEN: Yes

A sign on the wall reads: "God was the first potter and man his first work."

This huge warehouse space is filled with pottery and tiles, ranging in size and price from minuscule to mammoth. The feeling you get as you wander up and down the loaded aisles is that this must be a discount venue, but don't kid yourself, while the prices are competitively fair, there are no bargains. They will ship.

LA RODA (27)
C/ del Call 18, off Plaça de Sant Jaume

    TELEPHONE: 93 317 94 44
    FAX: 93 412 79 08
    METRO: Jaume I, 4, or Liceu, 3
    CREDIT CARDS: AE, DC, MC, V
    HOURS: Mon–Sat 10 A.M.–1:30 P.M., 4–8 P.M.
    ENGLISH SPOKEN: Limited

La Roda has a better selection of ceramics, including many you won't see in every other shop in town.

Clothing and Shoes

CAMPER (4)
C/ de València 249

TELEPHONE: Not available
METRO: Passeig de Gràcia, 3
CREDIT CARDS: AE, DC, MC, V
HOURS: Mon–Sat 9:30 A.M.–1:30 P.M., 5–8:30 P.M.
ENGLISH SPOKEN: Depends on the clerk, but usually yes

Spain's best buy in shoe fashions of the moment. There are three other locations in Barcelona, but this one is the most central. Camper shoes are also sold in general shoe stores and in department stores.

CREACIONS UMBERT (25)
C/ del Cardenal Casañas 19, off Plaça del Pi

TELEPHONE: 93 301 98 34
METRO: Liceu, 3
CREDIT CARDS: AE, DC, MC, V
HOURS: Mon–Sat 9:30 A.M.–1:30 P.M., 4:30–8:30 P.M.
ENGLISH SPOKEN: Enough

Loving grandmothers beware! You won't get out of this adorable shop with empty hands. It is not cheap, but the personalized children's clothing and accessories are wonderful. Buy only a bib, or go all out and have entire ensembles personalized for the special little ones in your life.

RAFA TEJA ATELIER (40)
C/ de Santa Maria 18

TELEPHONE: 93 310 27 86
FAX: 93 315 20 86
METRO: Jaume I, 4
CREDIT CARDS: AE, MC, V
HOURS: Tues–Sat 11 A.M.–2 P.M., 5–8:30 P.M.
ENGLISH SPOKEN: Yes

The shop features a stunning display of every type of scarf imaginable, to wear or to frame. Choices range from small hand-painted silk squares to cashmere wraps. There's also a selection of artistic jewelry and bargain baskets of some mighty fine leftovers you shouldn't miss pawing through.

LA MANUAL ALPARGATERA (36)
C/ d'Avinyó 7

TELEPHONE: 93 301 01 72
METRO: Jaume I, 4, or Liceu, 3
CREDIT CARDS: AE, DC, MC,V
HOURS: Mon–Sat 9:30 A.M.–1:30 P.M., 4:30–8 P.M.
ENGLISH SPOKEN: Yes

You haven't seen or experienced the true comfort of espadrilles until you have been to this factory/shop, where the hemp-soled sandals are made by hand and to measure. Cotton, suede, leather, lace . . . you name it, and they have it, or they will create it in any color or size you wish. They have been in business for generations and have shod many famous feet, including the pope's.

Computer, Email, and Internet Services

E-MAIL FROM SPAIN (34)
Rambla dels Caputxins 42
> **TELEPHONE:** 93 481 75 75
> **FAX:** 93 481 75 74
> **EMAIL:** info@emailfromspain.es
> **INTERNET:** www.emailfromspain.es
> **METRO:** Liceu, 3
> **CREDIT CARDS:** None, cash only
> **HOURS:** Mon–Sat 10 A.M.–8 P.M.
> **ENGLISH SPOKEN:** Yes

It is a little confusing to locate, but you can't miss the sign, which is visable from La Rambla. Walk through the archway at Rambla dels Caputxins 42; the offices are on the first floor of a lovely old building near Plaça Reial. Hotmail, Telnet, AOL, Yahoo, and much more are yours to surf. You can send and receive email and enroll in Spanish lessons. The staff is young, friendly, and oh, so computer savvy.

Cosmetics and Perfumes

LA CRIMA DEI (30)
C/ del Veguer 7
> **TELEPHONE:** 93 315 14 22
> **METRO:** Jaume I, 4
> **CREDIT CARDS:** MC, V
> **HOURS:** Mon–Sat 10:30 A.M.–1 P.M., 5–8 P.M.
> **CLOSED:** 15 days in Aug, dates vary
> **ENGLISH SPOKEN:** Yes

The sweet, perfumed air flows out to the street to beckon you into this fairyland of handmade soaps, perfumes, and colognes. The boutique is owned by three sisters and a designer who made their own soaps and perfumes as a hobby. Friends persuaded them to sell their creations, but by going public, so to speak, they have not compromised their high quality or standards. The name of their store, La Crima Dei, means "God's Tear," and suggests a love of nature. Their products are inspired by the Mediterranean and emit the fragrances of the flowers and plants of the entire region, with a few whimsical types such as chocolate and caramel made just for fun. Everything is artistically arranged by type: classics, the four elements, the sea, exotic blends, and fruits and floral. Their products make lovely, romantic gifts.

SEPHORA (9)
Plaça de Catalunya in the El Triangle Building (look for FNAC sign)
TELEPHONE: 93 306 39 00
INTERNET: www.sephora.com
METRO: Catalunya, 1, 3
CREDIT CARDS: AE, DC, MC, V
HOURS: Mon–Sat 10 A.M.–9:30 P.M.
ENGLISH SPOKEN: Yes

Everyone likes Sephora . . . even men. High tech has been raised to lofty levels in this wonderland of cosmetics and perfumes, which you have to see to believe. A ceiling studded with hundreds of hand mirrors leads you down an escalator to more cosmetics and beauty products than you ever thought possible. Go if only to admire the packaging, the layout, and the svelt fashion victims clad in black suits, who will wait on you with one black-gloved hand. Ask to have your purchase, no matter how small, gift wrapped. There are sofas in key postitions for shopping pals who need to sit down to absorb it all.

Department Stores

EL CORTE INGLÉS (10)
Plaça de Catalunya, 14
TELEPHONE: 93 302 12 12
METRO: Catalunya, 1, 3
CREDIT CARDS: AE, DC, MC, V
HOURS: Mon–Sat 10 A.M.–9:30 P.M.
ENGLISH SPOKEN: Yes

El Corte Inglés is one-stop shopping on nine levels, with a cafeteria on top that has a sweeping view of the city. There's a huge supermarket in the basement, a beauty shop, and a travel agency. Cheap Chic thrill seekers can venture up to the eighth floor and plow through the remainder bins of fire-sale goods. There is a smaller branch devoted to ear-splitting music, audio equipment, and books at Avenida del Portal de l'Angel.

MARKS & SPENCER (11)
Plaça de Catalunya 32
TELEPHONE: Not available
METRO: Catalunya, 1, 3
CREDIT CARDS: AE, DC, MC, V
HOURS: Mon–Sat 10 A.M.–9:30 P.M.

ENGLISH SPOKEN: Yes

Billed as Europe's biggest Marks & Spencer, it creates stiff competition for its neighbor, the monolithic El Corte Inglés, which also occupies a corner position on the Plaça de Catalunya.

MERCAT DE LA CONCEPCIÓ (5)
C/ d'Aragó, between C/ de Balién and C/ del Bruc

TELEPHONE: None
METRO: Passeig de Gràcia, 3
CREDIT CARDS: MC, V
HOURS: Mon–Sat 8 A.M.–8 P.M.
ENGLISH SPOKEN: Very little

This is Barcelona's answer to a miniature K-Mart with a supermarket in the basement. Good to remember if you are en route to La Sagrada Familia and want to pick up some snack foods. Forget the ready-to-wear department.

SIMAGO (16)
Rambla del Estudis 13

TELEPHONE: None
METRO: Catalunya, 1, 3
CREDIT CARDS: MC, V
HOURS: Mon–Sat 9 A.M.–9 P.M., bakery open same hours on Sun
ENGLISH SPOKEN: No

Simago is more of a dime store with a supermarket in the basement and a bakery selling freshly baked baguettes faster than they can make them. This location is great, especially if you are out of water, need another tube of toothpaste, or want to pick up a few snacks for your hotel or a picnic.

Fans

ALONSO (17)
C/ de Santa Anna 27

TELEPHONE: 93 317 60 85
METRO: Catalunya, 1, 3
CREDIT CARDS: MC, V
HOURS: Mon–Sat 10 A.M.–8 P.M.
ENGLISH SPOKEN: Yes

Victoria Alonso sells typical Spanish fans, purses that look like Judith Leiber designs, head-coverings for brides, shawls, and gloves in a pretty Art Deco shop on an interesting shopping street at the top of La Rambla. Almost everything is hidden in drawers, but take a seat and enjoy being personally waited on by charming Victoria.

Food

COLOMADO QUILEZ (8)
Rambla de Catalunya 14

> **TELEPHONE:** 93 215 23 56, 93 215 87 85
> **FAX:** 93 215 87 85
> **METRO:** Catalunya, 1, 3
> **CREDIT CARDS:** AE, MC, V
> **HOURS:** Mon–Fri 9 A.M.–2 P.M., 4:30–8:30 P.M., Sat 9 A.M.–2 P.M.
> **ENGLISH SPOKEN:** Limited

To prolong the savory tastes of your visit to Barcelona, treat yourself at this classic shop. The walls are lined with cans and bottles of vinegars and oils from all over the world, and the deli is filled with countless types of cheeses, hams, and sausages. Don't miss the wine and liquor department, which stocks every known type of alcohol. They have their own brand of coffee, Cafe Quilez, from Columbia, which can be ground while you wait.

Gifts

BOTIGA TÈXTIL (33)
C/ de Montcada 12

> **TELEPHONE:** 93 268 25 98
> **METRO:** Jaume I, 4
> **CREDIT CARDS:** AE, MC, V
> **HOURS:** Tues–Sat 10 A.M.–8 P.M., Sun until 3 P.M.
> **ENGLISH SPOKEN:** Yes

The Botiga Tèxtil and its adjoining café are on the same street as the Museu Picasso, and follow the same opening hours. The shop has an eclectic selection of books, clothes, tableware, jewelry, and watches. While the shoppers are busy, the less enthused can enjoy sitting in the café.

CAYETANA'S DOLLS HOUSE (3)
C/ de València 247

> **TELEPHONE AND FAX:** 93 487 76 27
> **METRO:** Passeig de Gràcia, 3
> **CREDIT CARDS:** MC, V
> **HOURS:** Mon–Sat 10 A.M.–2 P.M., 5–8:30 P.M.; closed Sat in Aug
> **ENGLISH SPOKEN:** Yes

If you ever had a dollhouse, or know anyone who loves them, please make a special trip to this tiny dollhouse-size shop, filled with everything for the miniature home. Everything is designed and made by the charming owner, who will be happy to sell you one piece, or to design and ship you the dollhouse of your dreams.

GANIVETERIA ROCA (24)
Plaça del Pi 3

TELEPHONE: 93 302 12 41
FAX: 93 412 53 49
METRO: Liceu, 3
CREDIT CARDS: MC, V
HOURS: Mon–Sat 10 A.M.–1:30 P.M., 4:15–8 P.M.
ENGLISH SPOKEN: Yes

This is the Tiffany's of scissors and knives, and it's been on this corner since 1911. The selection is staggering and the quality the best.

GARCIA (42)
Rambla de Santa Mònica 4

TELEPHONE: 93 302 69 89
FAX: 93 301 48 92
METRO: Drassanes, 3
CREDIT CARDS: AE, DC, MC, V
HOURS: Daily, winter 10 A.M.–8 P.M., summer 9 A.M.–9 P.M.
ENGLISH SPOKEN: Yes

It isn't the only Lladró game in town—El Corte Inglés carries it and so do many other small shops in the Barri Gòtic—but it is definitely a very worthwhile stop if you are on the Lladró trail in Barcelona. The stock includes one-of-a-kind pieces, and whatever you buy can be packed and shipped for you.

MUSEU D'ART CONTEMPORANI DE BARCELONA (MACBA) (13)
Plaça dels Àngels 1

TELEPHONE: 93 412 08 10
METRO: Catalunya, 1, 3
CREDIT CARDS: AE, MC, V
HOURS: Mon–Wed, Fri–Sat 11 A.M.–8 P.M., Sun 10:30 A.M.–3 P.M.; closed Thur, as is the museum

Contemporary is the operative word for the well-displayed selection of unusual gifts in the gift shop of Barcelona's stunning modern art museum. Look for great T-shirts and ties, umbrellas black on the outside and inside covered with bright-colored daisies, desk items, art books (a few in English), prints, postcards, and dramatic jewelry.

BRODATS GIRÓ SOLER (15)
C/ d'En Xuclà 16, off C/ del Pintor Fortuny

TELEPHONE: 93 318 58 34
METRO: Catalunya, 1, 3, or Liceu, 3
CREDIT CARDS: AE, MC, V
HOURS: Mon–Fri 10 A.M.–2 P.M., 5–8:30 P.M.
ENGLISH SPOKEN: Very limited, but the owner speaks French

Come here for laces, embroideries, sachets, and frilly lingerie to make you want to be a bride all over again. I also love the pink satin–trimmed slippers that come in an embroidered pouch with a delicate pink flower on the flap, as well as the adorable baby clothes and crocheted booties.

Herbalists

HERBOCAT (14)
C/ d'En Xuclà 23, off C/ del Pintor Fortuny
TELEPHONE: 93 301 14 44, 93 319 19 65
FAX: 93 414 49 33
METRO: Catalunya, 1, 3, or Liceu, 3
CREDIT CARDS: MC, V
HOURS: Mon–Fri 9 A.M.–2 P.M., 4–8 P.M., Sat 9 A.M.–2 P.M., 5–8 P.M.
ENGLISH SPOKEN: Usually in the afternoon only, but call to be sure

No matter what time of day I passed this herbalist, it was busy and people were waiting to be served. I didn't pay much attention until I developed severe allergies and needed some relief. After using the herbs prescribed by the knowledgeable young woman who helps in the afternoons, and speaks English, I was cured . . . and convinced that these people know what they are doing. In addition to herbs for any ailment, they handle natural beauty products. The shop is on a back street next to a cheese shop and across from Brodats Giró Soler, described above.

HERBOLARIA FARRAN (37)
Plaça Reial 18
TELEPHONE: 93 304 20 05
METRO: Liceu, 3
CREDIT CARDS: MC, V
HOURS: Mon–Sat 9:30 A.M.–2 P.M., 4:30–8 P.M.
ENGLISH SPOKEN: Yes

Herbolaria Farran has herbs, teas, and health foods for all reasons and seasons of the year. I thought the choice of supplements a bit thin, but the rest of the store stocks a well-rounded selection of dried fruits, honey, essential oils, beauty products, soy milk, spices, and Spanish books on health.

Housewares

VINÇON (1)
Passieg de Gràcia 96
TELEPHONE: 93 215 60 50
FAX: 93 215 50 37
METRO: Diagonal, 3, 5

CREDIT CARDS: AE, MC, V
HOURS: Mon–Sat 10 A.M.–2 P.M., 4:30–8:30 P.M.
ENGLISH SPOKEN: Yes

The latest designs for every aspect of your home and/or office are on display here. You are probably not going to buy a floor lamp or deal with the paint and wallpaper designers, but it is a very interesting look at what is available and popular with the Barcelona yuppies. There is a sale corner in the back on the right, and the upper floor is the former apartment of Santiago Rusiñol, one of the greatest *modernista* artists.

Jewelry

J. MIRÓ (28)
C/ de la Llibreteria 11

TELEPHONE: 93 319 04 09
METRO: Jaume I, 4
CREDIT CARDS: AE, MC, V
HOURS: Mon–Sat 9:30 A.M.–8:30 P.M., Sun 11 A.M.–6 P.M.
ENGLISH SPOKEN: Yes

Different artists are represented in this open shop where their work is displayed behind hanging glass cases. Many of the streamlined pieces are set with either amber or other semiprecious stones, and prices vary according to the artist and the intricacy of the design. Rings cleverly secured by a plastic string and rock allow customers to try them on to their heart's content.

Junk Shops

LA LIAR DEL COL. LECCIONISME (29)
C/ de la Llibreteria 13

TELEPHONE: 93 268 32 59
METRO: Jaume I, 4
CREDIT CARDS: None, cash only
HOURS: Mon–Fri 10 A.M.–1:30 P.M., 4:30–8 P.M., Sat 10 A.M.–1:30 P.M.
ENGLISH SPOKEN: Yes

Some might call the stock "antiques," but in my book I call it glorious junk. True, owner Jesús Torriente has some antique fans and decorative hair combs, but you really have to dig to come up with something that is both in good repair and an antique. However, if you are a dedicated accumulator, the shop is worth a look.

Leather

CALPA (31)
C/ de Ferran 53

> TELEPHONE: 93 318 40 30
> METRO: Liceu, 3, or Jaume I, 4
> CREDIT CARDS: AE, MC, V
> HOURS: Mon–Fri 9:30 A.M.–2 P.M., 4:30–8 P.M., Sat 10 A.M.–2 P.M., 5–8:30 P.M.
> ENGLISH SPOKEN: Yes

Calpa has beautiful leather bags in all sizes, styles, and price categories.

CASA ANTICH SCP (41)
C/ del Consolat de Mar 27–31

> TELEPHONE: 93 310 43 91
> METRO: Jaume I, 4
> CREDIT CARDS: AE, DC, MC,V
> HOURS: Mon–Sat 9 A.M.–8 P.M.
> ENGLISH SPOKEN: Yes

The big draw here is luggage . . . every type of travel bag you can imagine and some you never could. I like the long bags with hangers in the shape of a body and the skirt-hanging bags. If you don't see the bag you want and they don't have it in stock or cannot order it for you, they will make it. Umbrellas, belts, and wallets are also sold.

KASTORIA (23)
Avda. de la Catedral 6–8, corner of Via Laietana

> TELEPHONE: 93 310 04 11, 93 319 36 78
> FAX: 93 319 55 90
> METRO: Jaume I, 4
> CREDIT CARDS: AE, DC, MC, V
> HOURS: Mon–Fri 10 A.M.–7 P.M., Sat until 2 P.M.
> ENGLISH SPOKEN: Yes

Kastoria has two floors of fashions in leather for men and women plus Lladró porcelain, all sold by a multilingual sales staff. Quality is very high and the selection enormous.

NAGORE-SANCHO (18)
C/ de la Portaferrissa 9

> TELEPHONE: 93 317 29 89
> METRO: Liceu, 3
> CREDIT CARDS: AE, DC, MC, V
> HOURS: Mon–Sat 10 A.M.–8:30 P.M.
> ENGLISH SPOKEN: Yes

Bags, bags, and more bags are on offer here, plus a good selection of sport and everyday purses. Upstairs check out the discounted goods and the suitcases and backpacks.

Markets

ANTIQUES

MERCAT GÒTIC (22)
Avda. de la Catedral s/n
TELEPHONE: 93 291 61 00
METRO: Jaume I, 4
CREDIT CARDS: Depends on the seller, but generally none
HOURS: Thur 9 A.M.–8 P.M.
ENGLISH SPOKEN: Depends on the seller
Every Thursday in front of the cathedral antiques sellers lay out their special treasures. The bargains are long gone, but it is worth a thirty-minute browse, followed by a coffee at one of the cafés facing the cathedral.

ARTS AND CRAFTS

BROCANTERS DEL PORT VELL (43)
Portal de la Pau s/n
TELEPHONE: 93 317 01 12
METRO: Drassanes, 3
CREDIT CARDS: Generally none
HOURS: Sat–Sun 10 A.M.–10 P.M.
ENGLISH SPOKEN: Depends on seller
Look for sellers in stalls along the lower part of La Rambla and the waterfront before crossing the Maremagnum Bridge. Most of the items are new, and there is no end to the hawkers just back from Tibet who think they have something to sell, but it is definitely a place to check out if you are looking for inexpensive trinkets or basic leather goods. There are also several dealers selling coins, jewelry, and bric-a-brac of some merit.

PLAÇA DE SANT JOSEP ORIOL (26)
TELEPHONE: 93 291 61 00
METRO: Liceu, 3
CREDIT CARDS: Generally none
HOURS: First weekend of the month, Fri–Sat 10 A.M.–9 P.M., Sun until 3 P.M.
ENGLISH SPOKEN: Some

The market is laid out on a pretty square (near Plaça del Pi) and features homegrown and prepared herbs, honey, baked goods, wine, olives, jams, and beeswax products. Also here are amateur painters of varying talent. With careful looking, you can usually find a nice painting for a good price.

BOOKS, STAMPS, AND COINS

MERCAT DE SANT ANTONI (12)
Ronda de Sant Pau at Ronda de Sant Antoni

TELEPHONE: 93 423 42 87
METRO: Sant Antoni, 2
CREDIT CARDS: None, cash only
HOURS: Sun 9 A.M.–2 P.M.
ENGLISH SPOKEN: None

The locals turn out in full force, but it is a real yawn unless you are into coins, dusty books, old magazines, and video games.

PLAÇA REIAL (35)

TELEPHONE: None
METRO: Liceu, 3
CREDIT CARDS: None
HOURS: Sun 9 A.M.–2 P.M.
ENGLISH SPOKEN: Limited

This is aimed at the die-hard collector, so if you know your stuff, you could turn up something of great value. The setting on the Plaça Reial adds a bit of lustre.

FLEA MARKETS

ELS ENCANTS
End of C/ del Dos de Maig, near Plaça de les Glòries

TELEPHONE: 93 246 30 30
METRO: Glòries, 1
CREDIT CARDS: None
HOURS: Mon, Wed, Fri–Sat 8 A.M.–6 P.M., hours can vary slightly
ENGLISH SPOKEN: None

I thought I would never meet a flea market I didn't like, or that I couldn't find something of interest in, even if I couldn't get it home or afford it. Well, now I have in this vast collection of trash and just plain junk that includes rusty bent nails, broken radios, chipped china, cheap cookware, fifties' dial telephones, and flimsy clothing. UGH! I found absolutely nothing interesting. Period. I cannot imagine anyone wasting five minutes of time here . . . let alone making the effort to trek here from the city center. Obviously the locals do not agree with me because, as I approached it, I saw people walking back to the metro carrying bags full of goods.

ELS ENCANTS DEL GÒTIC (39)
Plaça George Orwell, end of C/ dels Escudellers
TELEPHONE: 93 412 13 31
METRO: Liceu, 3
CREDIT CARDS: None, cash only
HOURS: Sat 10 A.M.–9 P.M.
ENGLISH SPOKEN: Very limited

Lots of medals and badges are mixed in with the occasional rare find. It is small and very amateurish, with the sellers displaying what looks to be odds and ends from their own homes. However, if you are in the neighborhood and a real flea market aficionado, it is an amusing way to spend a half hour on a Saturday morning.

FOOD

LA BOQUERIA–MERCAT DE SANT JOSEP (20)
Rambla de Sant Josep 91
TELEPHONE: None
METRO: Liceu, 3
CREDIT CARDS: None, cash only
HOURS: Mon–Sat 8 A.M.–8 P.M.
ENGLISH SPOKEN: Don't count on it

There is no question about it: This fabulous food market is absolutely the best in Barcelona. In fact, it rivals many other city markets across Europe for quality, layout, unlimited variety, and the sheer beauty of its *modernista* building. No visitor to Barcelona should miss it. In theory, the market is open from Monday to Saturday from 8 A.M. to 8 P.M. In fact, Monday is a slow day, and many of the stalls are closed, especially the fish sellers. Afternoons are also slow. The best time to see it in its full glory is early in the morning, especially on Saturday. Bring a shopping bag, have your camera loaded with film, and plan to spend at least an hour admiring the rows of perfectly matched fruits and vegetables arranged with a jeweler's precision. Look for the pristine meat and fish stalls, where you will be waited on by painted ladies wearing white overalls. Sample the freshly baked pastries, marvel at the variety of mushrooms and herbs, or indulge in a ham or hot sausage sandwich washed down with a beer. There is indeed a method to what seems to be this madhouse of people and food. Fruit and vegetables ring the edge, meat and chicken are on one side, fish and seafood are arranged in a circle in the center. Toward the back, on the right, is a large parking lot where you will see farmers hawking their fruits and veggies at lower prices than you will pay inside.

MERCAT DE SANT ANTONI (12)
Ronda de Sant Pau at Ronda de Sant Antoni

TELEPHONE: None
METRO: St. Antoni, 2
CREDIT CARDS: None, cash only
HOURS: Mon–Sat 8 A.M.–2 P.M., 5–8 P.M.
ENGLISH SPOKEN: None

From Monday to Saturday the locals shop for food and cheap clothing; on Sunday they come in droves to comb through the book and coin stalls that ring the exterior. The food market doesn't compare with La Boqueria (see above), but it is an interesting sociological look at how the average blue collar–person does daily shopping. The clothing is a kick . . . especially the stalls selling one-piece girdles.

Shopping Malls

BARCELONA GLÒRIES
Avda. Diagonal 208

TELEPHONE: 93 486 04 04
METRO: Glorìes, 1
CREDIT CARDS: AE, DC, MC, V
HOURS: Mon–Sat 10 A.M.–10 P.M.
ENGLISH SPOKEN: Depends on shop

Take everything in a normal shopping mall and multiply it by ten to equal this huge shopping complex that seems to be a K-Mart, Walmart, and Target combined with fashion-of-the-moment boutiques and a giant supermarket in the basement. You will certainly never go hungry—there are countless fast-food and chain restaurants to satisfy every taste.

BOULEVARD ROSA (6)
Rambla de Catalunya 66, Passeig de Gracià 53-55

TELEPHONE: None
METRO: Passeig de Gracià, 3
CREDIT CARDS: Depends on shop, but generally MC, V
HOURS: Mon–Sat 10:30 A.M.–8 P.M.
ENGLISH SPOKEN: Depends on shop

This is Barcelona's first shopping mall and still going strong, with one trendy boutique after another.

LES GALERIES MALADÁ (21)
C/ de Portaferrissa s/n

TELEPHONE: None
METRO: Liceu, 3
CREDIT CARDS: Depends on shop, but usually MC, V

HOURS: Mon–Sat 10 A.M.–1:30 P.M., 5–8 P.M.

ENGLISH SPOKEN: Depends on shop

This series of boutique shops is clustered along one of the better shopping streets in the Barri Gòtic.

MAREMAGNUM (44)
Port Vell

TELEPHONE: 93 225 81 00

METRO: Drassanes, 3

CREDIT CARDS: Depends on shop, but usually MC, V

HOURS: Daily 10 A.M.–midnight, Sat till 1 A.M.

ENGLISH SPOKEN: Depends on shop or restaurant

This huge entertainment palace is open every day of the year until at least midnight for all your shopping, dining, and entertainment needs. It is dramatically located at the end of La Rambla, across a flying wooden walkway. While you are here you can visit the finest aquarium in Europe, see an Imax film, play miniature golf, indulge in electronic games in the fun center, eat every kind of fast food there is, sit at one of the waterside bars and enjoy tapas, or dance the night away. Oh yes, and there are shops galore.

Cheap Chic Shopping in Madrid

With more than fifty thousand shops in the city, you should be able to find whatever you want, and more. Classic buys in Madrid range from bullfight posters and espadrilles to ceramics, hams, olive oil, flamenco music, and handmade guitars. Fortunately for the Cheap Chic shopper, the shopping districts are defined and central.

The number in parentheses to the right of each business name is the Cheap Chic map key number for the Madrid city map.

SHOPPING STREETS

The exclusive Salamanca neighborhood northeast of the center has the highest number of designer boutiques, such as Chanel, Armani, and Versace, clustered along Calle de Claudio Coello, Calle de Serrano, Calle de Velázquez, Calle de José Ortega y Gasset, Calle de Goya, and Calle de Hermosilla. The shops on these streets are not cheap, but it doesn't cost a thing to join the well-dressed locals who are also here to look, admire, and dream. The best metro stops for these streets are Serrano and Velázquez (both line 4).

Kitsch central seems to be around the Plaza Mayor, along Gran Vía, and near the Prado. If you head south from the Plaza Mayor, Calle de Toledo has an amusing series of shops selling hairpins, surgical supports, and corsets that look as though they were torture instruments during the Spanish Inquisition. On the eastern side of Plaza Mayor are silversmiths and jewelers along Calle de Zaragoza. The heart of city-center shopping is around Calle de Preciados and along Gran Vía. For heavy-duty shoe shopping, walk along Calle de Augusto Figueroa in Chueca and check out the stores lining both sides of the street—lots of end-of-the-line shoes with Cheap Chic friendly prices. Chueca offers more alternative shopping along Calle del Almirante.

If you are here at Christmastime, make sure to visit the Plaza Mayor, which is dressed for the season and filled with stalls selling Christmas wares. At other times, the square is filled with artists selling their work; most of it is the usual color-by-number variety, but occasionally there is something worthwhile.

Antiques

One of the most interesting concentrations of antiques stores and auction houses (*almonedas*) is near El Rastro. Other good scouting grounds in the city center are on Calle de las Huertas and Calle del Prado. For top-end antiques and galleries, head for the Salamanca neighborhood and walk along Calle de Serrano, Calle de Velásquez, and Calle de Jorge Juan. The Sunday morning Rastro (flea market) is a fun place to shop for trinkets and trash, but don't expect to find any antique treasures. On some of the side streets there are some good shops, but few bargains.

GALERÍAS PIQUER (35)
C/ de la Ribera de Curtidores 29

TELEPHONE: None
METRO: La Latina, 5
CREDIT CARDS: Depends on the store
HOURS: Mon–Sat 11 A.M.–2 P.M., 5–8 P.M., Sun 10 A.M.–2 P.M., hours vary

This is a courtyard of twenty antique shops in the Rastro.

NUEVAS GALERÍAS (31)
C/ de la Ribera de Curtidores 12

TELEPHONE: None
METRO: La Latina, 5
CREDIT CARDS: Depends on shop
HOURS: Mon–Sat 9 A.M.–2 P.M., 5–8 P.M., Sun 9 A.M.–2 P.M.
ENGLISH SPOKEN: Usually

This is another arcade of antique shops in the middle of the Rastro.

Art Prints

MÉXICO II (27)
C/ de las Huertas 17

TELEPHONE: 91 429 58 12
FAX: 91 429 94 76
METRO: Antón Martín, 1
CREDIT CARDS: AE, DC, MC, V
HOURS: Mon–Fri 10 A.M.–2 P.M., 5–8 P.M., Sat till 2 P.M.; closed in Aug, one week at Easter
ENGLISH SPOKEN: Yes

Across the street is México I (Calle de las Huertas 20), where the originals are at least three times the prices you will pay for the prints at this location. The subject matter covers all the bases, from astronomy to zebras. Rafael Amievu García and his family have been in the business for decades, and know their subject well. Be sure to admire their interesting collection of old globes, which are, unfortunately, not for sale.

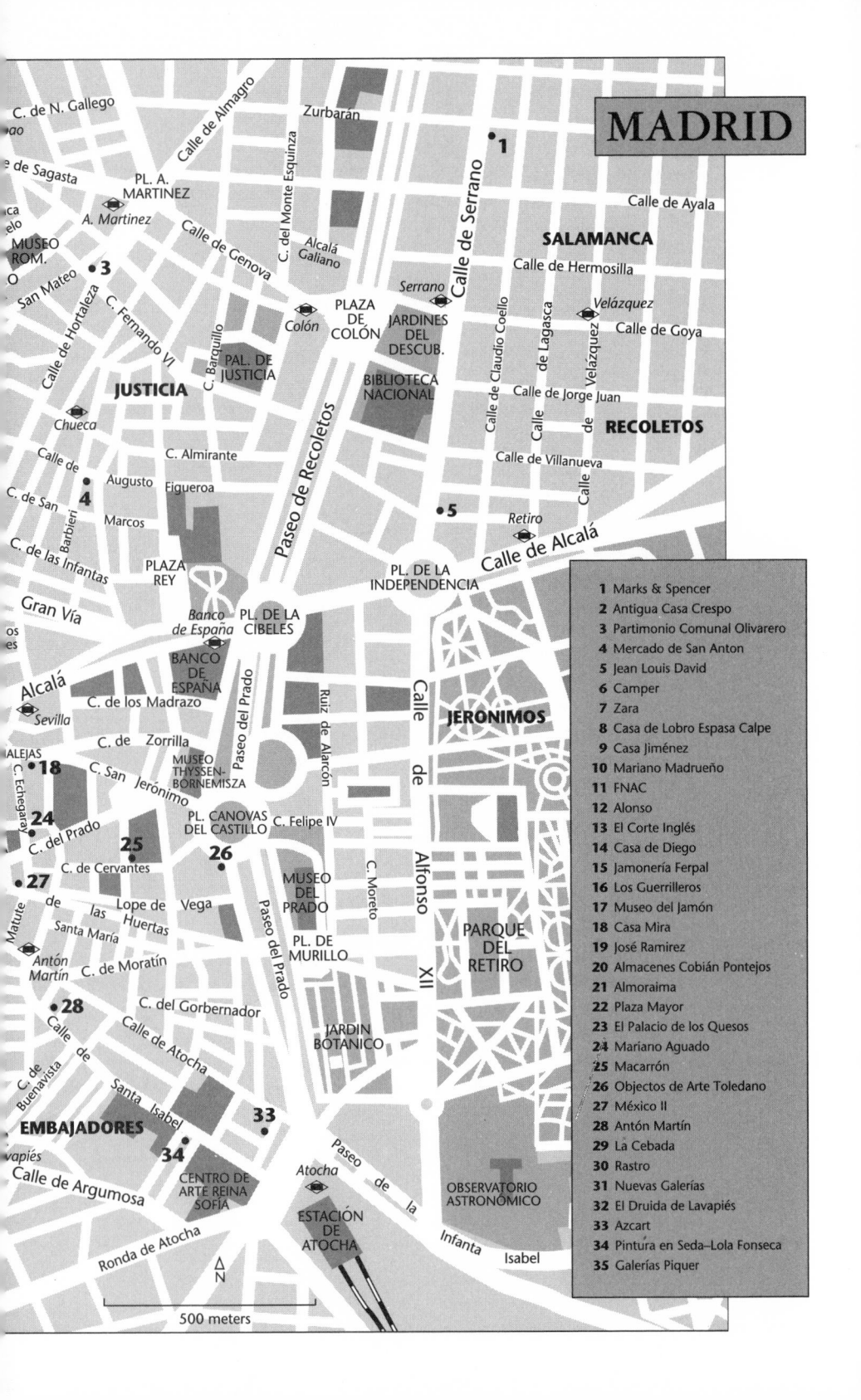

MADRID

SALAMANCA

RECOLETOS

JUSTICIA

JERONIMOS

EMBAJADORES

Zurbarán

Calle de N. Gallego

de Sagasta

MUSEO ROM.

San Mateo

Calle de Hortaleza

C. Fernando VI

Chueca

Calle de

C. de San

Barbieri

C. de las Infantas

Gran Vía

Alcalá

Sevilla

ALEJAS

C. Echegaray

C. del Prado

C. de Cervantes

Matute

Santa María

Antón Martín

Calle

C. de Buenavista

vapiés

Calle de Argumosa

Ronda de Atocha

PL. A. MARTINEZ

A. Martínez

Calle de Genova

Calle de Almagro

Calle del Monte Esquinza

Alcalá Galiano

C. Barquillo

PAL. DE JUSTICIA

Colón

C. Almirante

Augusto Figueroa

Marcos

PLAZA REY

Banco de España

PL. DE LA CIBELES

BANCO DE ESPAÑA

C. de los Madrazo

C. de Zorrilla

C. San Jerónimo

MUSEO THYSSEN-BORNEMISZA

PL. CANOVAS DEL CASTILLO

Lope de Vega

Huertas

C. de Moratín

C. del Gorbernador

Calle de Atocha

Santa Isabel

CENTRO DE ARTE REINA SOFIA

ESTACIÓN DE ATOCHA

Serrano

PLAZA DE COLÓN

JARDINES DEL DESCUB.

BIBLIOTECA NACIONAL

Paseo de Recoletos

Calle de Serrano

Calle de Ayala

Calle de Hermosilla

Calle de Claudio Coello

Calle de Lagasca

Velázquez

Calle de Goya

Calle de Jorge Juan

Calle de Villanueva

Calle

de

Retiro

Calle de Alcalá

PL. DE LA INDEPENDENCIA

Ruiz de Alarcón

Paseo del Prado

Calle

de

Alfonso

XII

C. Felipe IV

MUSEO DEL PRADO

C. Moreto

PL. DE MURILLO

Paseo del Prado

JARDIN BOTANICO

PARQUE DEL RETIRO

Atocha

Paseo

de

la

Infanta

Isabel

OBSERVATORIO ASTRONÓMICO

N

500 meters

1 Marks & Spencer
2 Antigua Casa Crespo
3 Partimonio Comunal Olivarero
4 Mercado de San Anton
5 Jean Louis David
6 Camper
7 Zara
8 Casa de Lobro Espasa Calpe
9 Casa Jiménez
10 Mariano Madrueño
11 FNAC
12 Alonso
13 El Corte Inglés
14 Casa de Diego
15 Jamonería Ferpal
16 Los Guerrilleros
17 Museo del Jamón
18 Casa Mira
19 José Ramirez
20 Almacenes Cobián Pontejos
21 Almoraima
22 Plaza Mayor
23 El Palacio de los Quesos
24 Mariano Aguado
25 Macarrón
26 Objectos de Arte Toledano
27 México II
28 Antón Martín
29 La Cebada
30 Rastro
31 Nuevas Galerías
32 El Druida de Lavapiés
33 Azcart
34 Pintura en Seda–Lola Fonseca
35 Galerías Piquer

Art Supplies

MACARRÓN (25)
C/ de San Agustín 7, at C/ Cervantes
  TELEPHONE: 91 429 68 01, 91 429 0672
  METRO: Antón Martín, 1
  CREDIT CARDS: AE, DC, MC, V
  HOURS: Mon–Fri 9 A.M.–1:30 P.M., 4:30–8 P.M., Sat 10 A.M.–1:30 P.M.
  ENGLISH SPOKEN: Yes
  The shop is the official supplier for the Círculo de Bellas Artes and in the past has supplied such illustrious names as Dalí and Picasso. The well-informed staff is very helpful, no matter what your level of artistic expertise is.

Beauty Services

JEAN LOUIS DAVID (5)
C/ de Serrano 4
  TELEPHONE: 91 575 51 31
  METRO: Retiro, 2
  CREDIT CARDS: AE, MC, V
  HOURS: Mon–Sat 8 A.M.–10 P.M.
  ENGLISH SPOKEN: Limited
  Great haircuts and long-lasting manicures for both men and women at very attractive prices are yours at this smart hair-styling salon in the best shopping neighborhood of Madrid.

Bookshops

CASA DE LOBRO ESPASA CALPE (8)
Gran Vía 29
  TELEPHONE: 91 521 21 13
  METRO: Gran Vía, 1, 5
  CREDIT CARDS: AE, DC, MC, V
  HOURS: Mon–Sat 9:30 A.M.–9:30 P.M.
  ENGLISH SPOKEN: Depends on clerk
  This is the largest bookstore in Madrid, and it carries a good selection of books in English on the street level toward the back, though you probably won't want to pay the prices.

FNAC (11)
C/ de Preciados 28

> **TELEPHONE:** 91 595 61 00
> **METRO:** Callao, 3, 5
> **CREDIT CARDS:** AE, DC, MC, V
> **HOURS:** Mon–Sat 10 A.M.–10 P.M., Sun and holidays noon–8 P.M.
> **ENGLISH SPOKEN:** Yes

FNAC is a popular French chain of stores that stocks an immense range of books (both Spanish and foreign), CDs, videos, magazines, periodicals, computers, and software. On the ground level is a ticket agency and a photo-developing service. Prices are said to be discounted, but that is by Madrid pricing, which tends to be high.

Clothing and Shoes

ALMACENES COBIÁN PONTEJOS (20)
Plaza de Pontejos s/n

> **TELEPHONE:** None
> **METRO:** Sol, 1, 2, 3
> **CREDIT CARDS:** MC, V
> **HOURS:** Mon–Fri 9:30 A.M.–2 P.M., 4:30–8:30 P.M., Sat 9:30 A.M.–4 P.M.
> **ENGLISH SPOKEN:** Limited

This place is amazing: three floors of ribbons, laces, DIY jewelry supplies, Spanish combs and tiaras, one room devoted entirely to needle-point threads, ropes, braids, and buttons, and another devoted only to zippers. Also for sale are patterns, trim, baby clothes, lingerie, and men's underwear (both long and regular). Who buys all this? Well, it is so jam-packed with shoppers that you have to take a number to be waited on. If this were the only place like it in Madrid, the crowds might be more understandable, but it is not. The whole square around Plaza de Pontejos is ringed with similar stores, but this one is the biggest.

ALONSO (12)
C/ de Preciados 24

> **TELEPHONE:** 91 522 07 21
> **METRO:** Callao, 3, 5
> **CREDIT CARDS:** AE, DC, MC, V
> **HOURS:** Mon–Sat 10:30 A.M.–1:30 P.M., 4:30–8 P.M.
> **ENGLISH SPOKEN:** Limited

Attention, doting grandmothers and indulgent aunties: Don't say I didn't warn you about this adorable children's shop, which has been here for one hundred years selling clothing for babies to ten-year-olds. It is almost impossible to leave without something, even if it is only a frilly little bib the mother will probably want to frame rather than use.

ANTIGUA CASA CRESPO (2)
C/ del Divino Pastor 29

> **TELEPHONE:** 91 521 56 54
> **METRO:** San Bernardo, 2, 4, or Bilbao, 1, 4
> **CREDIT CARDS:** None, cash only
> **HOURS:** Mon–Fri 10 A.M.–1:30 P.M., 4:30–8 P.M.; closed late Aug
> **ENGLISH SPOKEN:** Limited

If you missed buying your espadrilles (*alpargatas*) in Barcelona at La Manual Alpargatera (see page 196), here is your second chance. This museumlike shop is the most famous place in Madrid to buy these shoes, and they come in a dizzying range of colors, sizes, and materials.

CAMPER (6)
Gran Vía 54

> **TELEPHONE:** None
> **METRO:** Callao, 3, 5
> **CREDIT CARDS:** AE, DC, MC, V
> **HOURS:** Mon–Sat 10 A.M.–8 P.M.
> **ENGLISH SPOKEN:** Limited

Whatever your shoe pleasure, the Camper shoestore chain has shops in every major city throughout Spain with good prices on all the latest styles in footwear. Camper shoes are also sold in department stores and larger shoe shops.

LOS GUERRILLEROS (16)
Plaza de la Puerta del Sol 5

> **TELEPHONE:** None
> **METRO:** Sol, 1, 2, 3
> **CREDIT CARDS:** AE, MC, V
> **HOURS:** Mon–Sat 10 A.M.–2 P.M., 4:30–8:30 P.M.
> **ENGLISH SPOKEN:** Limited

"Don't buy here, we're very expensive" reads the stupid sign. The shoes are cheap, and sometimes even stylish.

ZARA (7)
Gran Vía 32

> **TELEPHONE:** 91 522 97 27
> **METRO:** Gran Vía, 1, 5
> **CREDIT CARDS:** MC, V
> **HOURS:** Daily 10 A.M.–8:30 P.M.
> **ENGLISH SPOKEN:** Depends on clerk

If you are a trendy fashion addict, Zara is your kind of store. With over a hundred outlets in Spain and abroad, you are never far from one. The big draw? Quick-fix copies of whatever top designers produce each season, which are made and on the Zara racks only a few weeks after they have been on the fashion runways. Prices are low by comparison, but quality can be spotty.

Department Stores

EL CORTE INGLÉS (13)
C/ de Preciados 3
> **TELEPHONE:** 91 556 23 00
> **METRO:** Sol, 1, 2, 3
> **CREDIT CARDS:** AE, DC, MC, V
> **HOURS:** Mon–Sat 10 A.M.–9:30 P.M.
> **ENGLISH SPOKEN:** Yes

The giant of Spanish department stores sells everything you could possibly want to wear, or to furnish your house, plus a wide range of services that includes multilingual directorial help, a grocery store, and shoe repairs.

MARKS & SPENCER (1)
C/ de Serrano 52
> **TELEPHONE:** 520 00 00
> **METRO:** Serrano, 4
> **CREDIT CARDS:** V
> **HOURS:** Mon–Sat 10 A.M.–8:30 P.M.
> **ENGLISH SPOKEN:** Yes

The popular British shop is a success selling its middle-of-the-road fashions to consumer-happy Spaniards. If you are out of Marmite, here's the place to restock.

Fans

ALMORAIMA (21)
Plaza Mayor 12
> **TELEPHONE:** 91 365 42 89
> **METRO:** Sol, 1, 2, 3
> **CREDIT CARDS:** AE, MC, V
> **HOURS:** Mon–Fri, 10 A.M.–2 P.M., 4–8 P.M., Sat 10:30 A.M.–2 P.M.
> **ENGLISH SPOKEN:** Yes

This is *the* shop for fans for all tastes and pocketbooks.

Food

CASA MIRA (18)
C/ de San Jerónimo 30
TELEPHONE: 91 429 67 96
METRO: Sevilla, 2
CREDIT CARDS: None, cash only
HOURS: Generally 10 A.M.–2 P.M., 5:30ñ9 P.M.
ENGLISH SPOKEN: Limited

This is the only place to go for the famous *turrón* (flavored nougat) that is eaten at Christmastime by everyone in Spain. They also sell marzipan and other sweet temptations. The family business was started as a small stall in the Puerta del Sol a 150 years ago by Luis Mira.

EL PALACIO DE LOS QUESOS (23)
C/ Mayor 53
TELEPHONE: 91 548 16 23
METRO: Sol, 1, 2, 3
CREDIT CARDS: None, cash only
HOURS: Mon–Sat 9 A.M.–2:30 P.M., 5:30–8:30 P.M.; May–Oct closed on Sat

As the name suggests, this is a *palace* of cheeses.

JAMONERÍA FERPAL (15)
C/ del Arenal 7
TELEPHONE: 91 521 51 08
METRO: Sol, 1, 2, 3
CREDIT CARDS: MC, V
HOURS: Mon–Sat 9 A.M.–8:45 P.M.; in Aug, Mon–Sat 9:45 A.M.–2 P.M., 5:30–9 P.M.
ENGLISH SPOKEN: Limited

They have one of the best selection of cheeses in the center of Madrid. They also sell hams.

MUSEO DEL JAMÓN (17)
C/ de San Jerónimo 6
TELEPHONE: 91 521 03 46, 91 531 57 21
METRO: Sol, 1, 2, 3
CREDIT CARDS: MC, V
HOURS: Mon–Sat 9 A.M.–midnight, Sun 10 A.M.–midnight
ENGLISH SPOKEN: Limited

This is the best place to sample, eat, and buy every variety of wonderful Spanish ham. They also have a restaurant and snack bar (see *Cheap Eats in Spain*). They have numerous locations throughout Madrid.

PARTIMONIO COMUNAL OLIVARERO (3)
C/ de Mejía Lequerica 1, at C/ de Hortaleza

TELEPHONE: 91 308 05 05
METRO: Tribunal, 1, 10, or Alonso Martinez, 4, 5, 10
CREDIT CARDS: None, cash only
HOURS: Mon–Fri 9:30 A.M.–2:30 P.M., 5:30–7:30 P.M., Sat 9:30 A.M.–2:30 P.M.; closed Aug
ENGLISH SPOKEN: Limited

Spain is famous for its olive oil, and there is no better place to find such a wide selection. They sell every kind of Spanish olive oil, including some exclusive to this shop, all grades, and in all price ranges.

Gifts

AZCART (33)
C/ del Doctor Drumen 7, at C/ de Atocha

TELEPHONE: 91 527 35 72
METRO: Atocha, 1
CREDIT CARDS: MC, V
HOURS: Mon–Sat 10 A.M.–2 P.M., 5–8:30 P.M., Sun and holidays 10 A.M.–2 P.M.
ENGLISH SPOKEN: Yes

Azcart is near the Reina Sofía art museum, which may account for its above-average selection of contemporary art–inspired gifts, posters, watches, tote bags, and very interesting silver jewelry.

OBJECTOS DE ARTE TOLEDANO (26)
Paseo del Prado 10

TELEPHONE: 91 429 50 00, 91 429 66 46
FAX: 91 420 16 19
EMAIL: odat@arrakis.es
METRO: Banco de España, 1
CREDIT CARDS: AE, DC, MC, V
HOURS: Mon–Sat 9:30 A.M.–8 P.M.
ENGLISH SPOKEN: Yes, and every other language a tourist might converse in

Touristy? And how! Kitschy? In spades! However, this supermarket dedicated to the pocketbooks of tourists does have some merit, especially if you are looking for little, inexpensive gifts, such as wooden filagreed fans, simple Majorica pearls, and the usual T-shirts. If you are shopping for Lladró, their selection is good. Since the prices are the same all over town, if you see something you like here, and have never seen it before, better snatch it before it's too late. If you are in the market for full suits of armor or like ceramic bulls trimmed with fur, you are also in the right place. The shop is across the Paseo del Prado from the Prado museum. As you walk there, notice the vendors selling posters announcing bullfighters and flamenco dancers—and upon which you can have your own name inscribed.

Guitars

JOSÉ RAMIREZ (19)
C/ de la Paz 8

TELEPHONE: 91 531 42 29
FAX: 91 571 59 45 (for the workshop and office)
METRO: Sol, 1, 2, 3
CREDIT CARDS: AE, MC, V
HOURS: Mon–Fri 10 A.M.–2 P.M., 4:30–7:30 P.M., Sat 10:30 A.M.–2 P.M.
ENGLISH SPOKEN: Yes

If you are looking for the finest guitars, look no further than this family-run shop, which has been in business since 1882. General Omar Bradley's wife bought a guitar here for her husband, and many others, both famous and not so, have purchased their wonderful instruments. They also sell guitar cases and can ship. Everything is done by hand, including manually typing out your bill while you wait.

Herbalists

EL DRUIDA DE LAVAPIÉS (32)
C/ de la Fé 9, corner C/ de Buenavista

TELEPHONE: 91 527 28 33
METRO: Lavapiés, 1
CREDIT CARDS: MC, V
HOURS: Mon–Fri 10 A.M.–2:30 P.M., 5–8:30 P.M., Sat 10 A.M.–2:30 P.M.
ENGLISH SPOKEN: Limited

Everything you expect in a herbalist and health food store plus a limited supply of tofu, biological yogurt, honey, eggs, bread, and a few tired fruits and veggies.

Markets

Most areas of the city have their indoor markets (*mercados del barrio*). A few are listed below, along with the famous El Rastro flea market. Remember that many food markets are closed on Monday and on Saturday afternoon, and the best time to go is on Saturday morning.

BOOKS, STAMPS, AND COINS

PLAZA MAYOR (22)

TELEPHONE: None
METRO: Sol, 1, 2, 3
CREDIT CARDS: Don't count on it
HOURS: Sun 9 A.M.–2 P.M.
ENGLISH SPOKEN: Depends on seller

A stamp, coin, and old-book market operates on the Plaza Mayor on Sunday mornings. Also for sale are old military regalia, postcards, and magazines.

FLEA MARKETS

RASTRO (30)
C/ de la Ribera de Curtidores

TELEPHONE: None
METRO: La Latina, 5
CREDIT CARDS: Don't count on it
HOURS: Sun 7 A.M.–2 P.M.
ENGLISH SPOKEN: Seldom

The teaming flea market is a must-see/must-do in Madrid even if you find shopping a bore. Stalls spread down Calle de la Ribera de Curtidores from the Plaza de Cascorro. Starting from the top you will find clothes, jewelry from Tibet and India, poor-quality leather, fifties furniture, fake antiques, religious paintings, spare car parts, hardware, porn videos, old books, and plenty of just plain junk. Sometimes the crowds of shoppers are more interesting than the goods being sold. Bargaining is expected, but because the seller's profit margin is low, don't look for much more than a 5 to 10 percent discount. Pickpocketing is rampant. Wear a money belt inside your clothes, and keep an eagle eye out at all times.

FOOD

ANTÓN MARTÍN (28)
C/ de Santa Isabel 5

TELEPHONE: 91 369 06 20
METRO: Antón Martín, 1
CREDIT CARDS: None, cash only
HOURS: Mon–Fri 9 A.M.–2 P.M., 5–8 P.M., Sat 9 A.M.–2 P.M.; closed in Aug
ENGLISH SPOKEN: None

This is a smaller, more manageable indoor food market with several levels.

LA CEBADA (29)
Plaza de la Cebada 15
TELEPHONE: None
METRO: La Latina, 5
CREDIT CARDS: None, cash only
HOURS: Mon–Fri 9 A.M.–2 P.M., 5–8 P.M., Sat 9 A.M.–2 P.M.
ENGLISH SPOKEN: Seldom
This is one of the more colorful and well-priced food markets.

MERCADO DE SAN ANTON (4)
C/ de Augusto Figueroa, between C/ de Barbieri and C/ de la Libertad
TELEPHONE: None
METRO: Chueca, 5
CREDIT CARDS: None, cash only
HOURS: Mon–Fri 9 A.M.–2 P.M., 5–8 P.M., Sat 9 A.M.–2 P.M.
ENGLISH SPOKEN: Very limited
Come here for a good look at a neighborhood food market.

Shawls

CASA JIMÉNEZ (9)
C/ de Preciados 42
TELEPHONE: 91 548 05 26
METRO: Callao, 3, 5
CREDIT CARDS: AE, DC, MC, V
HOURS: Mon–Sat 10 A.M.–1:30 P.M., 5–8 P.M., July closed Sat afternoon, Aug closed all-day Sat
ENGLISH SPOKEN: Yes
This is the most famous shop in Madrid specializing in *mantones* and *mantillas*, the traditional lace and embroidered shawls.

Silk

PINTURA EN SEDA–LOLA FONSECA (34)
C/ de Santa Isabel, 50
METRO: Antón Martín or Atocha, 1
CREDIT CARDS: AE, MC, V
HOURS: Mon–Fri 10 A.M.–2 P.M. 4:30–8:30 P.M., Sat 11 A.M.–2:30 P.M.
ENGLISH SPOKEN: Yes
Hand-painted ties, scarves, shawls—to wear or to frame—are sold at Lola Fonseca's atelier and teaching venue. Her unusual one-of-a-kind designs and stunning colors make her silks irresistible.

Umbrellas and Walking Sticks

CASA DE DIEGO (14)
C/ de la Montera 1
> TELEPHONE: 91 531 02 23
> FAX: 91 522 66 43
> METRO: Sol, 1, 2, 3
> CREDIT CARDS: AE, DC, MC, V
> HOURS: Mon–Fri 9:45 A.M.–1:30 P.M., 4:30–8 P.M.
> ENGLISH SPOKEN: Yes

The shop specializes in made-to-order umbrellas, fans, and walking sticks. Prices for the umbrellas range from a simple model at 2,000ptas to one made with silver and ebony that sells for 50,000ptas.

Wine

MARIANO AGUADO (24)
C/ de Echegaray 19
> TELEPHONE: 91 429 6088
> METRO: Sevilla, 2, or Sol, 1, 2, 3
> CREDIT CARDS: None, cash only
> HOURS: Mon–Fri 10 A.M.–2:30 P.M., 5–8:30 P.M., Sat 10 A.M.–2 P.M.
> ENGLISH SPOKEN: Limited

The shop sells only Spanish wines to serious connoisseurs at very reasonable prices.

MARIANO MADRUEÑO (10)
C/ del Postigo de San Martín 3, at C/ de Preciados
> TELEPHONE: 91 521 19 55
> METRO: Callao 3, 5
> CREDIT CARDS: MC, V
> HOURS: Mon–Fri 9:30 A.M.–2 P.M., 5:30–8:30 P.M., Sat 9:30–2 P.M.; closed Aug
> ENGLISH SPOKEN: Limited

The selection of wines is huge, and they come from all over Spain. Prices start at 150ptas and go up. The carved wooden shelves and wrought-iron columns have been in place since the bodega opened over a hundred years ago.

Cheap Chic Shopping in Seville

It seems that most of the shopping in Seville is geared to the tourist, with more ceramic and tile outlets than anyone could possible canvas in a short stay. Despite the sheer number of tile shops, these practical and decorative ceramics are good buys. Also look for handmade fans and *mantillas,* the lovely lace headdresses that hang over a large comb, as well as for food products like olive oil, sherry wine vinegars, and fragrant spices originally brought by the Moors. Many monestaries and convents are cooking for a profit: Try marmalade and jam from the Convento de Santa Paula, a convent that began in 1475 and is still home to a handful of nuns. The list of shopping possibilities below is by no means comprehensive, but as in Barcelona and Madrid, it provides a few key addresses and suggestions to get you started on your quest for shopping treasures.

Shopping hours are pretty much the same as in Barcelona and Madrid, generally from 9:30 or 10 A.M. until 1 or 2 P.M., then again from 5 until 8 or 8:30 P.M. Nothing much is open on Sunday, and many stores close Saturday afternoon. In July and August, shop closings can vary with the whims and heat tolerances of owners, but those in the major tourist areas and department stores will be open.

The number in parentheses to the right of each business name is the Cheap Chic map key number for the Seville city map.

SHOPPING STREETS

Outside the Barrio de Santa Cruz, the main shopping streets in Seville center around Calle Sierpes, a completely pedestrianized, awning-shaded shopping street. Parallel to Calle Sierpes is Calle Velázquez, which flows into Calle Tetuán. Everything is here: fans, shawls, Lladró by the barrelfull, flamenco costumes, leather, ceramics galore, jewelry, and plenty of places your nonshopping tagalongs can sit and have refreshments. Adorable children's clothes are concentrated in shops around Calle Alvarez Quintero. The best stores seem to be concentrated toward the Plaza de San Francicso end.

Antiques

ANTIGÜEDADES LOLA ORTEGA (10)
Plaza del Cabildo, Entrada Queipo de Llano 22

TELEPHONE: 95 421 87 71
CREDIT CARDS: AE, DC, MC, V
HOURS: Mon–Fri 10 A.M.–2 P.M., 5–8:30 P.M., Sat 10 A.M.–2 P.M.; closed Aug
ENGLISH SPOKEN: Yes

This family affair is headed by Lola Ortega, her daughter, and her two sons. They have been in business in Seville for years, and definitely have their collective fingers on the pulse of the antique world. In this shop, which is under the arches of the beautiful Plaza de Cabildo, just off Avenida de la Constitución, they must have something for everyone in almost every price range, from postcards, old laces, jewelry, shawls, and fans to furniture, original tiles, paintings, and religious sculpture. One of the sons runs a second shop in the Barrio de Santa Cruz at Jamerdana 2; tel: 95 422 36 06.

Beauty Services

YVES ROCHER (3)
C/ Tetuán 21

TELEPHONE: 95 422 57 77
CREDIT CARDS: AE, MC, V
HOURS: Mon–Fri 10 A.M.–2 P.M., 4–7 P.M.
ENGLISH SPOKEN: Yes

Yves Rocher is a chain of European beauty boutiques that offer beauty treatments designed to make you feel pampered and special. Prices are very good, especially when they are running specials. They also promote a line of good-value, modestly priced beauty products.

Bookshops

LIBRERÍA VÉRTICE (16)
C/ San Fernando 30

TELEPHONE: 95 421 16 54
CREDIT CARDS: MC, V
HOURS: Mon–Fri 9:30 A.M.–2 P.M., 5–8 P.M., Sat 10:30–1:30 P.M.; closed Sat in July
ENGLISH SPOKEN: Yes

American John Lilly runs this comprehensive bookshop across Calle San Fernando from the Hotel Alphonse XIII and close to the university. He stocks books, tapes, cards, dictionaries, and an excellent selection of books in English.

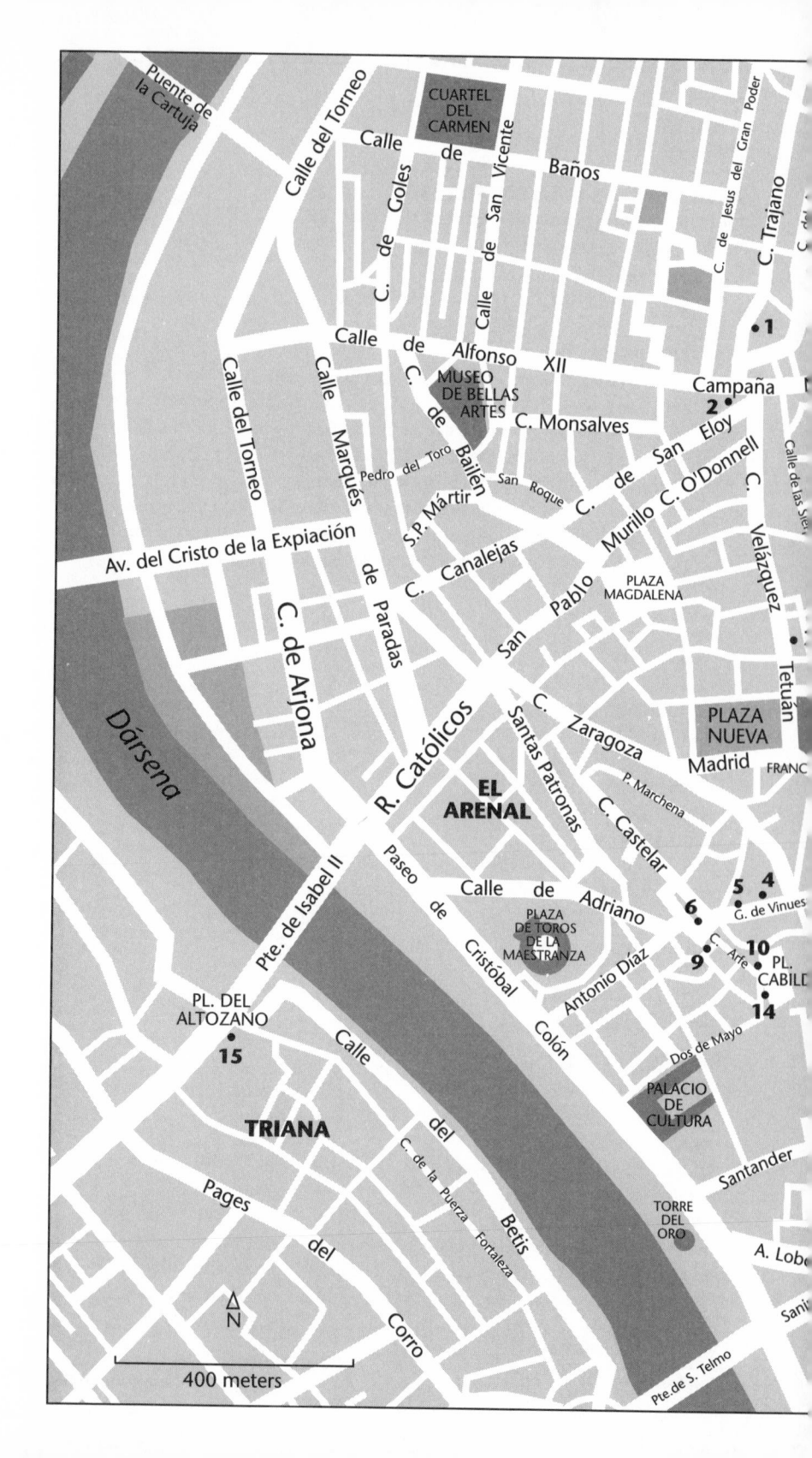

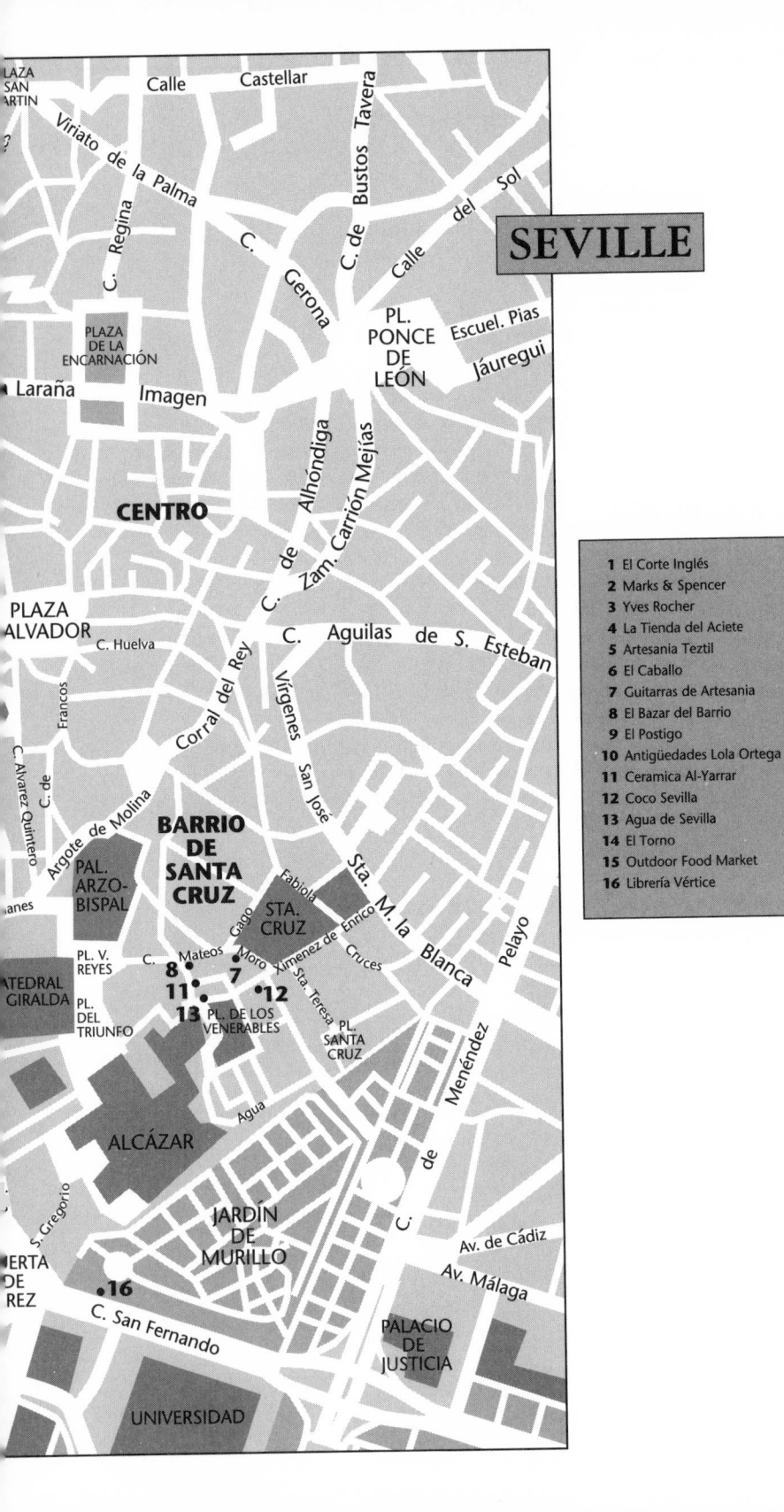

SEVILLE

1 El Corte Inglés
2 Marks & Spencer
3 Yves Rocher
4 La Tienda del Aciete
5 Artesania Teztil
6 El Caballo
7 Guitarras de Artesania
8 El Bazar del Barrio
9 El Postigo
10 Antigüedades Lola Ortega
11 Ceramica Al-Yarrar
12 Coco Sevilla
13 Agua de Sevilla
14 El Torno
15 Outdoor Food Market
16 Librería Vértice

Ceramics and Tiles

CERAMICA AL-YARRAR (11)
Rodrigo Caro 20, Esquina Plaza Doña
TELEPHONE: 95 422 85 68
CREDIT CARDS: MC, V
HOURS: Daily 10:30 A.M.–8 P.M.
ENGLISH SPOKEN: Yes

After a day or two on the streets of Seville, shops peddling ceramic jugs and colorful tiles seem to be a dime a dozen and located at almost every turn. Soon, everything begins to look the same. For a change of pace, and a much more interesting and unusual selection, make your way to this attractive shop in the Barrio de Santa Cruz. They also specialize in pictures taken of you and yours all dressed up as flamenco dancers: photos of men are 1,000ptas, women 2,000ptas.

EL BAZAR DEL BARRIO (8)
Mateos Gago 24
TELEPHONE: 95 456 00 89
CREDIT CARDS: AE, DC, MC, V
HOURS: Mon–Fri 10 A.M.–2 P.M., 5:30–9 P.M., Sat until 2 P.M.
ENGLISH SPOKEN: Yes

This is another colorful tile shop in the Barrio de Santa Cruz with a better selection than most. If you are worried about getting your treasures home, they will ship.

EL POSTIGO (9)
C/ Arfe s/n
TELEPHONE: 95 421 36 76, 95 456 00 13
CREDIT CARDS: AE, DC, MC, V
HOURS: Mon–Sat 11 A.M.–2 P.M., 3–8 P.M., Sun 11 A.M.–3 P.M.
ENGLISH SPOKEN: Yes

If you are in the market for any type of ceramic, this large artist's warehouse stocks a huge selection of all anyone could ever need or want.

Clothing

ARTESANIA TEZTIL (5)
C/ García de Vinuesa 33
TELEPHONE: 95 421 50 88
CREDIT CARDS: AE, DC, MC, V
HOURS: Mon–Sat 9:15 A.M.–1:30 P.M., 5–8 P.M.; closed Aug 15–22, dates vary
ENGLISH SPOKEN: Yes

If you are in the market for shawls, fans, or leather goods (including jackets, purses, and belts), be sure to take a good look at the wide-ranging selection here.

Crafts

COCO SEVILLA (12)
C/ Ximénez de Enrico 2

TELEPHONE: 95 421 45 32

CREDIT CARDS: MC, V

HOURS: Mon–Sat 10:30 A.M.–8 P.M., Sun 11 A.M.–8 P.M.

ENGLISH SPOKEN: Yes, and French

When I discovered this unique shop, the works of four talented textile and design artists had their work exclusively on display. By now there may be more, but quality will not be compromised. Featured are hand-painted silks made into shawls, pillows, and scarves and beautiful hand-made fans, jewelry, and many other items that you won't see anywhere else. Even the postcards and posters are unusual. It is a must if you are looking for something appealing but appreciate something different.

Department Stores

EL CORTE INGLÉS (1)
Plaza del Duque de la Victoria 10, off C/ Trajano

TELEPHONE: 95 422 09 31

CREDIT CARDS: AE, DC, MC, V

HOURS: Mon–Sat 10 A.M.–9 P.M.

ENGLISH SPOKEN: Depends on the clerk, but usually enough

This is Seville's branch of the nationwide department store, which has everything from food and footballs to a beauty salon, every type of cosmetic imaginable, clothes for the entire family, housewares, a good foreign exchange desk, and almost anything else you could want.

MARKS & SPENCER (2)
Plaza del Duque de la Victoria and C/ de San Eloy s/n

TELEPHONE: None

CREDIT CARDS: MC, V

HOURS: Mon–Sat 10 A.M.–9 P.M.

ENGLISH SPOKEN: Depends on clerk

England's great middle-of-the-road merchandiser has arrived in Spain. The Spanish are obviously enthusiastic about buying orange marmalade and Marmite along with the frumpy fashions and great underwear Marks & Spencer is known for in England.

Flea Markets

EL JUEVES
Alameda de Hercules s/n (follow C/ del Amor de Dios north)
> TELEPHONE: None
> CREDIT CARDS: None, cash only
> HOURS: Thur 9:30 or 10 A.M.–1 P.M., hours vary
> ENGLISH SPOKEN: Not much

Get here by ten to get the good stuff; by noon some sellers are folding up their tables and blankets. This is very, very local with vendors spread out along a dirt square displaying lots of just plain junk. It is small enough to go through carefully in an hour, and with perseverance and luck, you are bound to find a trinket or two.

Food

EL TORNO (14)
Plaza del Cabildo s/n
> TELEPHONE: 95 421 91 90
> CREDIT CARDS: MC, V
> HOURS: Mon–Fri 10 A.M.–1:30 P.M., 5-7:30 P.M., Sat–Sun, holidays 10:30 A.M.–2 P.M.
> ENGLISH SPOKEN: Limited

What a wonderful place! This is a holy boutique selling wares made and produced by nuns and priests in convents throughout Spain. In addition to tempting, homemade sweets, cookies, and candies, the sisters have created children's clothes and other small gifts you can tuck into a suitcase.

LA TIENDA DEL ACIETE (4)
C/ García de Vinuesa 31
> TELEPHONE: 95 421 30 30
> EMAIL: oliveoil@mizmail.com
> CREDIT CARDS: MC, V
> HOURS: Mon–Fri 10 A.M.–2 P.M., 4–7 P.M.
> ENGLISH SPOKEN: Yes

At this olive oil shop you can find a selection of extra-virgin Andalucían olive oils and balsamic vinegars in attractive gift bottles and boxes that make great gifts for yourself or friends.

OUTDOOR FOOD MARKET (15)
Triana section of Seville, just across the Puente de Isabel II
> TELEPHONE: None
> CREDIT CARDS: None
> HOURS: Mon–Sat, 9 A.M.–1 P.M.

ENGLISH SPOKEN: Not much

Seville's most central outdoor food market has better-than-average quality and competitive prices.

Gifts

AGUA DE SEVILLA (13)
Rodrigo Caro 16
TELEPHONE: 95 422 50 70
CREDIT CARDS: AE, DC, MC, V
HOURS: Daily 10 A.M.–8:30 P.M.
ENGLISH SPOKEN: Yes

The small shop in the Barrio de Santa Cruz is beautifully decorated in the warm colors of Andalucía and specializes in fragrances based on the flowers and fruits of Seville. In addition to the lovely fragrances, they feature dynamic, one-of-a-kind artist-designed jewelry and accessories. Definitely one of my favorite shops in Seville.

Guitars

GUITARRAS DE ARTESANIA (7)
C/ Mesón del Moro 12
TELEPHONE AND FAX: 95 422 78 98
CREDIT CARDS: AE, MC, V
HOURS: 11 A.M.–2 P.M., or ring the bell
ENGLISH SPOKEN: Yes

Here is your Seville address for handmade guitars.

Leather

EL CABALLO (6)
Antonia Díaz 7
TELEPHONE: 95 421 81 27
FAX: 95 421 12 29
CREDIT CARDS: AE, DC, MC, V
HOURS: Mon–Fri 9 A.M.–2 P.M., 5–8:30 P.M., Sat until 2 P.M.
ENGLISH SPOKEN: Yes

El Caballo is well known throughout Spain for selling fine leather goods, especially for horseback-riding enthusiasts. If they don't have it in riding gear, it doesn't exist. There are also branches in Barcelona and Madrid.

Glossary of Cheap Chic Words and Phrases

There are two lists below: one of terms in Castilian Spanish and Catalan (for use in Barcelona) to help you recognize items and shop names, and another of phrases in Spanish to help you while you're shopping.

CHEAP CHIC WORDS IN SPANISH AND CATALAN

English	Spanish	Catalan (Barcelona)
antique shop	anticuario	antitquari
bakery	panadería	forn
barber	barbero	barber
bookshop	librería	llibrería
to buy	comprar	comprar
cake shop	pastelería	pastissería
chemist	farmacia	farmacia
closed	cerrado	tancat
department store	almacenes	magatzems
dry cleaner	tintorería	tintorería
expensive	caro	car
hairdresser	peluquería	perruquería
jewelery	joyería	joiería
laundry	lavandería	bogaderia
market	mercado	mercat
mechanic	mecánico	mecànic
open	abierto	obert
sales	rebajas	rebaixes
shoe store	zapatería	sabatería
shop	tienda	botiga
size	talla	talla
supermarket	supermercado	supermercat
ticket	entrada	entrada
tobacconist	estanco	estanc

HELPFUL CHEAP CHIC SPANISH PHRASES

How much does this cost?	*¿Cuánto cuesta esto?*
I would like . . .	*Me gustaría . . .*
Do you have?	*¿Tienen?*
Do you take credit cards?	*¿Aceptan tarjetas de crédito?*
What time do you open?	*¿A qué hora abren?*
What time do you close?	*¿A qué hora cierran?*
this one	*este*
that one	*ese*
Anything else?	*¿Algo más?*
Nothing else, thanks.	*Nada más, gracias.*
money	*dinero*
cheap	*barato*
discount	*discuento*
free of charge	*gratis*
black	*negro*
white	*blanco*
red	*rojo*
yellow	*amarillo*
blue	*azul*
green	*verde*

Glossary of Spanish Words and Phrases

Whenever you are traveling in a foreign country, it pays to speak as much of the native language as you can. Your efforts will always be appreciated. This Spanish glossary is meant to help you become familiar with a few words and phrases to get you by in simple situations. Castilian (*castellano*) is the official language in Spain, and it is what we think of as the Spanish language, but there are also three other regional languages that are widely used in the country. Catalan is spoken in Barcelona, the Balearic Islands, and Valencia; Galician, similar to Portuguese, is spoken in Galicia; and Basque is spoken in the Basque country and Navarra. See the glossary in Cheap Chic, page 232, for a list of helpful shopping terms, and for a short Catalan glossary (for use in Barcelona), see page 100.

GENERAL PHRASES

Sir/Mr.	*Señor/Sr.*
Madam/Mrs.	*Señora/Sra.*
Miss	*Señorita*
yes/no	*sí/no*
okay	*vale*
please	*por favor*
thank you (very much)	*(muchas) gracias*
you're welcome	*de nada*
that's okay, don't mention it	*no hay de qué*
excuse me	*perdón/perdone*
excuse me (to attract attention)	*oiga*
hello	*¡hola!*
good-bye	*¡adiós!*
goodnight	*buenas noches*
good/bad	*bueno(a)/malo(a)*
well	*bien*
small/big	*pequeño(a)/gran, grande*
hot/cold	*caliente/frio*
fast/slow	*rápido*
enough	*bastante*
with/without	*con/sin*
more/less	*más/menos*
more or less	*más o menos*
here	*aquí*
What?	*¿Qué?*

When?	¿Cuándo?
Why?	¿Por qué?
Where?	¿Dónde?
Who?	¿Quién?
My name is . . .	Me llamo . . .
What is your name?	¿Como se llama usted?
I am American/English.	Soy americano(a)/ inglés(a).
How are you?	¿Cómo está usted?
Very well, thank you.	Muy bien, gracias.
Pleased to meet you.	Encantado de conocerle.
See you later.	Hasta luego.
That's fine.	Está bien.
Where is the nearest telephone?	Dónde está el teléfono más próximo?
Do you speak English?	¿Habla inglés?
I don't speak Spanish.	No hablo español.
I don't understand.	No comprendo/no entiendo.
Could you speak more slowly?	¿Puede hablar más despacio, por favor?
What is this called in Spanish?	¿Como se llama este in español?
Can you help me?	¿Puede usted ayudarme?
How much is it?	¿Cuánto cuesta? /¿Cuánto vale?
The bill, please.	La cuenta, por favor.
Do you have any change?	¿Tiene cambio?
I am hungry.	Tengo hambre.
I am thirsty.	Tengo sed.
I am sorry.	Lo siento.
I am tired.	Estoy cansado(a).
I am sleepy.	Tengo sueño.
I am ill.	No me siento bien.

EMERGENCIES

Help!	¡Socorro!
Stop!	¡Pare!
Call a doctor/police!	¡Llame a un médico/ a la policía!
Go away!	¡Vete!
Be careful!	¡Tenga cuidado!

AT THE HOTEL

Where is hotel/hostel . . . ?	¿Dónde hay un hotel/un hostal . . . ?
What is the address?	¿Cuál es la dirección?
I (we) have a reservation.	Tengo (tenemos) una habitación reserva.
Do you have a vacant room?	¿Tiene una habitación libre?
for one night/one week	para una noche/una semana
an inside/outside room	una habitación interior/exterior

I would like . . .	*Quisiera . . .*
a single room	*una habitación individual*
double, with double bed	*doble, con cama de matrimonio*
twin, with twin beds	*una habitación individual, con dos camas*
a room with/without a bath/shower	*una habitación con/sin baño/ducha*
breakfast included	*desayuño incluido*
How much is it per person, per night?	*¿Cuánto cuesta por persona, por noche?*
It is too expensive.	*Es demasiado caro.*
Do you have anything cheaper?	*Tiene algo más barato?*
I would like to see it	*Quisiera verla.*
Where is the bathroom?	*¿Dónde está el baño?*
Where is the car park?	*¿Dónde está el parking?*
This does not work.	*Esto no funciona.*
air-conditioning	*con aire acondicionado*
bed	*la cama*
lift/elevator	*el ascensor*
key	*la llave*
swimming pool	*la piscina*
price	*el precio*
discount	*el descuento*
free	*gratis*

SIGNS

entrance/exit	*entrada/salida*
full	*ocupado/completo*
rooms available	*habitaciones libres*
open	*abierto*
closed	*cerrado*
admission charge	*la entrado*
prohibited	*prohibido*
toilets	*servicios*

GETTING AROUND

right/to the right/turn right	*derecha/a la derecha/gire a la derecha*
left/to the left/turn left	*izquierda/a la izquierda/gire a la izquierda*
ahead	*todo recto*
far/near/close	*lejos/cerca/cerca*
up	*arriba*
down	*abajo*
to the end of the street	*al final de la calle*

I am lost	*Me he perdido.*
Where is/are . . . ?	*¿Dónde está/están . . . ?*
How do I get to . . . ?	*¿Por donde se va a . . . ?*
How far is it to . . . ?	*¿Cuántos metros/kilometers hay de aquí a . . . ?*
Is this the bus for . . . ?	*¿Es este el autobús para . . . ?*
What time does the . . .	*¿A qué hora . . .*
the next/first/last	*próximo/primer/último/*
metro/bus/train	*el metro/el autobús/el tren*
leave/arrive?	*sale/llega el?*
Where is the bus/metro stop?	*¿Dónde está la parada de autobús/ metro?*
Can you show me?	*¿Me puede indicar?*
a one-way/return ticket	*un billete sencillo/de ida y vuelta*
How much is the fare?	*¿Cuánto vale el billete?*

PLACES

airport	*aeropuerto*
railway station	*estación de ferrocarril*
metro station	*estación de metro*
bus stop	*parada de autobús*
the next stop	*la próxima parada*
I am looking for . . .	*Estoy buscando . . .*
a bank	*un banco*
a bookstore	*una librería*
the cathedral	*la catedral*
city center/old city	*el centro de la ciudad/la ciudad antigua*
the hospital	*el hospital*
my hotel	*mi hotel*
the market	*el mercado*
the main square	*la plaza mayor*
the palace	*el palacio*
the police	*la policía*
the post office/postcard/stamp	*los correos/un postal/un sello*
the toilet	*los servicios*

TIME

What time is it?	*¿Qué hora es?*
At what time?	*¿A qué hora?*
in the morning	*de la mañana*
in the afternoon	*de la tarde*
in the evening	*de la noche*
today	*hoy*

tomorrow	*mañana*
yesterday	*ayer*
noon/midday	*mediodía*
afternoon/evening	*la tarde*
night	*la noche*
midnight	*la medianoche*
now	*ahora*
later	*más tarde*
one o'clock	*la una*
two o'clock in the morning/afternoon	*las dos de la mañana/tarde*
five past one	*la una y cinco*
quarter past one	*la una y cuarto*
half past one	*la una y media*
twenty to one	*la una menos cuarto*
one hour	*una hora*
half an hour	*una media hora*
early	*temprano*
late	*tarde*

DAYS, MONTHS, SEASONS

Monday	*lunes*
Tuesday	*martes*
Wednesday	*miércoles*
Thursday	*jueves*
Friday	*viernes*
Saturday	*sábado*
Sunday	*domingo*
January	*enero*
February	*febrero*
March	*marzo*
April	*abril*
May	*mayo*
June	*junio*
July	*julio*
August	*agosto*
September	*setiembre*
October	*octubre*
November	*noviembre*
December	*diciembre*
winter	*invierno*
spring	*primavera*
summer	*verano*
fall	*otoño*

NUMBERS

0	*cero*
1	*uno*
2	*dos*
3	*tres*
4	*cuatro*
5	*cinco*
6	*seis*
7	*siete*
8	*ocho*
9	*nueve*
10	*diez*
11	*once*
12	*doce*
13	*trece*
14	*catorce*
15	*quince*
16	*dieciséis*
17	*diecisiete*
18	*dieciocho*
19	*diecinueve*
20	*veinte*
21	*veintiuno*
22	*veintidós*
30	*treinta*
31	*treinta y uno*
40	*cuarenta*
50	*cincuenta*
60	*sesenta*
70	*setenta*
80	*ochenta*
90	*noventa*
100	*ciento*
101	*ciento uno*
102	*ciento dos*
200	*doscientos*
500	*quinientos*
1,000	*mil*
1,001	*mil uno*
2,000	*dos mil*
1,000,000	*un millón*

Index by City

BARCELONA

Accommodations

Big Splurges in Barcelona

Cheap Chic Shops in Barcelona

SEVILLE

Accommodations

Big Splurges in Seville

Cheap Chic Shops

Readers' Comments

Every effort has been made to provide the reader with accurate information. The publisher and author, however, cannot be held responsible for changes in any of the listings due to price increases, inflation, fluctuations in the exchange rate, political upheavals, the passage of time, whims of owners, or changes of management. The publisher and author also cannot be held responsible for the experiences of readers while traveling.

Cheap Sleeps in Spain is revised and updated on a regular basis. If you find a change before I do, or make an important discovery you want to pass along to me, please send me a note stating the name and address of the hotel or shop, the date of your visit, and a description of your findings. Your comments are every important. I investigate every complaint, hand out every compliment, and personally answer every letter I receive. Because of this, I do not provide an email address, since the volume of mail it would generate would make it impossible to personally reply to each message. I hope you will understand and still take a few minutes to drop me an old-fashioned letter telling me about your Cheap Sleeps in Spain. Thank you, in advance, for taking the time to write.

Please send your comments to Sandra A. Gustafson, *Cheap Sleeps in Spain*, c/o Chronicle Books, 85 Second Street, Sixth Floor, San Francisco, CA 94105.